PERGAMON GENERAL PSYCHOLOGY SERIES

Editors: Arnold P. Goldstein, *Syracuse University*
Leonard Krasner, *SUNY*, *Stony Brook*

Counseling and Accountability: Methods and Critique

PGPS-30

Counseling and Accountability: Methods and Critique

HARMAN D. BURCK
HAROLD F. COTTINGHAM
ROBERT C. REARDON

Florida State University

PERGAMON PRESS INC.

New York · Toronto · Oxford · Sydney · Braunschweig

PERGAMON PRESS INC.
Maxwell House, Fairview Park, Elmsford, N.Y. 10523

PERGAMON OF CANADA LTD.
207 Queen's Quay West, Toronto 117, Ontario

PERGAMON PRESS LTD.
Headington Hill Hall, Oxford

PERGAMON PRESS (AUST.) PTY. LTD.
Rushcutters Bay, Sydney, N.S.W.

VIEWEG & SOHN GmbH
Burgplatz 1, Braunschweig

Library of Congress Catalog Card No. 72-75614

Printed in the United States of America
0-08-017029 3 (H)
0-08-017684 4 (S)

We dedicate this book to our:

. . . colleagues who may be surprised that we dared to do it,

. . . former students, clients, and subjects who continually motivated us to do it,

. . . future students who we hope will be pleased that we did it,

. . . families who wait to share any rewards of our doing it, and

. . . collaborators in Part II who are now anxious to do it to us.

Contents

Preface

Counseling and psychotherapy, as professional enterprises, are being provided to our society at an ever increasing rate. They are often provided on the assumption that if counseling is good, good counseling is even better. This provision of counseling and psychotherapy goes on and on, and too often professionals never ask the question: "What kind of counseling, provided by what kind of counselor, can be most effective at this time for this kind of population sub-group?"

Historically, the focus of counseling and psychotherapy research has been very diffuse. Each researcher seems to be doing his own thing. A glance at any recent research journal indicates a mosaic of studies, lacking any semblance of unity. There is a weak linkage between research findings and actual practice. In addition, innovative approaches to behavior change are constantly emerging. With their roots in new viewpoints on the nature of man, these methodologies have had a significant impact on counseling practices. Ironically, these recent developments in theory and practice have probably generated more changes in counseling strategies than much of the extensive research in the area.

We wrote this book for several reasons. First, as counselors, viewing the current scene, we felt a need to share with others our concerns about methodological problems and strategies of counseling and psychotherapy research. In this vein, we wanted a book which approached the problem in a very practical sort of way, rather than from merely a conceptual or theoretical point of view.

Second, students in social work, educational psychology, vocational rehabilitation, employment counseling, and others in the helping relation-

ships need practical, relevant information on research. Besides abstract ideas they need to see the concrete application of theoretical methods to actual research activities.

Third, there is a large and continuing need for professional workers in human behavioral change-producing relationships to evaluate and document their effectiveness. Accountability in personnel services is a fact which few practitioners have squarely faced, but which must be met head-on in the future. Perhaps this volume will assist those seeking to be more accountable for their efforts.

Finally, we feel that all professionals, involved in any central or tangential way with counseling and psychotherapy, have both a moral and an ethical responsibility to build evaluation and research strategies into their work.

In Part I we have attempted to set forth both conceptual foundations and working principles related to research on psychotherapeutic change. These include such features as theoretical bases, design, criteria, sampling, treatment, and measurement. Ethical and legal considerations are also discussed.

Part II follows naturally as an application of the principles and essential characteristics of research identified in Part I. As a basis for the critiquing process in Part II, thirteen examples of published counseling research are reproduced. These in turn are reviewed in the light of the previously described criteria from Part I. Thus in a departure from the usual research book, basic principles are applied directly to actual research efforts, with appropriate commentary.

We express appreciation to Ellen Amatea, S. Richard Sauber, Robert MacAleese and Alice Fernandez, all of whom have helped us along the way. A special word of thanks is due Dr. Arnold P. Goldstein and the folks at Pergamon Press who have been so very considerate.

Tallahassee, Florida H. D. B., H. F. C., R. C. R.

Part I Conceptual Foundations

CHAPTER 1

The Topic and the Book—Some Introductory Comments

Even the casual student of the literature in counseling or therapy research will recognize the pervasive, and curious, circularity in many writers' statements. The introduction and the conclusion of most articles have the same ring—the wail and lament of the shortcomings and problems of research in the area. Many counselors and therapists seem to find comfort in a kind of self-flagellation when it comes to research—they bemoan the lack of research but they do little about it. The present writers are not an exception, although this book does represent a departure from the usual indulgence.

THE BIG PICTURE

Examining the larger view for a moment, there is an urgent social need to deal with the question of behavioral change in the context of human relationships (Lennard and Bernstein, 1971). As far as counseling and psychotherapy are concerned, psychologists, at the general public's insistence, are being asked to respond to Raimy's twenty-year-old characterization of therapy: "... an undefined technique applied to unspecified problems with unpredictable outcome" (1950, p. 93). Money appropriated for the training of mental health professionals and for settings of therapeutic practice may not flow freely forever without some factual evidence of positive results. "Accountability" is in vogue. There is an urgent need for outcome research.

While it is true that psychotherapeutic practice has been little affected by research (Fiske, Hunt, Luborsky, Orne, Parloff, Reiser and Tuma, 1970), there is also some basis for hope and optimism. Meltzoff and Kornreich (1970) exhaustively reviewed the research literature, and concluded that some work has been surprisingly good, although there was plenty that was bad. And Goldstein (1971) has noted that effective change-producing elements, common to a variety of different kinds of human relationships (therapy, teaching, friendships, etc.), have been identified by researchers. He offers the notion of "relationship" as one aspect of effective behavior change.

In spite of the evidence (or lack of it), there is a rising demand for counseling and psychotherapeutic services. Wrenn (1962, p. 3) noted that the "counselor's role is one expression of our society's deep concern for the welfare of children and youth. So deep is this concern that families sacrifice themselves for their children in many ways." Hunt (1952) also discussed the social demand for professional help with personal problems. It is ironic that the practice of helping relationships is so insulated and autonomous that positive evaluation continues in spite of and without objective outcome research.

Given the need and expectation for helping relationship services, the economic strictures on the unlimited provision of such services, and the uncertain, often debated state of therapeutic practice, what should be done? The most socially responsible alternative for professional helpers involves scientific study of change-producing social relationships, whether they are labeled education, conversation, therapy, counseling, or whatever. Where, under what conditions, with whom does a person change his behavior? What are the parameters of change-producing human relationships, and, assuming some consensus in the characteristics of the healthy person, what outcomes might be expected from a change-producing relationship?

With this broad view, counseling and therapy research then becomes one facet of this bigger picture. "The essential ingredients," as Paul (1967, p. 110) says, "are at least one client and one therapist who get together over some finite period of time. Clients come to treatment in order to obtain help in changing some aspect of their behavior which they, or someone else, find distressing."

The questions and concerns noted above lead to the consideration of several basic notions about counseling-therapy research. In the following paragraphs, several observations, delimitations, and assumptions are offered which may help orient the reader to the scope and purpose of this book.

COUNSELING RESEARCH – SOME IMPORTANT POINTS

It was noted earlier that a basic problem in evaluation of counseling/psychotherapy centers around the problem of definition. But the spontaneous remission phenomenon, the need for long-term follow-up, the cooperation of clients and therapists, the availability of suitable criteria, replicability, costs, and the like combine together as formidable obstacles to effective evaluation.

In order to meet these problems, research in counseling has become more complex than it was, and the trend will undoubtedly continue (Goldstein, 1971). The problems of multifaceted independent variables, sometimes ignored in the past, are handled now in more sophisticated research designs. The reality today is that complex human change-producing relationships require complex research designs.

Moreover, the question is no longer whether or not counseling works. The real question today is WHAT treatment, by WHOM, is most effective in producing behavior change for THIS person(s) with THAT specific problem, and under WHICH set of circumstances (Paul, 1967)?

A useful distinction may be offered between the previously mentioned notions of research and evaluation. An unfortunate, naive belief about research is that one perfect, gigantic study can reveal whether or not counseling (or the counselor) is worthwhile. But value judgments about the most desirable cost-outcome ratio, the worth or justification of the provision of counseling services will necessarily continue to be made more on the basis of faith and pragmatic realities than scientifically accumulated evidence. Political, personal, and other value considerations, likely not included in a research study, are basic to any total evaluation of counseling. Scientific research, then, is simply one important facet of the broader process of evaluation.

As noted earlier, counseling and psychotherapy are viewed as one focal point for studying change-producing human relationships. Numerous authors have concluded, and we agree, that the basis for distinguishing between counseling and psychotherapy has little to do with the actual processes themselves. The "differences" which do exist between the terms do not make a difference in the conceptualization of human behavior change research.

There is an additional unnecessary distinction often made between process and outcome research. Outcome studies must no longer ignore process variables (Kiesler, 1966) if they seek to attempt to answer the real question of what outcomes are related to particular clients seen by counselors using various techniques. The greater number and complexity of variables in counseling-therapy research has led some investigators to focus exclusively on client–therapist interaction variables. The basis for such process research has been to find out what and how variables make a real difference in counseling. Our view, however, is that concurrent evaluation of counseling outcomes is necessary for any investigation of process variables. Process and outcome research have the most meaning in a mutual context of scientific inquiry.

One final point has to do with the high heat and faint light sometimes provided by widely quoted reviews of counseling research. Many carefully articulated claims and counter-claims of counseling are unfortunately based on research so poorly done that almost any conclusions are totally inappropriate (Meltzoff and Kornreich, 1970). Research with major errors in design or data analysis cannot be salvaged in the conclusions section of the report. Research carried out with fatal errors is only useful as a basis for improved research in the future – it can never stand on its own.

THIS BOOK

Earlier it was noted that counselors and others tend to talk and write more about research than they practice it. There are certainly many reasons for this: both counseling and research are difficult; counseling is generally socially accepted regardless of the research results; many counselors are not suitably trained to carry out research; the spirit of scientific inquiry is absent in the presence of dogmatic adherence to particular counseling theories; research is expensive and funds are scarce, etc., etc. The unspoken maxim is that counseling is good, and good counseling is even better.

This volume represents an attempt to bridge the gap between talk about research and its practice. Part I offers some general ideas about the theory, method and technique of research. Part II applies the generalizations to actual research reported in the literature.

Part I is organized around topics that have some homogeneity as basic, critical elements in a broad conceptualization of counseling research. Chapters on research design, the criterion problem, selection and sampling, counseling treatment variables, and measurement each touch on the more specific areas of research endeavors. Other chapters in Part I reflect on the broader issues, such as philosophical, theoretical, ethical, professional, and legal considerations, as well as the future of counseling-therapy research.

Counseling research, of course, is not something that can be neatly separated into ten discrete components. There is some overlapping of points and principles in the various chapters of Part I. Furthermore, several of the chapters offer a new emphasis or departure, while others focus on recurring, persistent problems.

Part II is an extension of research theory to the critique of specific, reported research studies. Each of the articles is reprinted in its published form, and then critiqued according to the research principles noted in Part I. Selection of the articles for inclusion in Part II was based on several simple criteria (see Introduction to Part II for details): (1) type; (2) theoretical basis; (3) setting; and (4) design.

The purpose of including articles in Part II was not to spotlight good, bad, mundane, or controversial research. Rather, the goal was to provide an illustrative collection of human behavior change research appearing in recent, appropriate journals, which could then be critiqued according to various methodological standards. It need not be emphasized that the articles included in Part II represent better than average research efforts—if this were not so, the reports would never have passed the journal editor's critical eye.

In summary, it should be reiterated that this volume seeks to bridge part of the gap between the rhetoric and practice of counseling-therapy research. The inclusion of critiqued research reports along with theoretical discussions of research topics is the means selected to help "bridge the gap."

CHAPTER 2

Philosophical and Theoretical Considerations

NEED FOR CONCEPTUALIZING BEHAVIORAL SCIENCE RESEARCH

Broadly speaking, education and the behavioral sciences both involve formalized and informal approaches to the modification of learning experiences. While learning as a component in the education change process is a natural phenomenon, such activities as instruction, therapy, and counseling are purposeful interventions and thus not subject to the natural laws found in science. Nevertheless, man's efforts to change the behavior of others by improving the conditions or methods for learning should have some design as well as an underlying rationale.

It may not be possible to predict and control various aspects of the behavior change process through scientific study involving nomothetic relationships comparable to research in physics and chemistry. It is, nevertheless, important as attempts are made to improve educational and social conditions and subsequently human behavior, that some implicit assumptions or basic viewpoints be formulated as guidelines for research. These guiding principles are even more necessary in social science than in pure science. Such is the case since many variables surrounding learning in practical situations preclude any direct causal or simplistic relationships. Only discovery, not invention, can reveal the fundamental interrelationships in the learning process. Similarly, discovery assumes an existence, as yet unconfirmed, of specific causal connections and response patterns, universally applicable.

Theoretical considerations may not always be formally labeled "theories." This is true due to the difficulty in identifying singular sets of constructs that lead to predictable outcomes in most instances. However, any systematic or empirical plan to change human behavior does have implicit assumptions or inherent philosophical beliefs even if more covert than stated. Formal theories have clearly identifiable features including stated postulates or assumptions, definitions of terms or concepts, and a formulation of hypotheses for prediction. These elements, when continued, help to organize present knowledge into a meaningful framework. Stefflre (1965) has suggested that good theories are clearly communicable, comprehensive, explicit, and parsimonious. Certainly, the conceptualization of research should enhance its broad goal, the ability to make probability statements about the nature of reality.

The function of formal theory or conceptualized bases for changing learning conditions is seen in the reciprocal relationship to practice. As practices are proposed or experimentally (or even intuitively) attempted, some theoretical assumptions are at work. Then the results of these actions are learned, replicated under other circumstances and hopefully proved to be generally consistent in their outcome. Subsequently new theoretical approaches or changes in current conceptualizations may be justified. Theories serve to generate research as well as to foster the implementation of practices dealing with changing behavior. Theories also assist in the discovery of relationships of operational truths (empirical constructs) as well as in the stimulation of ideas to solve new problems. Certainly, when possible, educational and psychological research should have theoretical origins. Such research should be based upon some aspect of behavior change and generalizations which have some degree of certainty or potential usefulness.

Several characteristics of theory building in relation to behavioral science research should be noted. A fundamental question that must be asked is whether or not one is concerned with basic research. Such research endeavors have as an immediate aim the quantitative formulation of variable general laws, and as an ultimate aim, the establishment of a system of concepts and relations in general principles (Ebel, 1967). On the other hand, applied research refers to the collection of data that offers assistance in the solution of some immediate practical problem. Presumably, theory building, although more directly relevant to basic research, is necessary in both instances.

Most educational theories do not form an adequate basis for research because they are vague and fail to identify variables as cues for measurement (Travers, 1964). Theories of behavior change appear to become more useful as they can be tied to observable conditions and controllable events.

As theories are evolved and applied to limited aspects of individual and system change, they serve primarily as a way of organizing knowledge so the known and unknowns can be recognized. Certainly the linkage between one idea and related concepts is necessary as relationships are established as a basis for generalizations and predictions. A reasonably simple theory that deals with relatively few major variables all of which are measurable, can be much more useful than a more comprehensive theory having many variables which cannot be measured.

THE PROCESS OF CONCEPTUALIZING COUNSELING RESEARCH

In examining the theoretical aspects of research on counseling, several points are relevant. To be useful, conceptual schemes must (a) broaden and deepen our understanding of the counseling process, (b) encourage critical research, and (c) permit the direct application of such research findings to subsequent counseling practice. Certainly the interrelationship of various kinds of theories must be recognized as the counseling process is studied. The place of information theory, role theory, personality theory, and learning theories as other intervening variables in human behavior change is obvious. The concern for single or discrete theories is a worthy objective. However, the complexities of man, the nature of personal disabilities, the philosophical issues in setting goals, and the lack of agreement on methodology for effecting behavior change appear to preclude developing explicit theories of a global nature. On the other hand various single theories relating to the different aspects of counseling, i.e., characteristics of clients, counseling processes or strategies, and outcome measures may be worthy of investigation.

While some counseling research should rest on conceptual foundations stated in precise language, other more broadly based empirical research is also justified. This latter approach, while not overlooking theoretical considerations would concentrate primarily on observable specifiable behaviors. These would include looking at the criteria measurement task first, the counselor's behavior for effecting changes second, and only subsequently attempting to conceptualize what actually happened.

Counseling theories as presently conceived have several limitations when applied to research designs and methodologies. Not only do these theories include constructs which are often untestable, but their assumptions may be complex or ambiguous. Often these conditions exist to such a degree that testable hypotheses are difficult to derive.

An examination of current literature on counseling research reveals other limitations. As Krumboltz (1968) points out, one basic weakness appears in the apparent ineffectiveness of most counseling research to answer the question, "As a result of this research, do counseling practices actually improve?" Another weakness of much research is the failure to consider the question, "To what extent does counseling research measure therapeutic benefits rather than simply outcome?" Rephrased, the question is, "To what extent will effective counseling add to (or subtract from) the degree of improvement the given type of client would otherwise show?" (Truax, 1968). Other controversial issues regarding quality of counseling research relate to such factors as homogeneity of patients (clients), spontaneous remission, and adequacy of research paradigms derived from present theories. Thus one must ask, "To what extent do theories specify patterns of independent, dependent, and confounding variables in sufficient detail for researchers to solve sampling and methodological problems?" (Kiesler, 1966).

Theoretical or conceptual bases for counseling can be grouped into two broad categories, (a) phases of the interaction and (b) emphases within the process. Sub-categories of interaction phases could include theories related to (a) the client and his characteristics, (b) the counseling process proper, and (c) outcomes resulting from counseling. In emphasis or approach, several sub-classifications are possible. Patterson (1959) has suggested the following: (a) learning theory approaches, (b) psychoanalytic approaches, (c) rational approaches, (d) perceptual approaches, and (e) existential approaches. A broad dichotomy, possibly subsuming the above categories offers another classification scheme. This system, a continuum, would postulate a directive, rational, highly cognitive position on the one end with a permissive, highly affective or conative approach on the other. Still another division is based on the contrasting underlying philosophical and psychological assumptions. This arrangement uses the labels of humanistic on the one hand, and behavioristic on the other. The former emphasizes man himself as the subject, while the latter stresses man as an object of knowledge in his environmental adjustment.

In the process of conceptualizing the counseling process for research purposes a desirable objective is some sort of broad theoretical structure or paradigm. Such paradigms conceivably should include such elements as characteristics of clients and counselors, specification of treatment methods, definition of outcome variables, and functional relationships among these components. Models of varying specificity for therapeutic study have been identified by both Allport (1955) and Colby (1964). The former suggested models of man as either a "reactive being" or as a "being in the process of becoming." Colby (1964), indicating that no single common paradigm commands consensus, observes that the current leading paradigms, overlapping to a degree, are the psychoanalytic, learning theory and existential.

Volsky, Magoon, Norman, and Hoyt (1965), drawing upon Carnap, propose a research structure which divides the language of science into two parts, observation language and theoretical language, along with correspondence rules for connecting the two. They also suggest a criterion of empirical meaningfulness for theoretical concepts. This criterion makes use of the smallest possible set of untested terms in the examination of each term as it arises. Finally, Volsky *et al.* recognize the role of the intervening variable or pure disposition concept, applicable to the set of responses elicited by certain stimuli or conditions.

Kiesler (1966) in an attempt to suggest minimum criteria for research paradigms for counseling (and psychotherapy) identifies the therapist and his behavior as independent variables. As dependent variables, Kiesler describes the various discussions of client behavior such as communication, experiencing, or the process of anxiety reduction and symptom removal. He also comments on the problem of confounding variables, i.e., contamination elements which make effects of independent variables ambiguous to evaluate. These may be subject, task, or environmental confounding variables.

In practical terms, the problem of constructing theoretical or conceptual bases for counseling research has several phases. Initially, a theoretical or symbolic language is necessary to describe the major components in counseling (clients, counselors, task, outcomes) and their interrelationships. Terms, definitions, and postulates are necessary to represent these elements. Secondly, some linkage must be provided between such symbolic schemes and observational data in appropriate input and output language. Using the terminology and assumptions, along with their interpretations, relevant hypotheses can then be proposed for testing. Finally, as results of research confirm or refute derived hypotheses, connections between observed data and theory enable researchers to modify relevant aspects of the proposed theory.

PROBLEM AREAS IN THEORY ORIENTED COUNSELING RESEARCH

Several sub-problem areas hamper the broad task of developing conceptual foundations for counseling research. These difficulties are of three types: (a) the classification and agreement on counseling goals, (b) the place of diagnosis or classification schemes, and (c) the question of theoretical structure undergirding counseling research.

Counseling Goals

Although little agreement exists on goal statements as such, Krumboltz (1966) has proposed three criteria for looking at outcomes in counseling research. These are (a) capable of being stated differently for each client, (b) compatible with, though not identical to, values of the counselor, and (c) degree to which counseling goals attained by each client should be observable. In examining attempts at categorizing or describing outcome goals of counseling, the wide divergence among both researchers and practitioners is clearly evident. These differences cover a wide range of bases for goal determination including time, source of goals, type of goal, single or multiple criteria, generality vs. specificity of goals, and responsibility for goals. The time basis, while not frequently considered, is reflected in Byrne's (1963) immediate, intermediate, and ultimate goal concept—although Byrne's first goal appears to be a process rather than an outcome type goal. Blocher (1968a), also in the same vein, is concerned with the chronology of goals in speaking of "action goals," "cognitive and perceptual changes," and "learning new instrumental behaviors," the latter being the central (and presumably ultimate) goal of counseling intervention.

Related to these classes of goals is the basic question of immediate as opposed to ultimate goals forming the criterion for researching the aims of counseling. At one end of a polarity scale are ultimate goals applicable to everyone expressed in such terms as self-understanding, self-acceptance, or self-fulfillment. At the other extreme are found immediate goals stated in the form of specific aspects of behavior, often in the language of the client himself. The basic issue here is whether counseling goals measurable by a gross criterion, and presumably a reflection of societal values, are more acceptable than immediately agreed upon client-counselor goals, evaluated in terms of externally observable behavior change. Thus the generality-specificity issue in assessing counseling outcomes is compounded by the question of the time sequence of goals as well as the responsibility for setting goals.

Another aspect of this problem is the question of goal source, whether it be the counselor, the client, or by mutual agreement. If *counselor* goals are primary, one must immediately raise the question of the basis for counselor objectives. Specifically, are they drawn directly from his own personal theory of man and society or are they inferred from what he assumes the client's society would expect that particular client to become immediately and/or ultimately? Thus the kinds of behavior change projected may clearly differentiate counseling outcomes as being much different from the outcomes of socialization and education in general. On the other hand, this condition may vary greatly from client to client. If *client* goals are to be accepted, how are these to be reconciled with the counselor's goals? Furthermore, should client aims be taken at face value, i.e., accepted as they are presented literally? Certainly the feasibility and genuineness of mutually agreeable goals is open to question. A related matter is the extent to which a client's "developmental contract" (Blocher, 1966), being ever changing, is as much a process as an outcome goal. Truax (1968) raises the intriguing possibility of examining *client benefit* instead of merely *client improvement* which might have taken place without counseling.

Another area of concern is the nature or type of goals to represent counseling outcomes. One of the more important aspects of this problem is the possible conflict between the single goal concept, where a subjective or abstract goal in terms of a socially meaningful criterion may be preferable to multiple, client expressed goals of greater objectivity. A facet of this dichotomy is the matter of internal (global) vs. external (objective) dimensions mentioned by Wellman (1968). Many authorities agree that a clearcut division is not the only alternative, that elements of both should be sought in counseling theory and research.

In summary, there are many factors that appear to influence both the setting of individual goals for counseling and the agreement upon general (or specific) goals for counseling research. Obviously little or no agreement exists on the theoretical structure regarding counseling outcomes as a basis for sophisticated, predictive research designs. Inevitably the ethical and moral elements of the criterion problem must be considered. Society and groups of therapists have identified, but not agreed upon, such general aims as removal of symptoms, reorganization of personality, curing of disease, and adjustment to the culture as broad counseling aims. But the translation of these or other outcomes into precise, convergent positions which represent commonly agreed upon evidence of counseling success does not appear to be possible. As Volsky *et al.* (1965) state, an acceptable conceptual framework for counseling research must include goals which even though elusive, are legitimate, desirable, and expected.

Diagnostic Schemes

Another problem area with many impinging variables is the matter of classification or diagnosis which theoretically and practically is implicit in counseling research. Allegedly, some sort of categorization or assessment scheme should serve as a basis for actions or movement during the counseling process proper, thus enabling the counselor to make predictions about client behavior. This same need for structure or diagnosis would seem to be a part of counseling research since replication and predictability are qualities sought. A secondary aspect of this question of classification is the function of diagnostic categories in process, as opposed to outcome research. As Kiesler (1967) points out, these have been traditionally distinguished by looking at *how* change took place in contrast to the end point or *what* changes took place. Kiesler (1967) also deplores this ambiguous distinction. He further states that to some extent process research involves outcome research and outcome research is equivalent to process investigation. Presumably, there are two distinct areas of client behavior change for study, i.e., (a) within the interview situation and (b) outside or beyond the counseling interaction.

Diagnostic schemes are probably more applicable to differential client behavior in the counseling session proper, than to any arbitrary pre-interview classification system for categorizing all types of clients. For example, Blocher (1966) uses the term "structuring" to refer to formulation of goals or "developmental contracts" with clients, a process of communicating and sharing expectations as to types of goals. Historically, Bordin (1946), Pepinsky (1948), Byrne (1958), and Callis (1965) have proposed at various times classes of diagnostic constructs for the counseling process, most of which were based on the criterion of type of problem. Robinson (1963), feeling that classification processes take place in the counselor's mind during interviewing, has suggested a modification of earlier constructs. He has proposed a two level process goal including both developing strengths and/or remedial goals with the former stressing the identification of areas of positive development.

Essentially diagnostic or classification systems are theoretical approaches to the question of selecting appropriate treatment for different psychological difficulties. It is hard to identify the extent to which these schemes are actually used in counseling practice or counseling research. In their own research, while not using the term diagnosis, Volsky *et al.* (1965) described as classification measures, "motivation to change self through counseling," and "perception of counseling," thus giving them a process label. Regarding the types of process research categories involving the client, Volsky *et al.* (1965) suggest three referent areas: the client's perception of his own role in the process, of the counselor's role, and of the characteristics of the process itself.

Theoretical Bases for Counseling Research

The problems of theory building and of conducting theory oriented counseling research are manifold. Looking at theory broadly, theories underlying counseling research should have practical value and be the point of departure for further study. They may also be derived from a number of sources in the behavioral sciences such as anthropology, psychology, and sociology. Essentially, as Scriven (1964) points out, psychological and other scientific research is interested in (a) prediction, (b) explanation, and (c) classification or "problems of static organization," i.e., a concern for variables, some of which are in part inaccessible. Back of this position is the strong likelihood, according to Scriven (1964), that a single law or fundamental discovery comparable to scientific laws may not be possible in psychological research. Kiesler (1966) too, referring to "The Definitive Study" which once and for all will prove the effectiveness of psychotherapy, is quite pessimistic about any single research package providing answers to a great many questions.

In the application of theory to counseling research the aim should be to identify small theories or limited conceptual positions rather than complex and comprehensive theories with many variables. Travers (1964) urges the use of even simple and incomplete theories which have a history of usefulness in the behavioral sciences. Suggestions for the use of theory by Scriven (1964) include (a) taking seriously the paradigms of informative partial descriptions, (b) mining the resources of ordinary language (i.e., do not proliferate technical jargon), and (c) abandoning the search for "super theories" of development, perception, or learning for example. Where possible, theory is posited as a basis for counseling research. As Magoon (1968) has indicated, however, an alternate model includes concentrating on criteria of observable behaviors, particularly as outcomes related to client changes. This could be followed by study of counselor behavior associated with changes. Finally, one might conceptualize what emerges from these efforts.

CHAPTER 3

Research Design

A pivotal point in any discussion of counseling research is the matter of design. In the following pages important aspects of the function and relation of design to a broad conceptualization of counseling research are explored. The chapter begins by analyzing some of the problems in the design of counseling research. Common sources of error and strategies employed to control error and strengthen designs are examined. The second part of the chapter analyzes examples of simple and complex designs which are often used or advocated.

The notion of design in counseling research involves many different things. Generally, the word may be used as a descriptive noun, a higher order abstraction, a modifier, or an active verb.

A descriptive noun A discussion of design may refer to a general, descriptive statement of WHAT was done. This nontechnical, informal description of the research activities might include virtually EVERYTHING the investigator did from the initial formulation to the final write-up.

An abstraction The concept of design also includes the researcher's higher level, abstract thinking about the problem and its relation to a variety of facts and knowledge in theory and related research. WHY is the study important? When the investigator thinks of research activity in terms of design, he cannot help but begin to explore possible interrelationships among variables. This is a creative, intuitive aspect of design. The identification, elaboration, and final delineation of theoretical hypotheses may suggest appropriate designs. Thus a research design may be thought of as an abstract statement of theorized relations among variables.

A modifier The term, design, embodies a scientific attitude, a predisposition, a way of thinking about the gathering of reliable and valid information to problems. As an attitude, design includes facts which the researcher may utilize in his attempts to control error and maximize the reliability and validity of his statements. But design also connotes a willingness to think in responsible, disciplined, analytical, calculating, rigorous ways about the research. Thinking about research in terms of design is a highly symbolic, personalized, conceptual process as well as a blueprint for action. The act of carrying out the research is thus primarily a matter of follow-through.

An active verb The term design may also be used in a more active, deliberate sense. HOW, WHEN, and WHERE is the study going to be carried out? Procedures for gathering data; timing of initiation of experimental effects and conclusion of the study; the strategy of obtaining instruments; the number of clients and counselors needed; methods of collecting and analyzing data; and so on. All of these aspects of design are the basic notion of planful, deliberate, concrete thinking about the counselor-researcher's activities.

DESIGN FACTORS IN COUNSELING RESEARCH

There are a variety of important, recurring factors to consider in counseling research: the complex sets of variables that affect counseling process and outcome; the common and recurring problems of control, such as pretest effects; and the conceptualization and control of error in counseling research. The following paragraphs examine these problems.

One problem in counseling research is the complex array of variables that impinge on counseling activities. While this is a fact of life in social and educational research and not unique to counseling, it is nonetheless a problem. Counseling theories of varying degrees of comprehensiveness and current research knowledge about counseling are often of limited usefulness in helping the researcher delimit and delineate the crucial, important variables. It is generally more important to incorporate a simple theory which utilizes a few measurable variables than a comprehensive theory including many variables which may innundate the researcher with data. It is important for the counselor-researcher to maintain his focus on the natural phenomenon that initially attracted his attention while attempting to simplify, delimit, and abstract the actual design of the research.

Numerous writers (Truax and Carkhuff, 1964; Voth, Modlin, and Orth,

1962) have discussed therapist, client, and situational sources of basic variables in counseling research. Therapist variables might include attitudes, personality characteristics, role perception, and preferred techniques. Client characteristics, e.g., counseling outcome expectations, anxiety, demographic characteristics, or personality traits may interact with therapist variables in complex ways. And, finally, situational variables such as intake procedure, setting for counseling, location and reputation of the agency, and nature of the referral may further complicate the process and outcome of therapy. Thus the design of research must delimit and narrow from among these sources of variables.

An important contribution to the literature on design and counseling research was made by Edwards and Cronbach (1952). They discussed three categories of experimental variables: stimulus, response, and organizmic. These three variables may also be thought of as situation, behavior and person categories. Of special importance are organizmic variables, which include any property or attribute of the individual, such as age, sex, race, personality traits, etc. On the one hand, the number of relevant variables to counseling outcome is so large that a sufficiently large number of cases to account for then is impossible (Chapter 5). On the other hand, carefully specified organizmic variables and clear hypothesizing can reduce the size of the sampled variables.

In all this discussion of the complexity of variables related to counseling research, one fact emerges clearly. The counselor-researcher must be able to formulate in advance a clear notion of the expected results. He must choose from among the different categories of variables those factors which are definitive, relevant, and measurable. Ignoring or missing important variables increases the probability of error and weakens the experimental design. Thus the formal design can only be as good as the hypotheses. An experimental design may facilitate answering hypothesized questions in a very efficient manner, but the responsibility remains with the investigator to move beyond the current study and hypothesize for the next experiment.

PROBLEMS OF CONTROL

The basic question in counseling research is *what kinds of counselor activity produce what kinds of change in what kinds of clients*. The problems of control in counseling research logically begin at the point when the researcher thinks that he knows some of the answers to this question. The simple purpose of controls is to enable one to determine the certainty that he really knows what he thinks he knows.

As noted earlier, these are common problems of control in counseling research. For this reason, certain designs are used more frequently than others. This is another way of saying that the problem and the design are interdependent. An adequate design will specify which variables to manipulate or fix, when and how observations should be made, the analysis of the data, and different conclusions that might be reached.

Among the common problems of control in counseling are the following:

Pretest effect A common problem is having equivalent groups of clients for various treatments or controls. A common design involves pretesting clients on variables directly relevant to subsequent counseling. The problem is that the pretest may sensitize clients to the treatment and thus confound the outcome measures.

Noncounseled controls In order to determine if counseling makes a difference in client behavior, it is logical to compare counseled and noncounseled groups. This involves the classical control strategy of withholding treatment from a control group in order to compare posterior measures with treatment group(s). Many writers have noted the virtual impossibility of isolating a client from other sources of help. For example, Orne (1962) has presented evidence which shows that people who need and want help get it from someone else, though it may not be a professional counselor. Such facts certainly qualify the ideal of a truly noncounseled control group.

Counselor cooperation One procedural problem relating to design is the researcher's need to involve other counselors in the project. For a variety of reasons, participating counselors may not carry out the previously specified treatment activities. Counselors may be incapable or unwilling to behave in the predetermined ways. In either event, the researcher is subverted and the outcomes of the study are jeopardized.

Hello-goodby effect In counseling research there is evidence of a natural regression phenomenon. Persons seeking help may overdramatize their problems in order to justify their need for help. At the outset or at the end of treatment, there may be another distortion in overestimating the benefits of counseling. This may stem from a desire to justify counseling or show gratitude to the counselor. Thus, clients receiving longer-term treatment may be inclined to report more positive improvement and results than those in a short-term treatment group or noncounseled, waiting-list control group. The operation of this artifact may have an obvious bearing on the comparability of various treatment groups, or of treatment vs. non-treatment groups. It is an example of the way in which an uncontrolled, regression variable operates as an artifact of the design and may confound the expected effects between other controlled, treatment conditions.

Situational variables In long-term research, Voth *et al.* (1962) and others have noted the importance of variables outside the treatment condition in outcome research. There is the need to view situational variables, e.g., attitudes of important others towards the client and his treatment, as a frame of reference in interpreting the interaction between counselor-client variables. Without including the broader context, there is a tendency to overdraw conclusions as based on change within the client or as a direct result of therapy.

Replication Historically counseling research has not been replicable. It has been manifestly impossible for one investigator to confirm or verify the work of another. Counseling research has been seen as a one-shot endeavor. The largest problem has involved the specification of the treatment—was client-centered counseling$_2$ really the same as client-centered counseling$_1$? The use of research designs in which variables have themselves been studied or specified is a major facilitator of replicability. Problems in the control of various sources and common types of error in counseling research have led to the thwarting of subsequent attempts to repeat the effort. More replication in counseling research can increase the external validity (Campbell and Stanley, 1963) of research which has not used adequate random sampling procedures for clients, counselors, or situations. Fiske *et al*, (1970) pointed out that science builds on replicated findings, which means that theoretically based studies, related to previous research, and characterized by considerable specificity are absolutely essential.

Interview topic One other feature which the counselor-researcher cannot control is the actual semantic content of the interview. It is impossible to dictate the subject matter for any period of time during the counseling hour. As noted later, simulated clients, counseling analogs, and programmed counselor responses are one attempt to deal with this control problem. As with other aspects of the treatment situation, this is a factor which the counselor-researcher must be resigned to minimally control.

In general, it may be said that any design may afford only slight control of many important variables in counseling research. The above problems comprise part of the nature of human research and attest to the fact that both clients and counselors have a subjective involvement in counseling.

From the preceding discussion it is obvious that one of the basic aims of scientific research is to control bias and error in the conclusions of a study. Campbell and Stanley (1963) have discussed error in terms of threats to the internal and external validity of the research design. The former refers to how well the design tests the experimental variable for which it was contrived, while the latter refers to the degree to which generalizations can be based on the experimental results. External validity may be best enhanced by sampling and selection controls of error (Chapter 5). Internal validity, including the hypotheses test, control of independent variables and extraneous variance, may be best controlled through selection of the experimental research design.

Design as a control of "internal error" in research may be elaborated in several ways. It is important to broaden the concept of "control" in research design. The basic notion is offered by Campbell (1954, p. 298): ". . . the minimum of useful scientific information requires at least one formal comparison." Control implies more than simply the use of a control group. It includes the idea of controlled phenomena – of an adequate accounting of variables presumed to be relevant to counseling. Thus, control in design more properly suggests comparison between groups that are systematically different on a dependent variable or criterion measure. The researcher might, therefore, obtain a better comparison by adding four counseling treatments to the design than analyzing differences between counseled and noncounseled groups.

The control of error through experimental design suggests that the researcher will manipulate at least one variable and exercise direct control over at least one variable. Unlike *ex post facto* designs where the researcher simply observed differences after the fact, the true experiment involves more control. Poor designs do not allow the researcher to adequately control variables or only to control the wrong ones (those irrelevant to the dependent variable); do not allow randomization of selection or assignment of clients or treatments; and do not identify or control extraneous, or miscellaneous variance.

Kerlinger (1964) suggested the maxmincon principle which identifies the variance in the design that should be maximized, minimized, or controlled. A good design should (1) maximize the experimental variance, (2) control the extraneous variance, and (3) minimize the error variance. There are a variety of ways this principle might be applied through a design; (1) eliminating the extraneous variable as a variable by not selecting clients on the basis of sex; (2) selecting clients, therapists; etc. randomly; (3) adding an extraneous variable to the design as a fixed independent variable; (4) statistical control; or (5) more rigorous instructions, measurement techniques, etc.

In the design of counseling research, the notion of control is inexorably intertwined. But a highly controlled study may not be a good one, because control is a relative value in any study. "What is most needed in research on psychotherapy is originality of thought and courage to grapple with important issues, setting up as much control as feasible. Each experiment should lead to another which is an improvement over its predecessor. In this sense a bad experiment is better than none, and several are better than one. Unless one makes the original crude experiments, no progress is possible" (Frank, 1962, p. 25).

SIMPLE, COMMONLY USED DESIGNS

The history of research in counseling has been ridden with ill-conceived, oversimplified, poorly designed studies. True experimental designs, however, are difficult to use because many of the independent variables defy control. In this section, many of the traditional, commonly used designs are briefly discussed. Beginning with preexperimental designs, the focus centers on the classical experimental design used in counseling research.

Preexperimental Designs

Designs, where all variables are assigned and fixed, where an effect is judged to vary discriminably with another variable, where variables are not manipulated, and where no randomization has occurred, are included in this discussion.

Correlational designs are typically historical because they involve analysis of the relationship among variables or facts which have already occurred. Causation is inferred and based on the magnitude of the relationship. Two response variables are analyzed with respect to covariation rather than the impact of a stimulus variable on a response variable. The lack of control means that obtained correlations could be the result of some unknown third variable. Correlational designs in counseling research are not meaningless or useless; they are simply inconclusive and indefinite.

Ex post facto designs are of a similar nature as correlational designs. These designs, however, allow the counselor-researcher to examine the interaction effects of factorial designs. A primary value of correlational and *ex post fact* research is that it may suggest hypotheses for future experimental designs.

Data analysis and statistical control provide another way to control variance. Frequently controls may be instituted where continuous measurement is involved through the analysis of covariance. In this case the initial known difference between experimental and control groups is partialed out and groups are equated by statistical means. Data analysis involves after the fact elaboration of specified observations in the data. For example, one might examine counseling protocols to see whether or not client-centered and rational emotive counselors were indeed different in respect to semantic content.

Classical Design

The most familiar experimental design is the *pre-post control-group design.* Clients are assigned to experimental or control groups randomly, or after initial matching procedure. In either case, there are at least two groups of clients, one experimental (treatment), and one control (no treatment). Each group is measured before and after treatment on a relevant criterion. The usual comparison is between post treatment measures for treated and nontreated groups, and the counselor-researcher may choose to omit pretesting.

The reason for using the classical design is obvious. To determine whether or not counseling has any effect, the researcher must compare those who have counseling with those who have not. This assumes, of course, that the two groups are similar on all important characteristics relevant to counseling outcomes.

While this appears to be a relatively straightforward procedure, it is infinitely more complicated than it may appear. One immediate problem is how to handle the desire for counseling by clients who are assigned to noncounseled control groups. It is not desirable to have control clients who do not wish counseling since motivation for treatment is an important variable in counseling effectiveness. Providing *delayed treatment groups* is one design alternative which avoids the distasteful matter of denying service to prospective clients. In this case one group is accepted for immediate counseling, and another group is placed on a waiting list. The procedural problem here, as noted before, is twofold: waiting clients may go elsewhere for counseling, or the mere anticipation of subsequent treatment may provide sufficient hope to result in some improvement.

A variation of this procedure is the *invited remedial treatment* design

(Paul, 1966; Spielberger and Weitz, 1964). In this approach, a specified counseling program is developed and prospective clients are invited to participate in the treatment. Several groups might emerge from such an approach: (1) clients invited who responded affirmatively and are accepted for treatment; (2) clients invited who responded positively but were refused treatment; and (3) uninvited control clients.

Finally, Goldstein, Heller, and Sechrest (1966) and Campbell and Stanley (1963) have suggested the liberal use of *patched-up* designs. In counseling settings, one might begin with a poor, inadequately controlled design. By being alert to various alternate hypotheses and adding control groups, additional treatment groups, clients, and other validity checks, the counselor-researcher can develop a better design. Because of the cyclical nature of most counseling center case loads, new variables and controls may be constantly integrated into the design, and rival hypotheses systematically investigated.

COMPLEX MULTIVARIATE DESIGNS

The use of preexperimental and classical experimental designs in counseling research has not escaped increasing criticism. Unfortunately the classical control-group design is plagued with practical difficulties, a ragged, piecemeal nature, and no utility in determining which kinds of counseling work best with which clients.

It is often noted that complex problems call for complex research designs. Thoresen (1969a) has concluded that one treatment, one control, one criterion research is inadequate because of problems with treatment-control groups, response artifacts, experimenter bias, client expectations, etc. What is needed is varied research with more complex designs, such as multiple criteria, measured sequentially over time, and taken from a variety of sources. For example, one important multivariate design is the factorial, where different types of clients and treatment conditions are compared. As with all designs, the aim is to make valid comparisons among variables. This section briefly presents and analyzes some of the more complex designs, including experimental analogs.

Multivariate, Experimental Designs

These true experimental designs are often referred to as cross-sectional, or classical control designs. As such, they are more powerful extensions of the pre-post control-group design noted earlier.

The first example is the *multiple treatment design*. In order to avoid denying counseling to any group of applicants, the researcher may design an experiment which offers differential treatment to various groups. Methods, techniques, duration, frequency, and other aspects of counseling treatment can be manipulated. By breaking the complex counseling situation down into component, identifiable, measurable parts and applying them to different groups, the contribution of each component to counseling outcomes can be evaluated. Obviously this design is significantly more complex than single treatment-control designs because the decision as to which ingredients in counseling should be controlled and manipulated is very difficult. This notion of control means the counselor-researcher must decide which independent variables are therapeutically significant and define those variables precisely and reliably.

One very powerful, important design, which is cumbersome because of problems in data analysis, is the *Solomon four-group* design. This multiple group factorial design assumes randomization, as do all other true experimental designs. Clients are assigned to four groups. Group 1 is the pretest, treatment, posttest; Group 2 is the pretest, posttest; Group 3 is treatment, posttest; and Group 4 is the posttest only. A variety of controls are employed in this design which permit the researcher to make a number of comparisons. Campbell and Stanley (1963) argue for a variation of the Solomon design which eliminates the pretest in Groups 1 and 2 but retains random selection and assignment. This design, the *posttest only control-group* design, includes at least two groups and involves one treatment/posttest group and one posttest only group. This is also a powerful design and quite applicable to counseling situations where a pretest is not possible or desirable.

Factorial designs are ideally the hardiest and most useful designs in counseling research (Paul, 1966). One factor which obviates factorial designs becoming extremely complex is the large number of clients that would have to be worked into the design. An example of a 2×2 factorial design is a comparison between behavioral and existential counseling for clients with high and low speech anxiety. If the researcher decided sex of client and counselor were important, he could easily build that variable into the design by adding a second level to both variables. Thus the design would be a $2 \times 2 \times 2 \times 2$ factorial, and the scope and complexity of the study multiplied significantly. A variation of the factorial design is the *repeated measures* design where a series of measurements are taken on the same clients. It is possible to examine interaction in this design. However, several important assumptions, e.g., no client learning on subsequent measures, must be met in using this design.

Functional Designs

The repeated measures factorial design has several things in common with what are sometimes called functional designs. This design includes the own-control, baseline, intensive longitudinal, and time series designs. Functional designs resemble process research because the experimental variable is designed to produce changes in client behavior—both inside and outside the counseling situation. By manipulating the injection of the treatment variable over time, the researcher assesses the process of change on various measures. Such within-patient controls are highly amenable in behavior therapy research. Thus the traditional control group is eliminated and comparisons are provided in other ways.

Counseling researchers have found that one way to avoid the control-group problem is to have the client serve as his *own control.* Basically, the design involves three measures at three times: (1) an evaluation after acceptance or application for treatment; (2) a waiting period and then a second evaluation before treatment begins; and (3) therapy and the final evaluation at the termination of treatment. Change between the first and second evaluations are compared with those between the second and third. Presumably, the differences would be a result of counseling. While this design avoids the problem of equivalent groups, it does not handle the changes in clients which result from the passage of time, and there is still the problem of withholding counseling services.

The elaboration of this design has received increased attention in recent years. Impetus has come from the verbal operant conditioning research paradigm and behavior modification research. By modifying reinforcement contingencies and other experimenter, subject, and situational variables, changes in frequency and intensity of verbalizations can be measured over time. Unlike the usual own-control design, these newer functional designs are characterized by small samples, including an N of 1 (Davidson and Costello, 1969). Thoresen (1969a), for example, has discussed the *empirical case study*, in which a high degree of control of environmental variables is exercised, and changes in client behavior are carefully measured. In all such designs, each client is his own control, and comparisons are made between measurements taken as variables are manipulated and as time passes. This intensive design (Chassan, 1967) could conceivably be extended over a considerable period of time in order to rigorously analyze intraclient behavior change. An attractive feature of this design is its compatibility with the 1–1 treatment interests of many counselors. Frequently noted limitations of this design include (1) generalization of individual data across subjects and (2) replication of treatment variables.

A variation of the own-control technique is the *time series* or *baseline design*. In this case a series of measurements of an individual or group are obtained prior to treatment, and/or the experimental treatment is interspersed between observations. There are measurement problems inherent in this design, e.g., instrument decay and client sensitization to testing, as well as the inability to control historical factors. In spite of these limitations of full control, significant empirical evidence can be accumulated. A variation of this time series design involves using another group which is also measured over time but does not receive the experimental treatment. In laboratory settings, this may be called a yoked control. Some writers (Guerney and Stollak, 1965; Gelfand and Hartman, 1968) have discussed the use of baseline data or autoanalytic methods. After obtaining a base rate on a client's verbalizations, the counselor might begin to vary the interaction, e.g., structuring, feedback, suggestions, interpretation in order to assess changes in subsequent client verbalizations. The criterion measures may be graphed in terms of frequency of occurrence of the criterion response.

Experimental Longitudinal

Because of the developmental nature of many aspects of counseling induced change, there is a great need for longitudinal, long-term research. Of necessity, these projects are large, ambitious, and expensive, and might well focus on programmatic changes. For example, changes in old programs could be monitored and new programs could be compared with old, established ones. Thoresen (1969a) has argued for experimental longitudinal projects. Such efforts, involving teams of counselor researchers, could combine the precision and control of more frequently used cross-sectional designs with the richness of description in longitudinal research. Hunt (1952) has presented a similar case for an integrated program of research in counseling.

Systems Approach

One of the most recent developments in the area of counseling research involves the "systems perspective." This view draws upon a variety of theoretical specialties, and Thoresen (1969b) has identified four aspects common in definitions of a systems approach: (1) objectives are specifically and objectively stated, often in behavioral terms; (2) there are interrelations of components in the system; (3) mechanisms for information flow throughout the system, e.g., feedback; and (4) the system may be composed of both men and machines. The complex phenomenon of counseling is well suited to the systems approach, because the research designs generated through systems analysis can more adequately process all the situation, behavior, and person variables related to counseling outcomes.

Analogs

Analogs, including computer simulation, client confederates, and social psychological laboratory studies, are used primarily to study counselor or client behavior in highly controlled, experimental situations. Such techniques involve the training of "clients" or "experimenter therapists" to perform in designated ways. While this research approach permits rigorous experimental control, the ultimate test of validity is the degree of relationship between the analog and the "real" therapeutic situation. Krumboltz (1968) and Whiteley and Jakubowski (1969) have discussed these problems.

Goldstein (1971) and Adinolfi (1971) suggested that meaningful research relevant to change-producing human relationship may be conducted in the laboratory. Social psychological research in person perception, dyadic communication, and interpersonal attraction has important implications for increased understanding of naturally occurring therapeutic social interactions. A basic notion in the use of experimental analogs is that counseling/therapy relations themselves are viewed as laboratory research, not that the former is "laboratory" and the latter "real life." It is clear that many process variables can be best studied by means of analogs.

SUMMARY AND CONCLUSION

The problems of design in counseling research are obviously traceable to problems in specifying the important relevant variables and the nature of their interrelationships. When treatment or process variables, criteria, and situation variables are defined and their influence on one another has been theoretically conceptualized, then design problems are no longer barriers to effective research. Kiesler (1966), for example, has noted that no one theory is comprehensive or explicit enough to permit adequate counseling research designs. Paul (1966) has suggested that simple pre-experimental designs should be used in the initial stages of research for hypotheses development. Complex factorial designs should be used in later stages, because they are the designs which will eventually answer the important questions about counseling/therapy. Thus, in conclusion, it is sanguine to say that research should be as well designed and highly controlled as possible. But no counselor-researcher should become so preoccupied with design and control that he fails to carefully think through the implications of good and bad design in relation to the problem he is investigating. More imprecise studies are better than abstinence from all research endeavors, especially if the commitment can be made to improve the quality of future research.

CHAPTER 4

The Criterion Problem

A major and persistent problem in counseling and therapy research is the identification, selection, definition, and measurement of the criterion. Too often in the evaluation of counseling, the criteria used are those most available and accessible rather than those most relevant to predetermined counseling objectives. Frequently the instruments dictate the criteria rather than the reverse. In this chapter, the criterion problem will be discussed under the following headings: (1) What is a criterion and what is the problem? (2) Levels and characteristics of criterion variables, (3) Some dimensions and issues of commonly used criteria, and (4) Some suggestions for selecting proper criteria. The problem of criterion measurement will be discussed in Chapter 7.

WHAT IS A CRITERION AND WHAT IS THE PROBLEM?

Simply stated, the criterion is an operationalized statement of the goal or objective of counseling. Jensen, Coles, and Nestor (1955) define a criterion as a behavior or condition, described in ideal terms, which develops as a goal of counseling. A criterion is a kind of behavior considered good or desirable, toward which a counselor works. It is determined by the questions asked by the researcher. English and English (1958) define it thus, "a comparison object, or a rule, standard, or test for making a judgment . . . a behavior goal by which progress is judged . . . the variable, comparison with which constitutes a measure of validity." The reader can immediately detect the quality of desirability within each of these definitions. This quality of the criterion is a direct reflection of the implicit, if not the explicit, value orientation of the researcher. For example, the criterion selected for use in a study with underachieving students may be improvement in GPA. This represents a social, if not personal, value implying that it is better for a client (and for society) to achieve at maximum potential.

In a plea for criterion-centered research, Astin (1964) describes the ecological nature of the criterion. He distinguishes between a pure psychological construct or trait and a criterion variable, which relates the person to his environment. It is obvious that a standard of performance or behavior cannot be described as desirable without specifying the social context in which the behavior is to occur. Most contemporary social problems are criterion problems. Typically, the problem with which the counselor-researcher is concerned is referred to as the *conceptual criterion*. This is a statement of meaningful, socially relevant outcomes based on the more general purposes of the researcher. It represents the lowest level of abstraction in the researcher's hierarchy of relevant goals. A measure of criterion provides the raw data (e.g., observations, reports of satisfaction with counseling, test scores, etc.) for exacting the criterion performance. The criterion performance "is any observable event which is judged to be relevant to the conceptual criterion" (Astin, 1964). The following examples illustrate these concepts:

Problem	Conceptual Criterion	Relevant Goals of Researcher
To compare different methods of counseling	Efficacy of counseling	Maximum development of human potential
To select engineering students	Proficiency (GPA) in engineering school and subsequent graduation	Decreases engineering student attrition

It is mandatory that the criterion performance be relevant to the conceptual criterion, but this relevance can be evaluated only by rational and logical analysis. It is in this area and its measurement, that the concept of criterion is a problem in counseling research. For example, there would be little disagreement that social adjustment is a beneficial and socially good conceptual criterion for measuring many of our counseling efforts. Disagreement arises, however, when we attempt to define the performance necessary to meet this conceptual criterion. Even greater disagreement occurs when we attempt to measure this criterion performance.

Thus we can see that the selection of criteria in counseling research involves value orientations and the researcher should not feel apologetic about this. Zax and Klein (1960) support such a conclusion: "Actually, the problem of making value judgments when one conducts research cannot be avoided. The very selection of the phenomena which will be observed and measured is in itself a judgment depending upon the values one holds."

LEVELS AND CHARACTERISTICS OF CRITERION VARIABLES

Thorndike (1949) distinguished three levels of criteria: (1) immediate criterion—a criterion measure which is immediately available, (2) intermediate criterion—a criterion measure which is available sometime after the activity or treatment, and (3) ultimate criterion—the complete or final outcome of a particular activity.

To illustrate how these levels might be applied in counseling research, a counselor-researcher might design a study to test the efficacy of counseling in relation to realism of vocational choice of college freshmen. Data on realism of vocational choice is secured prior to and immediately following counseling. Three to five years later, information on the vocation of each student is secured. Ten to fifteen years later this measurement is repeated. The ultimate criterion is the level of vocational success. Unfortunately, ultimate criteria are rarely available for counseling research due to the inaccessibility of data, population mobility, attrition, etc.

According to Williamson and Bordin (1941), the proper time interval for the evaluation of counseling is extremely important due to the possible effect of various factors operating during the period between counseling and evaluation. Sufficient time must be allowed to assess the effects of the treatment. This has been called the incubation effect. The longer the time interval, however, the greater the influence of extraneous factors confounding the conclusion that changes are a result of the treatment.

Warters (1954) found five-year and later follow-up studies more effective than a one-year study. Kaczkowski and Rothney (1956) felt that six months was not sufficient time for permanent effects of counseling to be demonstrated. Gonyea (1962), however, supported the use of immediate criteria because: (1) they expedited counseling outcome research, (2) they reduced the problem of selective attrition which complicates complex sampling problems, and (3) they resulted in experimental conclusions which could more quickly be incorporated into counseling practice. O'Dea and Zeran (1953) suggested that a practical solution to this problem was to evaluate both the delayed and immediate effects of counseling.

Jensen *et al.* (1955) discuss several characteristics which a good criterion variable possesses:

1. A criterion variable is *definable*. There should be a clear and understandable description of the criterion. It should be defined in such a way that the condition being measured can be known by any consumer of the research. Acceptable evidence that this standard is met is the description of the variable.
2. A criterion variable is relatively *stable*. Performance, behavior, or the condition with which the researcher is concerned is the same from time to time. If the criterion condition is highly unstable, the problem of measuring it meaningfully becomes more difficult. This characteristic is desirable but may not be known by the researcher.
3. A criterion variable is *relevant*. Accurate measurement of the variable will yield data pertinent to the problem. Acceptable evidence regarding relevancy consists of expert agreement and/or logical argument, since relevancy can be demonstrated in no other way than by resorting to the researcher's subjectivity.
4. Measures of the general population show *variability* on the criterion variable. Presence of variability is a basic assumption in studies involving measurement.

DIMENSIONS AND ISSUES OF CRITERIA

It is the purpose of this section to identify and summarize the dimensions in which criteria may vary, and to point out some issues.

1. Generality vs. Specificity (or Abstractness vs. Concreteness)

Criteria examples of the two extremes of this criterion dimension are "personal-adjustment" and "improved grade point average," respectively. It is at the generality end of the continuum, with the accompanying esoteric, vague, and abstract theoretical constructs, that many of the problems of developing a criterion have been created. In many situations, the counseling theorist is unsuccessful in specifying just what it is that one should attempt to measure. Schlien (1966) suggests that the solution is to move to a level of abstraction sufficiently high enough to encompass most of the differences in theoretical goals and objectives. Using self-esteem as an example, he suggests that if many criteria cannot meet the test of being raised to a higher level of abstraction, then perhaps they are transitory and insignificant. Even though some behaviors are easier to observe and describe (specific criteria), this does not necessarily mean that they are important.

Undoubtedly, the trend in counseling research is toward greater specificity of observable behavior as the criterion. This has been one of the avowed purposes of the behavioral counseling group. Krumboltz's (1966) position is clear: "However, in order to make such generalities (self-actualization, understanding, etc.) useful they must be translated into specific kinds of behavior appropriate to each client's problems."

2. Objective vs. Subjective

The differences here fall along the continuum of phenomenological kinds of self-reports of how the client feels about the counseling (subjective) to more objective measures which are observable through public consensus. Examples of subjective criteria are: postcounseling Q-sorts, self-rating scales, follow-up interviews, etc. The client-centered theorists have been most active in developing these subjective kinds of criteria since they more closely fit their particular theoretical approach. Travers (1959) feels that the chief difficulty in measuring subjective evaluations is that adequate instruments have not been developed and client responses too frequently have been influenced by immediate and transitory circumstances. Crowne and Stephens (1961) suggest that an understanding of phenomenal status is a problem of inference. Underwood (1957) feels that the basic problem of subjective criteria is the difficulty in moving from theoretical definition or constructs to operational definitions.

Examples of objective criteria are: reduction in scholastic failure, appropriateness of vocational choice, occupational performance, reduction of specific phobic reactions, etc. The emphasis here is on measuring crucial observable and inferable aspects of client behavior. These approaches vary from measuring very simple specific behaviors (e.g., change in GPA) to rather elaborate rating and observable scales which attempt to tap representative areas of client functioning. Objective criteria are certainly more difficult to obtain than are subjective criteria. Often it involves the counselor-researcher moving out of his natural habitat to secure criterion measures.

It is obvious that the current limitations of measurement promote the use of both subjective and objective criteria.

3. Single vs. Multiple

Should a single criterion or multiple criteria be used in counseling research? Most researchers seem to feel that multiple criteria should be used to evaluate counseling. Farnsworth (1966) points out that studies using single criteria have failed to show positive results. Truax and Carkhuff (1964) justify the use of multiple criteria on the basis that personality change is far from a unitary phenomenon. Wrenn and Parker (1960) suggest that multiple criteria be used since theoretical knowledge of the process of counseling is so limited. Strupp and Luborsky (1962) state: "No single measure of change even when repeated on the patient over time, is sufficient, since any change may involve altered interactions with other areas of the personality and with the environment." Goldstein *et al.* (1966) suggest that in using two or more measures, more information is gained about the limitations of therapy and about the relationship among the measures which allow better understanding of other research endeavors.

A few researchers tend to support the use of a single criterion. The behavioral counseling group, for example, demand greater use of observable, specific goals in counseling, and thus greater use of a single criterion measure. Indeed, sound behavioral research has made use of single kinds of criteria, viz., information-seeking behavior, decision-making behavior, etc.

4. Internal vs. External

Internal criteria are those manifested within the counseling session itself (intracounseling) as contrasted with external criteria which occur outside the counseling office (extracounseling). Examples of internal criteria are self-report inventories, counseling protocols, and most objective test data. Examples of external criteria are job stability and satisfaction, GPA, relationships with significant others, etc. There is often an overlap between the subjective-objective dimension and the internal-external dimension.

Shoben (1953) perhaps has been the most explicit in insisting that counseling studies include external criteria. He states, "until the operational criteria used in specific studies are related to the realities of the client's actual world, their meaningfulness remains moot and controversial." Zax and Klein (1960) feel that the most serious limitation of self-report measures of intra-therapy behavior is that they have not yet been related to everyday, external behaviors in the life of the subjects. Froehlich (1955) considers that immediate criteria, like satisfaction and counselor agreement, are important only if they are symptomatic of more ultimate criteria.

Thus one must conclude that there can be no justification for omission of the use of external criteria in outcome studies of counseling. Ideally, counseling research studies should include the use of both internal and external criteria.

5. Common vs. Individualized

Should the same criterion be selected for all subjects, or is it possible to establish separate and individualized criteria for each subject? Tiedeman (1960) comments that researchers should not wonder when little or no change appears after counseling when a few, long-range effects are expected for all subjects. He suggests instead that experiments in counseling should be designed in order to allow each counselor to specify the expected outcomes for each client.

Goldstein *et al.* (1966) state: "When we consider the great variety of complaints expressed by patients, of symptoms displayed, and the inclination of clinicians toward treatment of 'individuals,' it is rather surprising that psychotherapy researchers have not given more thought to the possibility of individualized measures of therapy outcome." The idea of target symptoms, suggested by Levitt (1959) applies here.

It is suggested that many of our studies have not yielded positive results because of what Kiesler (1966) refers to as the "patient uniformity assumption." This assumption refers to the misconception of many researchers who regard all clients at the start of treatment as more alike than they are different. Regardless of the stated initial problem, clients tend to be more different than they are alike. Therefore, it appears that a greater individualization of criteria for our research subjects will yield more meaningful results.

SELECTING THE PROPER CRITERIA

Viewed exclusively from a behavioristic approach to counseling, Krumboltz (1966) suggests that the following three conditions should be met in selecting counseling research criteria:

1. The goals of counseling should be capable of being stated differently for each individual client. A single set of goals cannot apply to all clients.
2. The goals of counseling for each client should be compatible with,

though not necessarily identical to, the values of his counselor. The counselor's own interests, competencies, and ethical standards should place limitations on what he is, and is not, willing to help his client accomplish.

3. The degree to which the goals of counseling are attained by each client's behavior provides the basis for the judgment.

Krumboltz's first point is well taken. Counselors do attempt, in practice, to tailor their counseling behavior to enhance and meet the needs of their clients. Individualization of the counseling process is a basic tenet of all theoretical approaches to counseling. Thus, it follows that in counseling research we should measure that precise behavioral condition we are trying to change, rather than some obscure and abstract goal common to all clients. One cannot disagree with Krumboltz's second point either. Certain professional and ethical standards help ensure the fact that the goals of counseling for each client should be compatible with, though not necessarily identical to, the values of his counselor. However, Krumboltz's third point might produce disagreement among researchers of differing theoretical orientations. Krumboltz states that the degree to which the goals of counseling are attained by each client should be observable. If one interprets behavior quite broadly (everything the client says or does), however, other theoretical orientations might be able to include this point.

Wellman (1968),† writing in reference to the broader problems of guidance research within a developmental framework, offers some excellent guidelines for use with counseling research criteria:

1. Criteria should be expressed positively and defined in terms of evidence of the achievement of, or movement toward, specific developmental objectives.

2. Basic criteria should be reduced to units of behavior that will permit reliable observation and reporting, and if global criteria are utilized and interpreted by inference, relationship with behavioral manifestations should be demonstrated as a basis for the inference.

3. Criteria should be defined precisely enough to permit scaling on a continuum, with the extremes of the variables easily identifiable; and

†From Wellman, F. E. The assessment of counseling outcomes: A conceptual framework. In J. Whiteley (Ed.), *Research in counseling: Evaluation and refocus*. Columbus, Ohio: Charles E. Merrill, 1968 © Central Midwest Regional Educational Laboratory, Inc., St. Ann, Missouri. With permission.

where discrete units are utilized, relationships to continuously distributed units should be investigated.

4. The developmental approach, which attempts to differentiate individuals and to account for environmental influences, dictates the establishment of multidimensional criteria.

5. Criteria should be structured to permit the estimation of criterion variables from two or more sources wherever possible.

6. Criteria capable of reflecting change in relation to a developmental model should permit repeated observations with appropriate attention to the time dimension.

7. Criteria requiring subjective estimations should be balanced with objective data at least inferentially related to the subjective criteria.

8. Combinations of internal criteria, intraindividual or intracounseling, with external performance criteria should be sought.

9. Operational definitions of criteria should provide the basis for instrumentation rather than the instrument providing the definition of criteria.

In summary, criteria (a) are generated by the theoretical goals and objectives of counseling, (b) involve value orientations of the researcher, (c) vary along temporal levels of immediate, intermediate and ultimate, (d) should be definable, stable, relevant, and variable among the general population, (e) range from general to specific, objective to subjective, single to multiple, internal to external, and common to individualized.

CHAPTER 5

Selection and Sampling Procedures

All inductive inferences are based on samples. Even a counselor's personal opinion about the worth of counseling is based on a sample of his experience. Our store of information about counseling can be traced to inferences based on some, not all, of the possible clients, counselors, counseling situations, treatment conditions, and so on. We want to know more about counseling, but we cannot observe and report on every experience, so we resort to a sampling plan. We have to depend on samples.

Counselors who have personal theories about counseling outcomes or effectiveness often base their conclusions on samples of observations and experiences which are both inadequate and unspecified. Worthwhile generalizations are based on relevant, systematic, stable, and unbiased samples of client, counselor, and situation variables.

This chapter explores the notion of sampling—one of two interrelated problems in the scientific investigation of counseling outcomes. Sampling and design, or the differential use of control procedures, are basic ways in which biased generalizations from counseling research may be controlled. Campbell and Stanley (1963) refer to "external validity" as one important criterion of an adequately designed study. Sample representativeness and generalizability is a part of external validity, but ecological and variable representativeness are also included. The latter two features refer to the social setting of the experiment and the constancy and stability of the variables respectively. "Internal validity" refers to the adequacy and appropriateness of controls of variables and error built into the research design. This chapter on selection and sampling, therefore, explores "external validity" while Chapter 3, Research Design, analyzes "internal validity."

Assumptions regarding uniformity among clients and therapists are explored, and basic procedures and principles of sampling are described. This chapter does not focus on statistical concepts, such as probability, or problems of experimental design.

GENERALIZATIONS FROM SAMPLES

Errors in generalizing or abstracting the results of counseling research are frequently traceable to improper use of samples and sampling procedures. Travers (1964) has noted the error of generalizing the results obtained from one representative sample to other, unrelated populations. Plutchik (1968) has also emphasized that the best and most useful generalizations are made when one has adequately sampled counselors, counseling situations, criteria, and counseling theories, as well as clients.

Many inconsistencies and contradictions in research generalizations can be traced to variations in client attributes among research samples (Chassan, 1967). Research generalizations also depend upon the assumption that the sample is representative of the larger population. If the smaller number of units drawn does not closely parallel the larger population of interest, at least regarding the important variables, then the resultant generalizations cannot help but be biased. There is a paradox here (Kaplan, 1964). While a sample must be representative of the population in order to be of any use at all, knowing that it *is* representative eliminates the need for the sample. The resolution of this dilemma involves the assumption, never a certainty, that a sample is representative when proper sampling procedures are employed. Experience has shown that certain methods for drawing a sample are useful in guaranteeing representativeness. Cochran, Mosteller, and Tukey (1954) have clarified the matter by arguing that representation should not be in any particular sample, but it should be in the sampling plan.

Some of the concepts used in this chapter are briefly defined as follows. *Sampling* may be functionally defined as taking any portion of a population, or well-defined group of people, events, or objects, as representative of that population (Kerlinger, 1964). A *population* is technically defined as a set of things that have particular characteristics in common. The definition of a population, or universe, is very important, because it determines whether or not an object does or does not belong to it.

THE IMPORTANCE OF SELECTION

Exposing people to counseling for research purposes is somewhat more complex than planting and watering seeds in the gardens of an agricultural experiment station. Counseling relationship relationships are unique ones, difficult to control, and the counselor-researcher must treat them as such. Meltzoff and Kornreich (1970) note that "it takes little talent to bias research in psychotherapy, so manifold are the opportunities for the unwary" (p. 28). In general, the client selects himself for treatment by determining his need for assistance with a behavioral problem, a decision, or troublesome feelings. This fact complicates obtaining the proper number, sex, age, etc. of clients for counseling research. The client may also have many stereotyped preconceptions about the nature of counseling, what it means to be a client, and what outcomes might follow the contact. There are probably as many idiosyncrasies associated with each person's reason for seeking counseling as there are clients themselves. Thus the simple fact that one becomes a client in counseling, and may be labeled as such, does not warrant an assumption of homogeneity in the population.

The unique differences among clients are sometimes ignored in counseling research due to the "patient uniformity assumption" (Kiesler, 1966). This myth of client uniformity, while facilitating simplified research efforts, has generally obscured many variables which are basic to a more complete understanding of counseling outcomes. Similarities consist of differences which do not make a difference, yet the counselor-researcher must acknowledge the fact that some differences among clients do make a difference in outcomes. Kiesler (1966) and others have referred to numerous studies which attest to this fact. Examples of manifest client differences which might confound outcome measures are verbal intelligence and verbosity, age, motivation for change, persuasability, level of general anxiety, history, referral source and procedure, intensity, and social acceptability of the problem, socioeconomic background, occupation, reference groups, education and philosophy of life. Furthermore, Truax and Carkhuff (1964) have found that the client's engagement in the process of deep interpersonal self-exploration is positively related to the degree of constructive personality change.

Thus the client uniformity assumption should be challenged. More careful attention must be directed to the selection and description of clients on the basis of historical characteristics which have some theoretical or previously identified relationship to the treatment and criteria. Client self-selection can create sampling problems, and alternative approaches, such as initial participation, should be used. Input variables, particularly those relative to client characteristics, must be considered with the same careful forethought as the longstanding, glamorous problems of criteria and treatment (see Chapters 4 and 6). Sprinthall (1968) has suggested that the attention focused in the past on treatment and criterion matters, or process and outcome, should now include "prior conditions and relevant pretreatment variables." A reconceptualization of counseling research, indeed counseling itself, is in order. Information about clients must be used to assign people to various treatment processes where the probability of desired client change can be maximized. The traditional psychopathological diagnostic nosology has little relevance to counseling; new dimensions must be employed. Blocher (1968b) has made useful suggestions in this regard.

Inappropriate assumptions of uniformity have also been made regarding other variables, such as counselors and situations. Reports by Rogers, Gendlin, Kiesler, and Truax (1967) and Truax and Carkhuff (1964) have underscored the need to sample and control these sets of variables. Future designs in counseling research must involve the selection of counselors, as well as clients, on the dimensions and variables which are crucial to differential counseling outcomes. Uniformity myths only serve to qualify many of the generalizations drawn about the results of counseling research, and such myths render the application of these results to particular counseling interactions virtually meaningless.

The discussion of selection procedures and counseling research invariably returns to the old and persistent question of ideographic vs. nomothetic models in psychological research. Allport's (1960, p. 31) ringing challenge—"the *personal nexus* wherein all variables are joined eludes every nomothetic approach"—is certainly relevant. Chassan (1967) also discusses the intensive design, or case study, as a prologue for more extensive or large-scale research efforts. Perhaps the reader should be reminded that a sample only provides information about large populations, not about individuals. By sampling, one learns more about population regularities and characteristics than idiosyncrasies of individuals in the sample.

SAMPLING PRINCIPLES AND PROCEDURES

Proper use of sampling techniques in research aids in controlling bias in conclusions or generalizations of the results in two ways: (1) the selection of units, clients, therapists, situations, from the larger population of interest; and (2) the assignment of units to various groups or categories in the experimental design. A biased sample is one where units differing from the rest of the population on some variable are preferentially selected without possibility of correction by statistical or other means.

An unbiased sample is a random one; therefore, the basic principle in any sampling plan is *randomization.* It may be procedurally defined as that method of drawing a portion or sample of a population so that each member of the population has an equal chance of being selected, and no choice affects subsequent choices. True randomization involves the use of mechanical procedures, i.e., dice, a table of random numbers, etc. Detailed discussions of randomization may be found in Guilford (1965), Garrett (1958), Kerlinger (1964), Cochran *et al.* (1954), and Volsky *et al.* (1965).

In counseling research it is desirable to control the variables which might affect the outcomes. Unfortunately, investigators do not know all the sources of error in counseling, much less how to control them, and under these circumstances the principle of randomization is used. By randomly drawing a sample or randomly assigning units to experimental groups, various characteristics of subjects which might bias the results are assumed to be generally counter-balanced. While complete randomization is desirable in counseling research, especially when the investigator does not know what effects certain uncontrolled variables might have, this ideal is not easily accomplished. For example, the counselor-researcher must make difficult and potentially biasing sampling decisions when he determines proper and improper reasons for dropping subjects from the sample (Meltzoff and Kornreich, 1970). The large number of fixed and mixed models in counseling research is probably an illustration of the problems of randomization. The hard rule, however, is that (1) generalization from nonrandomly selected samples to a population is not possible, and (2) differences among experimental groups which have not been "equalized," perhaps through random assignment, may not be taken as real. Of course, it must also be noted that the testing of any hypotheses involves clear assumptions about the way in which observations were recorded or data were collected. The application of sampling statistics and the inferences which might be drawn from the data depend on the conditions of sampling. Unless observations are randomly made, the use of statistical techniques is questionable, and resultant decisions or conclusions cannot be stated with any degree of assurance. While there may be limitations and weaknesses in sampling statistics and the inferences made from their use, biased sampling procedures can leave the researcher with conclusions which have no practical or scientific value.

TECHNIQUES OF SAMPLE SELECTION

In postcounseling follow-ups, the counselor-researcher may find it necessary to gather data on former clients. This data might consist of their reactions to counseling, current activities and adjustment, future plans, etc. Kerlinger (1964, p. 393) defines survey research as "that branch of social scientific investigation that studies large and small populations (or universes) by selecting and studying samples chosen from the populations to discover the relative incidence, distribution, and interrelations of sociological and psychological variables."

Because one seldom has the time or funds to gather data from an entire population, limited numbers of units are drawn. It is at this point that the investigator must decide on his "sampling plan" (Kaplan, 1964). The plan he selects will follow clearly proscribed procedures, and be based on considerations of randomness, representativeness, time, cost, and administrative procedures. The dilemma in choosing a sampling plan hinges on the following problem. Good counseling research includes a large number of clients chosen because of many person-variables related to counseling outcomes. But when a large N cannot be obtained and a small sample must be used, selection may be based on only a few criteria and other important client characteristics cannot be controlled through sampling. The matter of sample selection is discussed in this section, and five techniques, from least to most appropriate, are briefly presented.

1. Incidental Sampling

With this procedure the individuals drawn from a population are those which are most readily available. To illustrate, it might be supposed that data would be gathered from former clients of a counseling center who happen to eat lunch at campus cafeterias. Of course, generalization from such a sample to a larger population of former clients is warranted only if the sample can be shown to be similar to the larger group on significant variables. This *post hoc* analysis might involve categorizing variables as discussed under stratified sampling techniques.

2. Purposive Sampling

Much reported survey research has involved data gathered by this technique. While the sample is not random or representative, it may closely parallel the larger population if sufficient information is available prior to sampling. In counseling follow-ups, for example, it might be determined that on- and off-campus clients are highly similar in their reactions to counseling and other characteristics; thus, the more convenient on-campus group is used in the sample. Justification for this technique implies that the results will be valuable, although more appropriate techniques could have been used.

3. Cluster Sampling

This technique involves two stages. The investigator wants to obtain as large a sample as efficiently as possible, so he draws units into the sample in clusters rather than independently. Therefore, the counselor-researcher might first sample a group of counselors in an agency, and then sample the clients of those selected counselors in order to conduct a follow-up study. To illustrate further, if he wished to sample residence hall students who had received counseling, he might sample residence halls first, and then sample former clients in each hall.

4. Stratified Sampling

In counseling research, this technique is especially appropriate, although cumbersome. Assuming that the investigator knows something about the population of clients, sex distribution, age, etc., he may then (1) categorize the population according to unrelated variables which are relevant to the problem; (2) sample randomly within these categories; and (3) draw frequencies of cases within each category which are roughly similar to population frequencies. Stratification assures that the sample will be more representative of the population, and also controls the effects of certain variables. However, in most counseling agencies, it would be impractical to wait for a sufficiently large number of clients to accumulate before drawing a stratified sample. One would also have to assume that the time of the year for treatment requests was not a significant variable.

5. Random Sampling

The basic notions of randomization were discussed earlier, so only the means of obtaining a random sample are discussed here. The greatest degree of randomization is achieved by assigning a unique number to each individual in the population in sequence, and then selecting a sub-group of the population using a table of random numbers. It is necessary, of course, to follow the table of random numbers in a consistent way. Another commonly used method of random sampling involves arrangement of individuals alphabetically by name. Starting with a name taken at random, one simply selects every tenth or hundredth name, depending on the size of the sample desired. A caution about this latter procedure involves some unsuspected regularity in names, such as ethnic or regional frequencies. While selection of a random sample necessitates a minimum of prior knowledge of the population, it has the possible limitation of not being as representative of the larger population as desirable. This is especially true if only a small sample is drawn.

While this discussion of sampling techniques does not exhaust the possible different sampling methods, it does cover many of the more frequently used plans. The procedure chosen depends on the problem and total research situation. There is no uniform sampling plan, but some degree of randomness is a property of every procedure. It is entirely appropriate, moreover, for the investigator to admit the existence of bias or error in his sample, and on the basis of his general knowledge about the relation between the sampled and target population, adjust and weigh his sample accordingly. The primary concern is to warn the reader about a lack of representativeness, randomness, or whatever.

RANDOM ASSIGNMENT AND EXPERIMENTAL CONTROL

As noted earlier, a variation of the random sampling approach involves assignment of members, clients or therapists, to experimental groups. In random assignment, as well as in random selection, the purpose is to control variables which might bias research results. Variables may also be controlled through manipulation of the experimental design; delimiting the sample to a restricted, homogeneous group of clients; or by statistical procedures, such as the analysis of covariance, partial correlations, factor analysis, etc. In the following paragraphs, however, several methods of sampling as they relate to the assignment of individuals to experimental groups are presented.

Random Assignment

When control of relevant variables is not possible, or where they are unknown, experimental groups may be made equivalent through a process of randomization. In this way the personal bias of the investigator is greatly reduced. It should be clear that this is not a haphazard or grabbag procedure, such as assignment by simple alternation, birthdate, or student identification number would be. As discussed earlier, the essence of proper randomization involves rearranging a sequence of numbered units, e.g., clients, into a "random order." Volsky *et al.* (1965) have carefully discussed the construction of "random serial assignment schedules" for use by intake supervisors or receptionists who may be responsible for assigning clients to experimental groups. The groups may be either treatment (counseling) or control (no counseling), time-lapse (wait) controls, or other groups.

Matched Groups

When the investigator is aware of several relevant variables, but is limited by a small number of cases, he may utilize this information to form equivalent groups matched on the basis of relevant variables. Groups, rather than individuals, are usually matched because the latter requires a large number of clients. This procedure is very difficult, if not impossible, to put into practice (Frank, 1962). Though randomization is eliminated in matching, the usual statistical techniques are still used. Edwards and Cronbach (1952) suggest that single effect research efforts utilizing clients could give maximum value if the counseling treatment was described in detail and a homogeneous group of clients were matched on as many variables as possible.

Client Confederates

One possible approach in the assignment of clients to various groups involves the use of actors. They would be carefully trained to simulate counseling relationships with different counselors, treatment techniques, etc. Schmidt (1968) has reported on the use of this procedure.

In summary, the assignment of units to various treatment categories, as with the actual selection of those units, is best done according to random procedures, especially where relevant variables are unknown or uncontrollable. But it may also be advantageous for the counselor-researcher to combine several selection assignment procedures in order to facilitate control.

SAMPLE SIZE

The size of the sample is certainly related to the kind of research design used, as well as the quality and precision of judgments to be made. In counseling/therapy research the *N* frequently varies from one to several hundred. Travers (1964) notes that when differences are not readily apparent with fifty cases, then a larger *N* will probably not increase existing differences. But there is obviously no simple answer to this problem, and antecedent information gathered from prior research about the most advantageous *N* may assist in the determination of the proper sample size.

Chassan (1967) notes that the selection of various null hypotheses is in many ways influenced by sample size. Guilford (1965) has presented formulae for determining the necessary sample size, and has generally observed that the sample *N* should be as large as practicable. Kaplan (1964) suggests that the sample must be large enough to allow for gross differences among subjects to reveal themselves—that sample and population variance should be similar. He also notes that a small sample can be an unstable one.

In a similar vein, Edwards and Cronbach (1952) point out that a complex, multivariate study also requires a proportionately large number of clients for any statistical validation. However, with a small *N* the counselor-researcher can develop new hypotheses for future research—even if the statistical tests do not refute the null hypotheses.

SUMMARY

This chapter has called attention to the dependency of generalizations in counseling/therapy research on the sampling of events or experiences. In counseling research, the application of sampling techniques may diffuse the importance of differences among clients, counselors, and other relevant variables. Mere randomization of selection and assignment may not provide controls, unless other significant variables are incorporated into the design. Traditional techniques and procedures for drawing a sample and assigning units to experimental groups were presented and briefly discussed.

CHAPTER 6

Counseling Treatment: The Independent Variable

The single most difficult and complicated problem in all counseling and therapy research is the specification, control, and measurement of specific ingredients of the treatment process. The client comes to counseling with certain expectations, past behaviors, presenting problems and concerns. The counselor enters with his expectations, knowledge and experiences, values, etc. What actually happens in this verbally-mediated situation we call counseling or therapy. This is a highly complicated, vague, and subtle happening. What exactly happens when two people, one a counselor and one a client, meet for a certain length of time, in an interpersonal relationship? What is it that the counselor actually *does* (not what he says he does, or believes, or knows) in this relationship which promotes behavioral change in the client? The unraveling of this intricate phenomenon will be the subject of this chapter.

The solution to this problem lies in the counselor-researcher specifying as accurately and precisely as possible, the nature and the salient characteristics of the treatment variable. According to Volsky and associates (Volsky *et al.,* 1965), an adequate definition of the independent variable includes description of the qualifications and characteristics of the counselor, the attitudes and behaviors he displays, and the techniques and devices he employs in the process of treating the client. This solution sounds deceptively simple. However, it raises a host of problems for the researcher at a time when only a few possible solutions can be offered. Through the remainder of this chapter, many of these problems will be explored, along with reported ways of handling them. In pointing out the many and varied ways in which counselor-researchers have attempted to handle the problem of treatment explication, we will move from least rigorous (and least acceptable) to more rigorous (and more acceptable) procedures.

INDIRECT APPROACHES

1. Counselor Characteristics

The most simple and widely used manner of explicating the counseling treatment has been the description of certain counselor-experimenter characteristics, such as age, sex, years of experience, professional standing or status, professional setting, and brief comments about professed theoretical orientation. Another approach utilizes test scores to describe the counselor-experimenter (MMPI, intelligence, EPPS, CPI, etc.). Unfortunately, this tells us little about which counselor behaviors did, in fact, appear in the counseling. Many counselors are unwilling or unable to implement treatment as specified by the research plans. Also, many counselors are not very enthusiastic about participating in research themselves. In pointing out the problem of enlisting the research help of practicing counselors, Volsky *et al.* (1965) mention that the research aims may be foiled by counselors who must make changes in their preferred methods of operation, and who must participate in addition to handling an already burdensome caseload.

2. Case Notes and Professional Judgment and Opinion

Another common way of specifying the treatment variable is to rely simply on the counselor-experimenter's expert judgment and opinion as to what happened in counseling and its success, or to infer from the counselor's notes about what happened. This may be done either by the counselor himself, or by independent judges. Since case notes typically are highly interpretive (rather than descriptive) in nature, perceptual bias and distortion is introduced in an unknown direction and by unknown amounts through this procedure.

3. Theoretical Orientation Scales and Questionnaires

There is a long list of scales, typically of the self-report variety, which are used in attempting to explicate the counseling treatment variable. These scales attempt to tap the counselor's theoretical orientation and preferences. They are usually completed outside of the counseling context.

Sundland and Barker (1962) have studied differences in therapist orientation using the Therapist Orientation Questionnaire which contains sixteen sub-scales. Wallach and Strupp (1964) have constructed the Usual Therapeutic Practice Scale which was factor analyzed. McNair and Lorr (1964) modified the Therapist Orientation Scale, hypothesizing three dimensions of orientation: analytic, impersonal, and directive. The Fiedler Q-sort (1950) uses preselected items purporting to measure ability to establish a good therapeutic relationship.

Campbell and Kagan (1956) developed the Affective Sensitivity Scale; Arbuckle and Wicas (1957) the Test of Counseling Perceptions, a free response test of counseling perceptions; and Porter (1950) a test to tap counseling attitudes and perceptions.

Hopke (1955) and Van Zelst (1953) have reported the development and use of instruments to measure attitudes and empathy. Cottle (1954) has devised the Scale of Attitudes. Anderson and Anderson (1962) have a scale for measuring rapport. Two objective instruments purporting to measure empathy are the Kerr-Speroff Empathy Scale, and Cartwright and Lerner's (1963) adaptation of the Kelly Role Construct Repertory Test.

A group of scales which require the counselor-experimenter to respond to simulated counseling and therapy situations via films or taped counseling segments, are: O'Hern and Arbuckle's Sensitivity Scale (1964); Rank's Film Test of Counseling Perceptions (1966); and Strupp and Luborsky's (1962) series of brief film segments. A live interview using a standard "coached client" has also been used.

4. Supervisory and Peer Ratings

The approach here is to use supervisory ratings of counselor competency, categorizing the counselor-experimenter as more or less effective, more or less competent, etc. Sometimes the counselor's peers do the ratings. These ratings are usually secured before the research study is implemented, and do not rate the counselor *in situ*. Unfortunately, the criteria for separating the groups of counselors have not been adequate, and contradictory results may be attributed, in part, to differing conceptions of what comprises a good counselor or therapist (Patterson, 1968).

5. A final indirect approach lies in the client's perception of the process

These are usually assessed thru Q-sorts or other self-report questionnaires and forms. Gilbreath (1967) used a twenty-four point client questionnaire to distinguish leader-structured from group-structured methods of counseling. One of the most notable instruments here is the Barrett-Lennard Relationship Scale (1962) which attempts to tap client perceptions of counselor offered conditions derived from client-centered theory.

The above indirect approaches, in part or together, are necessary in attempting to describe the treatment variable. They are helpful in isolating and describing some of the important attributes of counseling and therapy. Yet they are insufficient and limited for the following reasons: (1) frequently they are self-reports rather than direct measures of counselor behavior, (2) they are typically taken before or concurrently with the treatment, seldom from the treatment process itself, (3) they lack logical and statistical relationships with actual, *in situ* counselor behavior and counseling outcomes, and (4) they lack validation.

DIRECT APPROACHES

This section looks at direct approaches which attempt to measure what actually happens in counseling sessions. These approaches deal with various systematic and categorical ways of handling the content material of counseling, or the interactions between counselor and client. They may use verbal content only or combine it with nonverbal aspects of the counseling session. Such categorical approaches may be applied directly to counseling sessions via typed verbatim transcripts, tape recordings, or sound/movie recordings.

1. Critical Incident Technique

This is a method of observation involving judgment concerning what should be observed and recorded. It is an observed counselor behavior or aspect of his behavior which is judged to make the difference between success and failure in counseling. The method describes what some person or group considers to be crucial matters in judging counseling success. The best summary of such work is reported in a book by Standal and Corsini (1959). Rogers (1963) however, summarizes the difficulties: "An experience which is seen by one therapist as healing, growth-promoting, helpful, is seen by another as none of these things. And the experience which to the second therapist is seen as possessing these qualities is not so perceived by the first. We differ at the most basic levels of our personal experience."

This approach has, thus far, contributed little to our knowledge of the counseling process. Travers (1964) notes these limitations: (1) it provides samples of rarely occurring behaviors, (2) this infrequency makes them extremely difficult to classify, (3) lack of substantial agreement among participants, and (4) the fact that the procedure is very laborious and time-consuming.

2. Content and Interactional Analysis

Kerlinger (1964) defines content analysis as a method of studying and analyzing communications in a systematic, objective, and quantitative manner for the purpose of measuring variables. It is a method of observation as well as a method of analysis. The main problem lies in setting up a workable category system. Trained observers code persons and actions to the categories, and the results are reported in frequencies or percentages. A more advanced approach is the counting of contingencies which takes into account the context in which certain words or ideas are expressed.

Marsden (1965) feels that the basic contribution of content analysis to psychotherapy research has been that it makes public the bases on which investigators make inferences about the importance and significance of a body of communication. He categorizes all content-analysis studies into three broad procedural models: the classical, the pragmatic, and the nonquantitative.

a. Classical model Quantification and objectivity are extremely important in this approach. Units are coded to categories descriptive of the content itself. It is designed so that workers with only a little special training can reliably perform the analysis. The intent is to limit content analysis to the semantic and syntactic aspects of communication.

Much content-analysis research has focused on *patient characteristics*, attempting to assess change or movement toward greater psychological health as a result of treatment. Auld and Murray (1955) have conducted excellent studies along these lines. Rogers *et al.* (1959), using a formulation of the process of personality change during treatment, developed a content-analysis system for measuring the degree of such change. Matarazzo, Saslow, and Matarazzo (1956) have conducted a series of studies using Chapple's Interaction Chronograph, a recording and computing instrument operated by an observer, which facilitates measurement of various behaviors and their relationships in time.

Research has also focused on the *therapist characteristics* in the therapy process. Strupp has published several papers pointing out the procedure he used in investigating therapist characteristics and their relation to therapist behavior in the interview (1957, 1962). His approach is unique since the system was intended to be sufficiently general to make comparisons across theoretical orientations and to be relevant to psychotherapy as a special kind of communication. Howe and Pope (1961) developed scales for measuring therapist activity level. The Wisconsin group have been most active developing scales to measure sympathy, warmth, and genuineness on the part of the counselor (Rogers *et al.*, 1967), indicating that evidence of their presence to a high degree is related to the client's personality with schizophrenics as well as college students.

Relatively new and intriguing efforts are being made to investigate *client-counselor interaction*, applying content-analysis categories to both participants. Based on a theory of small group behavior, Bales (1950) has developed a general purpose process analysis system. Twelve categories of group member behavior are represented (evaluation, control over others, tension management, etc.), and the simple sentence is the unit of observation. Both content and interaction processes are observed and categorized. Jaffe (1961) in expanding on this approach, feels that when a counselor and client come together in a therapeutic session, their verbal content ought to be treated as a single interpersonal system, the dyad. Although developed primarily for teaching situations, Flanders (1964) has also developed an interactional analysis system which quantifies selected qualitative aspects of verbal communication between teacher and student. Seven categories of teacher (counselor) talk are used (accepting student feelings; giving praise; accepting, clarifying; etc.). It measures the teacher's verbal influence and verbal flexibility, and is adaptable to counseling situations.

Finally, content-analysis studies have looked also at the *internal states* of the client. These studies have attempted to specify changes in both lexical and nonlexical communication content; such changes are then interpreted as indicative of changes in internal states. Best known here is the work by Dollard and Mowrer (1947) measuring the Discomfort-Relief Quotient. Other states which have been studied include, hostility, anxiety, drive, tension, speech disturbances, etc. Mahl (1959) has discussed the philosophical and methodological problems inherent in studying emotional and other internal states through classical content analysis.

b. Pragmatic model According to Marsden (1965), the pragmatic model was developed because the classical model was considered deficient in studying the themes found in verbal content. It attempts to realize psychological meaningfulness by working directly with complex clinical constructs for which behavioral cues and manifestations cannot be specified. Units are coded to categories descriptive of some condition of the communicator or of the relationship between him and his communication. The scoring unit is usually the grammatical clause, and each unit is coded to all categories to which it is relevant. As Marsden (1965) points out: "Relevance is a highly inferential matter, requiring a clinical judgment concerning the suppressed or repressed meanings of the unit to the patient. Here, the strategy is to infer the patient's needs, motivations, and conflicts from conscious or face-value, or unconscious meanings of the patient's speech." Murray (1956), Gottschalk and associates (Gottschalk, Gleser, and Hambridge, 1957), and Dollard and Auld (1959) have been most active in working from this model.

c. Nonquantitative model This model lacks methodological homogeneity. The one approach which has been extensively applied to therapeutic interviews is linguistic analysis. Some writers feel that content analysis and linguistics are different since the former is concerned primarily with meaning, while the latter is concerned with the properties of language as a code for the transmission of communication. Yet, Marsden (1965) feels that "if linguists have pursued a strategy of emphasizing structural considerations, linguistics is nonetheless ultimately concerned with meaning." As contrasted with the pragmatic model, linguistic analysis hopes to make possible identification of behavioral cues through a basically nonquantitative approach. This approach looks not only at linguistic, but also paralinguistic behavior (facial expressions, body movement and position) and other kinesic and tactile modes of communication. Pittenger (1958) and Scheflen (1963) have reported research in this area.

Marsden (1965) in summarizing content-analysis studies over a ten-year period, notes the relative infrequency with which any of the developed systems have resulted in more than an initial thrust at a given research problem. Ford and Urban (1967) also feel that attempts to get at behavioral changes by way of content analysis of therapy protocols have been most discouraging. They point out the following unresolved problems in this area: (1) interrelatedness of unit and category selection, (2) the absence of logical or theoretical rationale for the selection of units, and (3) continued infrequent use of content-analysis systems.

3. Other Direct Approaches

At least two other interesting approaches to explicating the treatment variable deserve special mention here.

The first emanates from direct, descriptive behavioral-theoretical models of counseling and psychotherapy. This group of counselor-researchers have best been able to explicate the treatment variable. They have demanded precision and rigor in their research designs, coupled with an emphasis on dealing with specific, observable behaviors. The task for the researcher operating from either a classical or operant conditioning model is to establish baseline data, to discern which stimuli are serving as reinforcers to maintain behavior, and to change both the nature and contingencies of reinforcement. Dealing with observable behavior rather than inner-determining hypothetical constructs, the researcher can be more precise in translating what the counselor is, in fact, doing in the counseling process. There are, however, still problems in selecting the appropriate reinforcer and isolating and describing the response class. Two references which deal with the contributions and limitations of this approach to counseling research are Breger and McGaugh (1965) and Burck (1968).

A second new approach to the analysis of the counseling treatment is the Interpersonal Process Recall (IPR) technique developed by Kagan and his associates (Kagan, Krathwohl, Goldberg, Schauble, Greenberg, Danish, Resnikoff, Bowes, and Bondy, 1967). Through the use of videotaping and immediate playback of counseling, the counselor and/or the client are directed to relive and report recalled thoughts and feelings experienced during the interview under the direction of a specially trained "interrogator." The role of the "interrogator" is to probe and push the client into exploring his feelings and actions in the taped interview. In this manner much of the nonverbal behavior of the individual client, largely ignored in traditional counseling analysis, also can be explored at great length. Significant outgrowths of this new technique have been: the development of a counselor verbal response scale which measures the extent to which counselors are characterized by affective, understanding, specific, exploratory, and effective responses; the development of an affective sensitivity scale; and the development of a classification scheme of client nonverbal behaviors which is significant in producing new insights into client intracounseling behavior. Such an innovative approach is quite significant in helping to unravel the many facets of the treatment variable.

SUMMARY

For entirely too long, we have viewed the counseling process as if it were a unitary phenomenon. Only lately we have begun to see the necessity of specifying in greater detail and in a much more precise fashion just what is happening. Explicating the process, however frustrating, helps to lessen the mystery of the nature of counseling and therapy. The resolution of this problem challenges the imagination and ingenuity of every researcher in this area, and presents methodological difficulties requiring bold, inventive speculations and attacks.

CHAPTER 7

Measurement

This chapter brings us to the complex and intricate problem of measurement in counseling and clinical research. Essentially, the problem is one of measuring in a rigorous scientific way the meaningful phenomena which make a difference in the clinical setting. Here we will attempt to formulate proper concerns, questions, and resolutions for the counselor-researcher as he asks the questions: What is measurement? Why, What, How, and When does one measure?

WHAT IS MEANT BY MEASUREMENT?

In most simple terms, measurement is the assigning of numbers to events, situations or objects, according to some rule. Magnitude or the measure is determined by properties of the objects or events; the number assigned is called its measure. To be sure, there are different levels of description and measurement in counseling research, ranging from simple, direct measures of number of therapy sessions, to more intricate attempts to measure the amount of client self-exploration during counseling. The more narrow, specific, and explicit the focus of activity, the easier it is to measure. Measurement of an object, event, or an individual in terms of a given attribute assumes that the individual or object can be described appropriately in terms of that attribute.

There appear to be at least two dichotomous, opposing attitudes about measurement, neither of which are helpful or conducive to good counseling research (Kaplan, 1964, p. 210). The first is the *mystique of quantity* in which the researcher responds to numbers as if they have occult powers or are omnipotent. As Kaplan states, "the mystique of quantity is an exaggerated regard for the significance of measurement, just because it is quantitative, without regard to what has been measured or what can subsequently be done with the measure." A number in this case is treated as if it had some intrinsic scientific value. The other attitude is the *mystique of quality* which views the power of numbers as a kind of witchcraft, good only for evil ends. The feelings here are that as we assign a number to some aspect of behavior, we thereby rob the behavior (or event) of its human significance. Measuring a certain value does not necessarily reduce it to a number only. Of course, there is nothing either mystical or magical about measurement. It only helps us to evaluate the effects of our labors. It is a man-made, arbitrary but logical, scheme of manipulation.

In counseling research, measurement is no simple matter. The task of the researcher is to select or construct assessment devices which most clearly capture the essence of the theoretical concept he has in mind, and the phenomena which occur in the process of counseling. Certainly there are many counseling outcomes and processes which are extremely important, but which we cannot now measure with any great degree of precision. Also, many of the theoretically expected outcomes and processes cannot be defined in clear and specific ways which would facilitate their measurement. Kiesler (1966) suggests that most counseling and therapy theories are crude and inprecise, and do not provide the researcher with concrete measures in any clear way. Yet, Goldstein *et al.* (1966) do not feel that the researcher should feel apologetic about this, but should take a straightforward operationalist's position and adopt likely measures for the concepts, with the appreciation that the operations may not really capture the essence of the concept. They feel that it is the critic's responsibility to specify a better set of operations.

Conceptual problems of counseling research measurement include: reliability (homogeneity, stability, equivalence, etc.), validity (concurrent, predictive, content, and construct), situational and population differences in performance, instrument sensitivity and the intended function of the instrument. Some of these problems will be discussed in this chapter, but the reader should refer to basic tests in psychological and educational measurement to grasp firm meanings.

WHY MEASURE?

Tersely put, we measure our efforts simply to gain feedback on how well we are doing our job (counseling), or to check out hunches and speculations about counseling processes and outcomes. At a more sophisticated level, effective measurement is mandatory in helping us to arrive at repeatable and verifiable observations, in order that we may precisely identify characteristics and attributes of the counselor, the client, their interactions and effects. It is not too difficult to state counseling goals and objectives, and their concomitant criteria, but until we formulate exacting measurement procedures, we will never know how close to the target we are coming.

WHAT TO MEASURE?

Quantification itself, in counseling research, is not so much a problem. Statistical procedures and techniques are available to correlate and test significant differences in any phenomenon which can be classified, numbered, or counted. Rather, a much more important question has to do with what to quantify. Quite often we see elaborate counseling research studies which make use of powerful statistical techniques, but which fail to measure the appropriate concepts and phenomena in terms of the stated theory, goals, and objectives, or what might logically be the proper criteria. For example, it would not be appropriate to measure and test the significance of differences in Grade Point Average changes in a study which provided *n* number of sessions of undefined client-centered therapy.

All too often we are confronted with the student who has just discovered a new test and wants to use it in a research project—any project. He has selected the measuring device before he asks himself the more important question of what it is he wants to measure. Too often, in counseling and therapy research, it is difficult to ascertain whether it is the counseling or the test that is being evaluated.

The answer to the question of what to measure must be found in the theoretical design of the research proposal itself. Whether the study is one of counseling process or outcome, the counselor-researcher must attempt to measure those phenomena which are dictated and generated by stated goals and objectives of the study. This can be done by logical deductive analysis only—it is a subjective process, not an objective one. Generally, deciding what to measure is to be found in the theoretical base and rationale of the study. The phenomena to be measured should be presented in clear, precise, and crisp language.

,v TO MEASURE?

After the counselor-researcher has answered the more basic question of what is it he wants to measure, he is then ready to select or devise methods of measuring it. Whereas the first three sections dealt with conceptual problems of measurement, this section will deal with methodological dimensions. This section is not meant to be inclusive of ways of measuring, but only suggestive of some of the more commonly used measuring procedures and devices in counseling and therapy research.

1. Expert Judgment

One of the oldest and simplest ways of measuring counseling outcomes is to have the counselor or therapist or others read case notes, typescripts, or listen to tape recorded segments of interviews, and to classify the counseling or the client into "successful-unsuccessful," "improved-unimproved," or other similar categories. Because of obvious counselor bias it is understandable why this is not desirable when the person who does the counseling also does the classifying. It is much more acceptable to use a group of independent judges, who know neither the counselor nor the client.

2. Psychological Tests

The use of psychological and educational standardized tests to measure changes resulting from counseling and therapy is one of the most common and prevalent. Unfortunately, assessment and measurement are too often equated with administering a printed test of some kind. The most popular kinds of personality tests used to assess counseling are the self-report and the projective.

Self-report tests such as the Minnesota Multiphasic Personality Inventory, Mooney Problem Checklist, California Psychological Inventory, Edwards Personal Preference Schedule, State-Trait Anxiety Inventory, etc., are easy to administer. The client checks certain items which are used to disclose his feelings and attitudes. At least two disadvantages of self-report devices are (1) the test may not necessarily be related to changes which would be expected from the treatment received, and (2) the client may distort his profile because he anticipates the purpose of the research or he wishes to project an image of himself.

Projective tests, such as the Rorschach, Thematic Apperception Test, Sentence Completion Technique, House-Tree-Person Test, Szondi Test, etc., may be used to minimize the client's deliberate distortion.

Projectives do focus on the psychodynamics with which counseling is usually concerned. Unfortunately, the projectives do not lend themselves easily to quantification, and their validity remains in question.

Too frequently, the selection of psychological tests is influenced by availability, acquaintance, newness, or because they are very commonly used in similar research. In searching for a test to measure the criteria performance, the counselor-researcher should ask himself, "What will be done in the counseling treatment that would suggest changes on this particular test?", and "Realizing the goals and objectives of this research, and the nature of the treatment variable, does this test significantly tap those phenomena which are logically expected to change?" Before using any test, the counselor-researcher should study carefully critical discussions of the instrument as found in *Buros Mental Measurement Yearbooks* and in test review sections of many counseling journals.

3. Behavioral Referrents

Another approach to measuring counseling process and outcome is the use of specific, observable behaviors which the client displays either inside or outside of the counseling process. An age old question in counseling is whether the client is, in fact, getting better, or whether he is just learning to play the "therapeutic game" expected by the therapist. Is he just verbalizing better feelings and attitudes or does his extra-clinical behavior, in fact, show changes in desired ways? Depending on the goals and objectives of the treatment, some examples of behavior referrents are: number of cigarettes smoked, absenteeism, amount of time spent studying, number of dates, amount of social interaction, school grades, examination scores, amount of talking in class, frequency of sexual contact, number of spouse quarrels, number of positive self-referrents, etc. Generally, behavioral referrents have to do with behavior displayed outside the counseling office, and may be more difficult to measure. Yet, with the use of personal diaries, logs, and similar accounting methods this may be partially overcome, particularly as the counselor-researcher enlists the help of significant others (parents, teachers, employers, siblings, spouses, etc.) to help report the behavior of the client outside of the counseling office.

4. Rating Scales

Rating scales are measures of individuals, their actions and reactions, characteristics, and behaviors, by observers (Kerlinger, 1964). They may be either categorical, numerical, or graphic. Since it appears that there will be greater use of rating scales to tap the intricacies of counseling and therapy, the following are some of the problems and cautions which must be taken into account by the researcher:

a. Operational definitions of the variables to be rated must be established.
b. Appropriate units of observation must be defined.
c. Good inter-rater and intra-rater reliability must be obtained.
d. The scale must tap unidimensions of the counseling process, rather than several.
e. Variables should be selected such that for a particular unit a reasonably complete picture of the interactions of counselor and client results.
f. The scale must have face validity and be concerned with construct validity.
g. The sampling problems must be resolved (i.e., sample size, location).
h. Differential results obtained when using different data media (typescripts vs. tape-recordings vs. sound movies) must be assessed.
i. The client's and the counselor's viewpoints of what is occurring in counseling must be assessed, as a check on the viewpoint arrived at by judges (Kiesler, 1967).

5. Physiological Correlates

The physiological measures of therapeutic change offer some promising measurements. They are usually correlated with other psychological changes and are, at best, inferential information. A number of researchers have attempted to utilize peripheral measures of autonomic functioning such as heart rate, skin temperature, muscle potentials, and skin resistance to measure the course of counseling and therapy. For example; Panek and Martin (1959) synchronized galvanic skin response (GSR) measures with verbal recordings of therapy; Dimascio and associates (Dimascio, Boyd, Greenblatt, and Solomon, 1955) correlated affect valence with level of heart rate; Shagass and Malmo (1954) found muscle tension (EMS) to be associated with certain themes in therapy; Anderson (1956) found that emotional, physiological and cognitive speech processes varied together during client-centered therapy.

There are many methodological problems unique to this kind of research. Difficulties arise in attempting to compare individuals' reactions to various stimuli since their initial prestimulus level of tension is so varied both among and within stimulus situations. Also shifts in autonomic responding may occur spontaneously. As the specific stimulus situation is such a powerful determinant of autonomic responding, the subject's response cannot be used as a criterion of effectiveness of therapy. Research has also been confounded by the inability to differentiate what the autonomic response is reflecting at any particular time. At one time it may be a reaction to the therapist; at another, to the therapeutic material. Thus, Lacey (1959) concludes: "The somatic process is not a suitable index of psychotherapy (as an outcome measure), but can be used to study psychotherapy as a process."

6. Some other Measures

This section will briefly discuss some other approaches to measuring change which may take place during counseling. The first is that of Q technique which involves the sorting of decks of cards (called Q-sorts); the correlations are computed among these responses of different individuals. The Q-sort usually consists of various descriptive statements which are empirically arrived at from positive and negative kinds of things clients say about themselves. In the influential studies by Rogers and Dymond (1954), clients showed increasing congruence between their ideal and real selves, as indicated by how they sorted self-descriptions about themselves over therapy.

Another measurement approach which may be fruitful in helping us more accurately assess counseling phenomena is the use of the semantic differential (SD), a method of observing and measuring the psychological meaning of things. Since counseling is concerned with attitudes, learning, and change, it seems the SD can be a potent measure of these. Certainly in studies concerned with communications in counseling (concepts, semantics, linguistics, meanings, etc.) the SD can be a sensitive and helpful measuring device.

Although we have discussed a few of the more commonly used approaches to measurement in counseling research, we feel the counselor-researcher should not feel constrained by tradition as he attempts to measure the criterion of his research. Reliability and validity are certainly important in the construction of measuring devices. Yet, the researcher should consider this area a wide open field and tackle the problems in imaginative sorts of ways. We feel that, in addition to the above, very promising avenues include direct and indirect observation schedules, structured and semi-structured interviews, checklists, participation flow charts, sociograms, analyses of open-ended questions and biographical statements and unobtrusive measures.

Finally, what seems to be needed in counseling research at this time, are measuring instruments which attempt to tap the strengths of charactero-logical attributes of clients, rather than their deficiencies or weaknesses. As Jahoda (1958) so forcefully puts it, "psychology (and counseling and therapy) traditionally has emphasized deviations, illness, and mal-functioning" rather than healthy functioning. Counselors, theoretically, pay heed to developmental theories rather than remediative ones; the same is fast becoming true of clinical psychology. Most instruments measure client pathologies rather than promises. Measuring devices which get at the strength of personality are sorely needed. The Personal Orientation Inventory by Shostrom (1963), which derives from human-istic conceptions of personality is one such instrument. Another is the Interview Relationship Inventory (Lorr and McNair, 1964), which shows promise in understanding the client and assessing therapy changes.

WHEN TO MEASURE?

Of course, the answer to this question depends entirely on the experi-mental design. Using the empirical case study (Thoresen, 1969a), the counselor research can obtain criterion measures over a period of time (e.g., pre therapy, several times during therapy, post therapy and various follow-up periods of time). More elaborate designs call for measuring at various other points of time. Typically, most counseling studies are of the pre-post variety and do not include a follow-up. This is unfortunate because of (1) many personality changes which do not show themselves unilaterally (that is, they may be curvilinear), and (2) the lack of stability of many changes induced during treatment. Ideally, counseling research studies should use repeated measures.

Repeated measures may have the disadvantage of sensitizing the sub-jects to the measure itself (Goldstein *et al.*, 1966). Some clients may learn certain things from a pretest which actually interacts with the treatment (i.e., counseling) itself. Reactivity may be handled by including a non-pretested, but treated, group of subjects. Another way of controlling for this phenomenon is to use measures which do not require the awareness of the subjects. These measures are naturally occurring events which can be obtained without the knowledge of the subject, and include such meas-ures as school grades, disciplinary offenses, job absenteeism, dates, etc.

In summary, then, several sequential points need to be made about measurement in counseling and therapy research. The phenomena to be measured are generated and dictated by the research proposal itself—

the theoretical rationale, the goals and objectives, the established criteria, and the logical expectations of the treatment itself. This must be established before the researcher selects or constructs the measuring device. Unfortunately, the devices and instruments which meet scientific requirements are rarely found ready-made. Particularly in the area of counseling research measurement there is great room for imagination, ingenuity, and creativity in developing instruments which more adequately tap the vague constructs found in the counseling theories and processes. The researcher should use the best measurements now available but should not feel bashful or apologetic about developing and building his own.

CHAPTER 8

Ethical, Legal, and Professional Considerations in Counseling Research

IMPORTANCE OF ETHICAL AND LEGAL RELATIONSHIPS

The practitioner engaged in counseling research in most instances is also likely to be either offering counseling services or be in the business of preparing counselors. Under these conditions, the interrelatedness of providing counseling as a practice and conducting counseling research is obvious. For this reason all of the concerns and problems in the area of ethical, legal, and professional relationships with counselees and the public associated with the conduct of counseling practices apply equally well to counseling research. Furthermore, it is difficult if actual clients are used, to conduct counseling research apart from a counseling center.

In any setting where human relationships are subject to change, either for research or service purposes, certain multiple obligations prevail. As Patterson (1959) points out, the counselor has responsibilities to the client, to the client's family, to his employer, to the referring source, to the profession, to society, and to himself. These obligations are compounded, yet just as basic when counseling research is superimposed or combined with the provision of counseling services.

The responsibility of professional groups in the counseling field to provide codes or guides for making ethical decisions is seen in action taken by the American Personnel and Guidance Association, the American Psychological Association, and the National Education Association. As one mark of a profession, these ethical codes have five major purposes, according to McGowan and Schmidt (1962):†

†McGowan, J. F. and Schmidt, L. D. *Counseling: Readings in theory and practice.* New York: Holt, Rinehart and Winston, 1962, 583–604. With permission.

1. Provides a position on standards of practice to assist each member of the profession in deciding what he should do when situations of conflict arise in his work.
2. Helps clarify the counselor's responsibilities to the client and protect the client from the counselor's violation of, or his failure to fulfill, these responsibilities.
3. Gives the profession some assurance that the practices of members will not be detrimental to its general functions and purposes.
4. Gives some guarantee that the services of the counselor will demonstrate a sensible regard for the social codes and moral expectations of the community in which he works.
5. Offers the counselor himself some grounds for safeguarding his own privacy and integrity.

This history of ethical, legal, and professional considerations in relation to counseling practice has a direct application to counseling research. Early in American history, society expressed its concern for the privacy of the individual through the Fourth Amendment to the Constitution. This same right is reflected in either laws or policies, and through codes which have developed as a result of public and professional interest in this matter. These types of concern can be classified as legal, ethical, or professional. In interpreting these areas Schmidt (1965) explains legal concerns over counseling (and hence counseling research) as what society expects from the counselor or limits him to in his work with clients. Similarly, he also defines ethical as related to what the counselor (or researcher) morally, philosophically, and otherwise expects from himself as a counselor or limits himself to in his work with clients. Finally, professional concerns, according to Schmidt (1965), are those that affect what one's colleagues expect from him as a counselor or limit him to in his work with clients.

With this backdrop, it can be seen that the conduct of counseling research, relating as it necessarily does to counseling practice, poses many practical and potential problems. Because of the extremely limited ethical or legal guidelines pertaining to research in counseling *per se*, the responsibility of the researcher for proper conduct of his own behavior is great. While codes of ethics are helpful, even essential, and legal decisions sometimes relevant, these do not serve adequately to solve individual problems. As Beck (1967) points out, quoting Titus, mature counselors, and by implication those engaged in research, must rely upon their own value judgments or a reflective morality in ethical matters. These judgments, in the absence of directly helpful training and experience, can only be based on an examination of relevant factors, an evaluation of the total situation, then a careful decision, supported by clear reasons for the decision.

The balance of this chapter will be devoted to two aspects of ethical and legal considerations for those engaged in counseling research. One aspect will briefly describe typical areas of counselor responsibility having ethical or legal implications. The other section will identify and illustrate various kinds of professional responsibilities having ethical and legal aspects of direct relevance to counseling research.

TYPICAL LEGAL AND ETHICAL CONCERNS FACING COUNSELORS AND THOSE IN COUNSELING RESEARCH

Legal Considerations

One of the difficulties faced by counselors in connection with establishing their legal status is the problem of role or professional recognition. The recency of the counselor on the educational scene has resulted in a few court cases as well as some ambiguity as to what counseling is. Other factors confusing the image of the counselor's function are lack of clarity among educators as to the nature of counseling, disagreement as to appropriate background preparation, and varying job functions of counselors. The current status of counseling, to say nothing of counseling research is without clear legal recognition in most states. To a degree, however, state certification and court decisions have given the psychologist a somewhat more favorable state of professional identity.

1. *Confidentiality and privileged communication* This status, not yet accorded to counselors generally, precludes a professional, under certain prescribed conditions, from being subject to arrest or prosecution for withholding information needed by the court in its determination of truth. Privileged communication, as used in the law of evidence, is a right of clients of professional persons to prevent the professional person from revealing communication of the client in legal proceedings.

2. *The counselor as expert witness* An expert witness, legally, is one qualified to give testimony requiring special skill, knowledge, training or experience. Counselors, by and large have not gained this status. On the other hand counselors may have some degree of legal protection in that generally they cannot be made to release confidential informa-

tion to the court. Since most of the information a counselor obtains is known as hearsay evidence—evidence that rests on the honesty of a person other than the witness—and thus is not admissable in a court of law, use of such facts can be more of an ethical than a legal problem.

3. *Libel and slander* Libel and slander are types of defamation, i.e., invasion of an individual's interest in his reputation and good name, causing others to shun him or to have unpleasant or derogatory feelings about him. Defamation in written or printed form is libel; in spoken form, slander. Counselors should be aware that in communicating knowledge about clients at times, the law sanctions dissemination of defamatory material in oral or written form if such statements are of social importance.

4. *Right of privacy* The right of privacy, the absence of undue interference in the affairs of an individual is a freedom, i.e., the right to be left alone, to be exempt from the inspection and scrutiny of others. The client's right of privacy may be impinged upon by either (1) a counselor's own revealing of confidences from counseling relationships or (2) a counselor's releasing confidential information at court request when a court decision is pending. Client privacy may also be at stake in the use of certain personality measures or in the forced disclosure of student personnel records (as opposed to a counselor's private notes).

5. *Malpractice* Malpractice generally is interpreted to include any professional misconduct or any unreasonable lack of skill or fidelity in the performance of professional or fiduciary duties (Schmidt, 1962). Counselors, by negligent acts might be held liable under two legal interpretations: criminal liability, being charged for failure to exercise certain responsibilities explicitly demanded by law; and civil liability, deriving from negligence in carrying out responsibilities.

6. *Criminal liability* Some psychologists are subject to criminal liability as in states where psychologists must be licensed, and one practices without such a license. Where no state certification laws exist, criminal liability can arise from engaging in activities belonging exclusively by law, to another profession.

Ethical Considerations

Ethical considerations are involved when situations develop which require decisions "in accordance with formal or professional rules of right or wrong" (Schmidt, 1965). Such rules are often, although not exclusively in the form of professional codes or standards. These codes, or systematized outlooks of professional groups are based on the experiences of members, and give sanction as well as obligation to the membership. Counselors and individuals engaged in counseling research are constantly facing challenges which call for a reexamination of professional goals, procedures, and professional actions in the light of their ethical obligations.

1. *Conflict in responsibilities* The multiple obligations of the counselor or researcher will frequently result in conflicts in responsibilities. While each section of a code of ethics may refer to a single or primary obligation, in actual research or counseling practice the professional person cannot ignore responsibilities to other individuals or groups. Unquestionably the counselor's values and his reasons for supporting them must be reexamined as he makes choices between two or more competing interests or demands.

2. *Confidentiality* The issue of confidentiality is one of the more complex concerns facing the counselor due to his obligations to the institution, to the client, and to the profession. Although no clear-cut ethical standards offer a final answer, several factors may affect the counselor's response to confidentiality in a specific situation. One point of view holds that the nature of the information imparted and the effect its revelation would have upon the client are the two most important elements. These criteria would seem to be even more significant when research data were being obtained, studied, and possibly published.

3. *Limits of competence* While referred to in the APGA Code of Ethical Standards (1961), this consideration may be a very subtle one in a counselor's own behavior pattern. Many factors, along with the counselor's professional and personal qualifications are at work here. Such elements as the time factor, the personal strain, the concern for sustained sensitivity and the need to continually be self-disclosing may be difficult to face. In counseling research one may have the added burden of pervasive doubts about the soundness of the design, client

mortality or lack of response, inadequate effectiveness measures and other external pressures.

4. *Referrals* Though not usually as important to those doing counseling research, the question of referral issues is persistent. Essentially, the concern is an ethical one of, at what point to refer, to whom, and under what circumstances. This issue may be complicated by other conditions such as lack of available resources, financial considerations, and lack of professional knowledge about the skills of resource agencies. Another inherent difficulty, intrinsic to the counseling process is the proper manner of involving the client in such a decision so that self-growth and confidence are not lost in the transition. In research, where referrals may not be anticipated, the effect on the project as well as on the counselor's continuing responsibility for the client are ethical matters.

5. *Use of taping equipment for recording interviews* While professional counselors seem to agree that counseling sessions should not be taped without the client's knowledge and permission, other concerns may arise. For example, if for some reason the material has research or training value, or the pending session may have potential use in in-service training programs, the counselor indeed has some ethical problems. The increasing use, based on micro-counseling research and the teaching value of videotapes, will tend to aggravate the pressures on counselors to use client material, recorded or confidential, for purposes other than counseling research *per se*.

PROFESSIONAL CONSIDERATIONS DIRECTLY RELATED TO ETHICAL AND LEGAL ASPECTS OF COUNSELING RESEARCH

The Institutional Setting

A number of potential problems, directly related to the institution or its policies as they affect counseling research work have ethical overtones. One area of basic conflict may be the institutional guidelines under which research is conducted. While many institutions have no released time policy for other than sponsored research a related ethical issue arises when the would be counseling researcher is employed primarily as a service person or practicing counselor. Similarly, the full-time college teacher faces a difficult decision in time management when contemplating the submission of research proposals or projects.

Other institutional policies may also bring about situations involving personal ethics. The problem of financing non-grant research may involve the proper use of graduate assistants, computing center services, or colleague time for professional advice. Even if research is conducted under outside funding arrangements or external sponsorship, frequent conflicts between university practice and government policy place the researcher in an awkward position. These difficulties usually center around such matters as use of personnel, property acquisition and accounting, time allocation, and budgeting freedom. On a larger scale the area of counseling research may not fit into the type of investigation firmly endorsed by some psychology departments, behavioral science programs, or student personnel administrators.

Within the locale of a department or teaching unit, the researcher often faces problems. Again, must he adapt his research to on-going programs, certain philosophical structures, or methodological designs, or does he have complete freedom to be creative and still get institutional backing? Many beginning instructors, seeking to be productive for professional advancement, are forced to "bootleg" or conduct research work surreptitiously until formal grants are obtained. In the designing of research projects, the director is faced with the question of source of subjects, i.e., should he use captive students from classes when funds are lacking, if this policy is discouraged by the department? A very subtle influence here is the attitude of departmental administrators who may frown on certain types of research efforts or program designs. Does the young researcher tend to jeopardize his professional status by conducting counseling research under these circumstances?

Client Relationships and Obligations

The broad area of subject involvement and responsibility poses many ethical concerns for the counseling researcher. While many of these are similar to ethical and legal considerations faced by practicing counselors, the research element often injects new considerations with serious professional and ethical implications.

In the selection and briefing of subjects to be used for research, the project director has certain obligations. The researcher's response to each of these concerns represents a difficult decision. Initially, the subjects should know about the nature of the study and the director's expectations of them as participants. They should also be aware of the circumstances, experimental conditions, and planned outcomes related to the study. Here, honesty in communicating with clients, in their language, the exact processes and types of experiences projected is essential. This is a particularly sensitive area because of the emotional meanings often attached to such expressions as "therapy," "diagnosis," "testing," "personality," and "sensitivity." Likewise, clients should be informed fully as to their prerogatives with respect to continued participation in the study.

In identifying and selecting subjects, other ethical issues arise in the matter of fees or monetary rewards, time expectations, freedom to vary response patterns, and anonymity. Additional problems may arise if clients are obtained from a captive source such as a class, and yet are expected to perform in an experiment in a "voluntary" manner. The question of client selection, where from a large voluntary sample one group is given counseling immediately while work with another group is deferred may be open to question. Some authorities, however, feel that this ethical issue is overemphasized simply because "treatment" has never been satisfactorily demonstrated. One underlying concern here is the basic criteria for client selection as related to subjects needed for the research. Can a researcher at one and the same time choose clients who profess needs (varying as they are), and in the same setting also meet the research conditions imposed by his study as to type of client, kind of problem, previous counseling experience, and similar factors?

Another area of client relationships involves agreements with subjects and post research activities of the researcher. For example, if agreements are made to subjects in return for their cooperation, what assurance can they be given of intention to fulfill this commitment? Likewise, credit and recognition may be due clients or contrariwise, complete anonymity demanded. A delicate question is the matter of withholding information or providing misinformation to subjects only when such action is essential to the investigation. Also, the director of the study should assume responsibility for corrective measures later to reconcile his client-counselor obligations. Though unlikely in most research there should be avoidance of injurious after-effects and recompense if such conditions should be clearly attributable to the research activity.

Counseling Research Activities and Outcomes

The conduct of counseling research brings about numerous occasions where ethical and professional judgments are difficult. In the initial stages of process research, certain conditions, if artificial or contrived, should be explicitly stated to all participants, unless justification for withholding these conditions is ethically sound. Such circumstances as quasi-counseling or conditional relationships should be clearly specified. The counseling researcher should recognize both in the research process and analysis the personal element. There is also the possibility of conflict in dyadic relationships between personal client growth goals and research design or procedural goals. This is especially a concern if a single therapist plays different roles in the research. Another process condition necessitating professional action based on ethical factors is the clear specification of client behaviors; often this is done in vague or ambiguous terms that defy interpretation for the subjects or the reviewers of the research. In regard to outcomes, here too the researcher should make explicit the criteria for judging behavior changes in clients.

With respect to the counselor's responsibilities, the research should describe in obvious terms the types, frequency and character of the counselor-client interactions. If multiple counselor contacts are expected, as part of the design or method, these should be detailed and their rationale presented, whether the same or different counselors are involved. One area calling for ethical responsibility is the task of identifying as explicitly as possible the qualifications, preparation, and viewpoint of those individuals in the experiment doing actual counseling. Every effort should be made through the use of models, training tapes, experienced judges, and rating schemes to characterize in as precise terms as possible the orientation of the "counselors."

In counseling research, the design, apparatus, and research conditions can easily affect the professional judgment of those supervising the research. Basically a question often arises as to the soundness or scientific character of the design: Will conformity to a predictable experimental design preclude imaginative research often vital in counseling studies? It should be recognized that tape and videotape equipment violate client privacy and the nature of the therapeutic relationship, and hence potentially research outcomes. When analogues or role playing are part of the experiment, is full recognition given to loss or distortion with this medium? Is the time control so gained, worth the actual client growth loss? Due to the pervasive nature of the counselor as one variable in counseling research every effort should be made to examine any undue influence the counselor's own personality and needs may have on the counseling process proper. Ethical concerns appear also in data analysis when inferences must be drawn from analogues, actors, or other artificial sources within the experiment.

The whole area of data analysis, reporting and use of results raises many professional problems of an ethical nature. One concern raised frequently is the question of use of research findings, tapes and interview exchanges for training purposes when this was not originally intended. Such a problem may bring into focus the broader issue of training goals vs. research goals for the individual or the department sponsoring research. The Code of Ethics of the American Personnel and Guidance Association sets forth several additional guidelines for reporting and publication of research findings:

3. In reporting research results, explicit mention must be made of all variables and conditions known to the investigator which might affect interpretation of the data.
4. The member is responsible for conducting and reporting his investigation so as to minimize the possibility that his findings will be misleading.
5. The member has an obligation to make available original research data to qualified others who may wish to replicate or verify the study.
6. In reporting research results or in making original data available, due care must be taken to disguise the identity of the subjects, in the absence of specific permission from such subjects to do otherwise.
7. In conducting and reporting research, the member should be familiar with, and give recognition to, previous work on the topic.
8. The member has the obligation to give due credit to those who have contributed significantly to his research, in accordance with their contributions.
9. The member has the obligation to honor commitments made to subjects of research in return for their cooperation.
10. The member is expected to communicate to other members the results of any research he judges to be of professional value.

Schwebel (1955) has cited three causes and has proposed three possible cures for unethical behavior in counselors. They are equally applicable to those engaged in counseling research. Schwebel's causes are: (a) self-interest of professional worker as expressed in personal profit, self-enhancement, and maintenance of security and status; (b) poor judgment, due in part at least to inexperience in problem solving counseling; and (c) ignorance of technical knowledge and one's own values. His cures, modified to apply to counseling research, might be stated as follows: (a) intensive personality research to screen out potentially unethical graduate students and professionals from research responsibilities, (b) more varied and independent supervision of those expecting to do counseling research, and (c) increasing academic requirements as well as self-awareness experiences for counseling researchers. A fourth and fifth cure could also be added: (d) make available and apply in training programs and job settings current guidelines for counseling (and research), and (e) adhere to codes and legal standards in counselor education research programs as implicit bases or models for future research workers.

CONCLUDING STATEMENT

This chapter has reviewed the importance of legal and ethical considerations in counseling research. It has also focused on (1) areas of counselor responsibility having ethical and legal implications and (2) professional considerations directly related to the ethical and legal aspects of counseling research.

As with the counselor, no single code of ethics or legal basis exists to provide direction for those engaged in counseling research. There are, and will continue to be, many sets of guidelines or even moralities by which man examines his behavior. The prime responsibility of the research worker is not only to investigate, but to understand, and when feasible, accept the most relevant guides as bases for his professional decision making. An inherent assumption underlying all counseling research is that those responsible for conducting research have a serious continuing obligation to be aware of and guided by the best available ethical codes and legal practices of the profession. They must also be aware of their own moral principles as related to on-going search for ultimate truth.

Persons engaged in research on counseling or therapy face a serious dilemma in ethical matters. Essentially the researcher has divided loyalties, or value areas involving the client, the helping agent, his employer, his colleagues, and society in general. While codes of ethics are available, their existence does not automatically give the researcher answers to the more personal questions he may face. He must in the final analysis resort to his own value structure as a recourse in each circumstance. This personal value structure, while it may reflect society's current standards, should also include a highly internalized system which draws upon the researcher's relationship with a Greater Being (Wrenn, 1952).

CHAPTER 9

The Future of Counseling and Therapy Research

This final chapter will examine several aspects of the future of research in counseling and therapy. Two broad categories will be used, unanswered questions and recommended changes in counseling research. Unanswered questions relate to the nature of human interaction, research designs and procedures, and evaluation of research. Needed improvements in counseling research include theoretical origins, programming for research, and features of research designs and methods. The chapter will conclude with a brief view of promising areas of counseling research.

UNANSWERED QUESTIONS

Nature of Human Interaction

One area in which many questions are without answers pertains to the components of the counseling process or more literally, the nature of human interaction. Fundamental to this issue is the need to demonstrate that there is such a thing as therapy (or counseling) as a basis for research; so far, this is an unconfirmed assumption. Several other equally challenging questions relate to the dynamics of the interaction process. For example, is the process so complex that "problems" or the identification of desired behavior change are impossible to reduce to researchable elements? Likewise, is it feasible to assume that a helping person can completely adopt the theoretical position, including assumptions, goals, and methodology of Ellis, or Rogers, or Wolpe? Similarly, if such an introjection is possible, is the facilitating person still genuine?

In examining the components into which interpersonal relationships can be divided, what combinations appear most appropriate? Choices range from Bierman's (1968) two orthogonal dimensions of active expressiveness vs. passive restrictedness and acceptance vs. rejection to the seven factors found in the Carkhuff–Truax (Truax and Carkhuff, 1967) scales. Allen and Whiteley (1968) have proposed the parallel elements of cognitive flexibility and psychological openness. In a similar vein Hobbs (1962) raises the question of the actual sequential relationship between self-understanding and affective behavior as phases of growth.

The counseling process, to be the subject of research, needs operational definition as to goals, or outcomes, and assessment of growth toward goals, including the use of criterion instruments which will measure the counselee's extra-clinical behavior. In addition, the helping process or treatment used must be conceptually known and operationally described, as it contributes to the defined goals. The criterion problem remains unsolved. It may hinge on a combination of goals, behavioral objectives for overt actions, and proximate criteria which examine therapeutic conditions associated with verbal insight or client identity.

There are other therapeutic issues stemming from past research which impinge upon future conseling research efforts. One basic question which remains unclear in answer is the extent to which counseling and psychotherapy produce any positive values not more easily accomplished by other more economical and efficient methods of human assistance. As Bergin (1967) indicates, if spontaneous remission is confirmed by research, what then is the status of professional therapy? An accompanying question relates to the types of therapist characteristics which are most productive of client self-exploration and ultimate change. A corollary issue is whether a global self-enhancing outcome, if attained, will observably "free" a client to change his overt behavior. Unknown at the moment is the significance of such factors as counselor personality traits, counselor-client similarity, and counselor experience level on process and outcome of helping. Similarly, what is the role of variable client characteristics on the results of therapy? Finally, little is known about the comparative effectiveness of various "approaches," particularly some of the behavior therapies.

Research Design and Procedures

Questions requiring answers in research design and methodology are numerous. One area in which doubts persist is whether the basis for diagnostic schemes, either theoretical or practical, should be process data or the therapeutic experience itself. Again, the exact connection between diagnostic classifications and therapeutic gains has no clearcut answer. In a broader context, the extent to which modification of symptomatic concerns in research efforts really results in a basic change in beliefs or attitudes is yet to be resolved.

Relating theories to research studies, the specific interrelationship between theoretical approaches followed, process actions, and client outcomes is far from clear. Basic to this issue is the assumption held by some and rejected by others that a single comprehensive theoretical basis for counseling research on process is possible. Some authorities question whether broad theories make adequate use of empirical data in research. A concomitant problem involving both theory and research design entails a study of ways to differentiate counselor from techniques or methodology, if possible.

In more practical terms, control of variables in counseling research remains elusive. Essentially the question is what manipulations lead to what changes? Similarly, how can one ascertain when an independent variable is really independent? In the dependent variable category one must ask how single and multiple dependent variables can be more closely related to molecular and molar constructs. Other specific problems of continuing difficulty are establishing internal and external validity and clarifying the function of control (no treatment groups).

The question of identifying and specifying outcomes remains one of the most difficult aspects of counseling research. Essentially what is lacking is a rationale for the relationship between counseling process objectives and outcome measures in specific research situations. Outcomes are often assessed inadequately through irrelevant means. Such factors as temporal changes, classification schemes for process outcomes, and multiple criteria for actual client behavior are rarely taken into account. Variations in style of counselor approaches as independent variables seem to be relatively unrelated to multiple measures on a variety of dependent variables. Basically little agreement exists on what outcomes to measure and how to measure them.

The lack of a disciplined research tradition in counseling investigations is both an asset and a liability. The complexity of counseling research, the blurring of traditional paradigm concepts as indicated by Kuhn (1962), and the need to relate them to the hows and whys of dyadic behavior change constitute persistent challenges to those seeking elegant and sophisticated research designs. Innovations are certainly in order as answers to questions are sought. An important issue, for example, is how to develop integrated or synthesized research that relates specific findings to the whole or to unified theory. Specifically, can the assumption "all other things being equal" be met so that the interaction issue can be dealt with in a clear manner? Until multidimensional theory based studies using multiple criteria are developed numerous questions will remain unanswered.

Evaluation of Research

The critical review of research investigation is often difficult because of the deficiencies in information describing the assumptions, procedures, and results of counseling research. The principle of symmetry, as enunciated by Goldstein *et al.* (1966) is important. They stress the need to apply the same standards of relevance to both sides of a research question. For example, methodological flaws which disqualify research results on one side of an issue also disqualify research on the other side. In reporting the analysis of data statistically, frequently too few tests are completed (or all reported) and conversely *post hoc* explanations are employed to justify main findings. Data reported also may be in terms of group trends, ignoring the regression phenomenon; with small groups individual case data may be more significant, especially if change on one variable can be directly related to an independent predictor of change.

Other aspects of counseling research difficult to evaluate involve verification of findings, i.e., when the same results are produced again. Similarly, few hypotheses are verified by new lines of supporting evidence. Hypotheses are verified only to the extent that methodological independence exists between observations leading to the formation of the hypotheses and observations leading to the verification of the hypotheses. Rigorous research, assumed to include appropriate design, suitable measurement, and execution of treatment procedures, is not easily discernable among counseling investigations. Questions not answered for evaluators include adequate description of conditions, justification of instrumentation, and explanation of rationale for process-goal relationships.

In the available outcome research, as Wellman (1967a) has reported, numerous questions remain unanswered. The nature of the counseling intervention is often vaguely or poorly described. Client populations, too, are not given adequate description in terms of variability, since homogeneity cannot be assumed. Generally speaking, the manageable criteria for outcome research are less than thoroughly justified, described, and followed. Unfortunately, few evidences of adherence to an adequate research paradigm in the framework of existing theory are found. Instead of the emphasis being upon imaginative or creative approaches the stress is more traditional; on design, instrumentation, controls, sampling, and data analysis.

RECOMMENDED CHANGES IN COUNSELING RESEARCH

Theoretical Origins

The conceptual bases for behavior research in the counseling area have been undergoing close scrutiny in recent years. One change that is evident is the emphasis on studying whole theories with respect to part-whole relationships. As Sanford (1965) points out, this attempt must continue even though the neatness of laboratory designs may be lacking in field settings. The underlying assumptions of research in psychology do not include a unifying paradigm but rather a series of prescriptions (antithetical pairs of assumptions) or complementarities. This notion, stressed by both Dreikurs (1966) and Watson (1967), carries the implication that all researchers must state their biases or assumptions regarding the aspects of behavior being investigated. Hopefully, in this manner counseling studies will be based upon a broader concept of research, moving away from reductionistic assumptions to holistic notions which for each investigation identify the prescriptions that affect the selection, formulation, and methodology of problem solving.

Another change proposed for theoretical bases of counseling research is a broader idea of the nature of research and its accompanying implementation. The scientific research in the behavioral sciences of the future according to Polanyi (1968) must include value judgments about the total human being not merely objective data. In no other way can researchers get an authentic image, an interpretation, and complete knowledge of living beings and of the universe in which they exist. Murphy (1969) in forecasting the nature of research in the year 2000 mentions a greater concern with man's inner experiences or unconscious world. Such investigations may take the form of studies of encounter groups, parapsychology, and the examination of free human situations in the community. In this process the term "experimental" may well be replaced by new language descriptive of a broader yet more systematic perception of the human animal in his ecological setting.

Programming for Research

An overview of projected changes in the programming of future counseling research reveals numerous innovations. As a basis for the theoretical structuring of research efforts Thoresen (1969c) suggests a fresh perspective and a clear departure from not only previous personal convictions but from dogmatic traditional models and procedures. Future research, as disciplined inquiry, will not only have a firmer theoretical base but will draw upon a new concept of research having a broader linkage with the behavioral sciences. In addition greater use will be made of the systems approach, the use of computer techniques, and of operational definitions at all points. A more imaginative posture will be taken in not only seeking meaningful questions to answer, but in being creative in planning research efforts which will produce valid methods of obtaining answers.

Taking a broad look at future counseling research models one finds several features not now evident in research structures. The concept of multivariate comparative studies, where two or more treatment variables are examined in relation to a variety of criterion measures, is also suggested by Thoresen (1969c). Greater use will be made of the case study using live clients, in field settings with the focus on observable changes, over time, studied as to frequency and magnitude. These developments may well be incorporated into experimental-longitudinal designs having both cross-sectional and time sequence features.

The "systems perspective," where input, processes, and output are not only carefully identified and controlled but are examined in observable performance terms, will prevail. The overriding plan could be one of interdependent elements, both theoretical and practical, and could provide for closely synthesizing and analyzing alternate ways of attaining clearly stated objectives. The primary research goal according to Thoresen (1969c) will be to identify all relevant factors and variables as well as their interaction, hoping to answer the question: What treatment, by whom, is most effective for this individual with that specific problem?

Characteristics of Research Design and Methodologies

Several features of specific designs for future counseling research endeavors have been proposed by Whiteley (1968). The salient characteristic of future designs could be described as a conceptually sound simultaneous consideration of client traits, counseling approaches, and outcome measures. The purpose of such complex structures would be to provide a kind of taxonomy of counselor strategies as a basis for an experience table for future selection and implementation of treatment approaches. In process research of this type careful coding systems would classify counselor actions, both verbal and nonverbal, and record the frequency, duration, and session length for study purposes. By careful use of concepts and operational terms, possibly even a new data language, the present loose (often mystical) vocabulary of counseling research could be avoided. Another modification would include tighter, more precise data on performance of subjects and definitions of what constitutes practical and meaningful change. Further refinements in future research designs may also include greater use of miniature therapy or analogues for therapy, and microcounseling procedures as a testing ground for specific research propositions.

The improvement of outcome research is also in prospect if Whiteley's (1968) recommendations are followed. In the future, greater attention should be paid to within-group differences, i.e., an analysis of individual characteristics as opposed to the traditional experimental-control design. This effort could well include, as a simultaneous consideration, the psychological characteristics of the client, relevant demographic data, and a classification of the presenting problem as seen by the client himself.

Research on the assessment of counseling outcomes also needs strengthening, according to many authorities. One of the important changes hoped for, according to Whiteley (1968), is a more effective way to relate in a systematic way, the measurable and definable goals of the behavioral counselor to the self-enhancement objectives of the preceptually oriented counselor. Future counseling outcome research, according to Krumboltz (1968) should: (1) be designed to discover improved ways of helping clients, (2) be designed so that different outcomes can be related to different counseling practices, and (3) be designed around outcome criteria tailored to what the client and counselor regard as desirable behavior changes.

In counseling process research the optimal experiment of the future may have certain features. A sample of expert therapists will be identified and described. The counselor-therapist may well select his own clients for research purposes. He will also set and specify the treatment conditions, as well as carefully describe the methods used and the results intended. This precise description of the nature of the counseling intervention is crucial. Results of the research might be reviewed in typescript, tape, or videotape form by an independent panel which could describe the outcomes or evidence of therapeutic gain for each client. The significant quality of future counseling process research would appear to be the extent to which adequate use is made of explicit operational definitions in clear performance terms. As Chenault (1969) has pointed out, there are multiple meanings of "help," as a goal, as a process, and as a consequence. Without the researcher's definition of "help" clearly established, any particular investigation is hardly meaningful to the consumer.

PROMISING AREAS OF COUNSELING RESEARCH

As counseling research is reviewed and future possibilities are examined, several aspects of human interaction in the community offer special appeal. This appeal stems partially from what research has accomplished in these areas, but also from kinds of investigation that are needed to further the impact of the helping person on our society.

One type of investigation that may prove valuable is that dealing with a study of both global and microcosmic characteristics of apparently successful helping persons and their interpersonal relationships. Such research might lead to the proposal of models and training programs to apply varying features of successful helpers to new counselors, clients, and situations.

Another area of process research which needs further exploration is a closer examination through multi-media devices and equipment of the elements of helping relationships which seemingly are characteristic of various levels of human interaction. Specifically, data might be obtained particularly with videotape approaches on a variety of counseling relationships. This material could then be analyzed by judges or panels using predetermined criteria to look at such elements as skills employed, affective atmosphere, movement, cognitive-affective balance, attending behavior, response patterns, and other factors.

A third type of study which the future may bring is some form of investigation which combines the microcosmic or action consequences of behavioral counseling with the self-concept, personal identity goals of a humanistic, therapeutic emphasis. These are not necessarily mutually exclusive and should be examined together, recognizing varying application with counselors, clients, and settings.

The area of exploration involving particular experiences for different consumer groups receiving counseling demands new research attention. Studies are needed to examine differential emphases and procedures with various social groups and educational levels. Current research has indicated new findings as to client needs but greater examination of operational modifications is required. Society's increasing concern for help with the culturally atypical person should give impetus to such investigations. One rich resource for such research are the many available examples of ineffective help with some islands of success.

As counseling is reperceived as a spirit of "community," in a literal sense, the individual's own social or geographical community can have a greater responsibility for effecting this personal growth. Future research could well focus on the growth-producing potential and output of the community self-help center. This center could be studied as a sociological instrument through such functions as group awareness experiences, and self-initiated use of programmed learning resources.

Finally, a frontier of counseling research exists in the area of syntheses of computer resources and human interaction procedures. While the potential of computerized guidance systems is yet unknown, the concept of freeing the counseling person for maximum interpersonal helping is accepted. Innovative research efforts which examine the interrelationships, the balance, and the relative effect of these two complementary approaches is an exciting prospect. Solid research is needed to determine how the counseling person can fuse or integrate his strengths with other client-developed external resources.

References

Adinolfi, A. Relevance of person perception research to clinical psychology. *Journal of Consulting and Clinical Psychology*, 1971, **37**, 167–176.

Allen, T. W. and Whiteley, J. F. *Dimensions of effective counseling*. Columbus, Ohio: Charles E. Merrill, 1968.

Allport, G. W. *Personality and social encounter: Selected essays*. Boston: Beacon Press, 1960.

Allport, G. W. *Becoming: Basic considerations for a psychology of personality*. New Haven: Yale University Press, 1955.

American Psychological Association. *Ethical standards of psychologists*. Washington, D.C.: *Journal*, 1961, **40**, 206–209.

American Personnel and Guidance Association. *Ethical standards casebook*. Washington, D.C.: American Personnel and Guidance Association, July 1965.

American Psychological Association. *Ethical standards of psychologists*. Washington, D.C.: American Psychological Association, 1961.

Anderson, R. P. Physiological and verbal behavior during client-centered counseling. *Journal of Counseling Psychology*, 1956, **3**, 174–184.

Anderson, R. P. and Anderson, G. V. Development of an instrument for measuring rapport. *Personnel and Guidance Journal*, 1962, **41**, 18–24.

Arbuckle, D. *Counseling and psychotherapy: An overview*. New York: McGraw-Hill, 1967.

Arbuckle, D. S. and Wicas, E. S. The development of an instrument for the measurement of counseling perceptions. *Journal of Counseling Psychology*, 1957, **4**, 304–312.

Astin, A. W. Criterion-centered research. *Educational and Psychological Measurement*, 1964, **24**, 807–821.

Auld, F., Jr. and Murray, E. J. Content-analysis studies of psychotherapy. *Psychological Bulletin*, 1955, **52**, 377–395.

Bakan, D. *David Bakan on method*. San Francisco: Jossey-Bass, 1967.

Bales, R. F. *Interaction process analysis*. Cambridge: Addison-Wesley Press, 1950.

Barclay, J. *Counseling and philosophy: A theoretical exposition*. New York: Houghton Mifflin, 1968.

Barrett-Lennard, G. T. Dimensions of therapist response as causal factors in therapeutic change. *Psychological Monographs*, 1962, **76**, (43), (Whole No. 562).

Beck, Carlton E. Ethical aspects of change in counselor education. *Counselor Education and Supervision*, 1967, **6**, 216–221.

Bergin, A. E. An empirical analysis of therapeutic issues. In D. S. Arbuckle, *Counseling and psychotherapy: An overview*. New York: McGraw-Hill, 1967.

Bierman, R. Dimensions of interpersonal facilitation in psycho-therapy and child development. *Psychological Bulletin*, 1969, Vol. **72**, No. 5.

Blocher, D. *Developmental counseling*. New York: Ronald Press, 1966.

Blocher, D. Developmental counseling: A rationale for counseling in the elementary school. *Elementary School Guidance and Counseling*, 1968, **12**, (3), 163–172. a

Blocher, D. What counseling can offer clients: Implications for research on selection. In J. Whiteley (Ed.), *Research in counseling*. Columbus, Ohio: Charles E. Merrill, 1968, 5–20. b

Bordin, E. S. Diagnosis in counseling and psychotherapy. *Educational and Psychological Measurement*, 1946, **6**, 169–184.

Breger, L. and McGaugh, J. L. Critique and reformulation of learning theory approaches to psychotherapy and neuroses. *Psychological Bulletin*, 1965, **63**, 338–358.

Burck, H. D. The counseling revolution: Promises and problems. *Guidance Journal*, 1968, **6**, 389–400.

Byrne, R. H. Proposed revision of the Bordin-Pepinsky diagnostic constructs. *Journal of Counseling Psychology*, 1958, **5**, 184–187.

Byrne, R. H. *The school counselor*. New York: Houghton Mifflin, 1963.

Callis, R. Diagnostic classification as a research tool. *Journal of Counseling Psychology*, 1965, **12**, 238–243.

Campbell, D. Factors relevant to the validity of experiments in social settings. *Psychology Bulletin*, 1954, **57**, 297–312.

Campbell, D. and Stanley, J. *Experimental and quasi-experimental designs for research*. Chicago: Rand McNally & Co., 1963.

Campbell, R. and Kagan, N. The affective sensitivity scale. Unpublished, 1956.

Carkhuff, R. B. Counseling research. *Journal of Counseling Psychology*, 1966, **13**, (4), 467–472.

Carkhuff, R. and Berenson, B. G. *Beyond counseling and therapy*. New York: Holt, Rinehart and Winston, 1967.

Carter, T. M. Professional immunity for guidance counselors. *Personnel and Guidance Journal*, 1954, **33**, 130–135.

Cartwright, Rosalind Dymond. Psychotherapeutic processes. *Annual Review of Psychology*, 1968, 387–416.

Cartwright, R. D. and Lerner, B. Empathy, need to change, and improvement with psychotherapy. *Journal of Consulting Psychology*, 1963, **27**, 138–144.

Chassan, J. *Research design in clinical psychology and psychiatry*. New York: Appleton-Century-Crofts, 1967.

Chenault, Joann. Help giving and morality. *Personnel and Guidance Journal*, 1969, **48**, 89–96.

Client-centered therapy. In T. W. Allen (Ed.), *The Counseling Psychologist*, 1969, Vol. 1, No. 2.

Coan, R. W. Dimensions of psychological theory. *American Psychologist*, 1968, **23**, 715–722.

Cochran, W., Mosteller, F., and Tukey, J. Principles of sampling. *Journal of the American Statistical Association*, 1954, **49**, 13–35.

Colby, K. M. Psychotherapeutic processes. *Annual Review of Psychology*, 1964, **15**, 347–370.

Cottle, W. C. Personality characteristics of counselors: II. *Journal of Counseling Psychology*, 1954, **1**, 27–30.

Coulson, W. E. and Rogers, C. R. *Man and the science of man*. Columbus, Ohio: Charles E. Merrill, 1968.

Crowne, D. P. and Stephens, M. W. Self-acceptance and self-evaluative behavior, A critique of methodology. *Psychological Bulletin*, 1961, **58**, 104–121.

Daubner, E. V. and Daubner, E. S. Ethics and counseling decisions. *Personnel and Guidance Journal*, 1970, **43**, 433–442.

Davidson, P. O. and Costello, D. G. (Eds.) *N = 1 Experimental studies of single cases*. New York: Van Nostrand Reinhold, 1969.

Dimascio, A., Boyd, D. W., Greenblatt, M., and Solomon, H. C. The psychiatric interview: A sociophysiologic study. *Diseases of the Nervous System*, 1955, **16**, 2–7.

Dollard, J. and Auld, F., Jr. *Scoring human motives: A manual*. New Haven: Yale University Press, 1959.

Dollard, J. and Mowrer, O. H. A method of measuring tension in written documents. *Journal of Abnormal and Social Psychology*, 1947, **42**, 3–32.

Dreikurs, R. The scientific revolution. *The Humanist*, January–February 1966, **28**, 8–13.

Ebel, R. L. Some limitations of basic research in education. *Phi Delta Kappan*, 1967, **48**, 81–84.

Edwards, A. and Cronbach, L. Experimental design for research in psychotherapy. *Journal of Clinical Psychology*, 1952, **8**, 51–59.

English, H. B. and English, Ava C. *A comprehensive dictionary of psychological and psychiatric terms*. New York: McKay, 1958.

Farnsworth, K. E. Application of scaling techniques to the evaluation of counseling outcomes. *Psychological Bulletin*, 1966, **66**, 81–93.

Fiedler, F. The concept of an ideal therapeutic relationship. *Journal of Consulting Psychology*, 1950, **14**, 235–245.

Fiske, D., Hunt, H., Luborsky, L., Orne, M., Parloff, M., Reiser, M., and Tuma, A. Planning of research on effectiveness of psychotherapy. *American Psychologist*, 1970, **25**, 727–737.

Flanders, N. A. Some relationships among teacher influence, pupil attitudes, and achievement. In B. J. Bidde and W. P. Ellena (Eds), *Contemporary research on teacher effectiveness*. New York: Holt, Rinehart and Winston, 1964, 196–231.

Ford, D. H. and Urban, H. B. Psychotherapy. *Annual Review of Psychology*, 1967, **18**, 333–372.

Frank, J. Problems of controls in psychotherapy as exemplified by the psychotherapy research project of the Phipps Psychiatric Clinic. In E. A. Rubenstein and M. B. Parloff (Eds.), *Research in psychotherapy*, Vol. I. Washington, D.C.: American Psychological Association, 1962, 10–26.

Froehlich, C. P. Bedrock for vocational guidance. *Journal of Counseling Psychology*, 1955, **2**, 170–171.

Garrett, H. *Statistics in psychology and education*, 5th Edition. New York: David McKay Co., Inc., 1958.

Gauerke, W. E. *Legal and ethical responsibilities of school personnel.* Englewood Cliffs, N. J.: Prentice-Hall, 1959.

Gazda, G. *Theories and methods of group psychotherapy and counseling.* Springfield, Illinois: Charles C Thomas, 1966.

Gelfand, Donna and Hartman, D. Behavior therapy with children: A review and evaluation of research methodology. *Psychology Bulletin,* 1968, **69**, 204–215.

Gendlin, E. and Rychlak, J. Psychotherapeutic processes. *Annual Review of Psychology,* 1970, **21**, 155–190.

Gilbreath, S. H. Group counseling with male underachieving college volunteers. *Personnel and Guidance Journal,* 1967, **45**, 469–476.

Goldman, L. Privilege or Privacy: I. *Personnel and Guidance Journal,* 1969, **48**, 88.

Goldstein, A. P. *Psychotherapeutic attraction.* New York: Pergamon Press, Inc., 1971.

Goldstein, A. P., Heller, K., and Sechrest, L. B. *Psychotherapy and the psychology of behavior change.* New York: John Wiley & Sons, Inc., 1966.

Gonyea, G. G. Appropriateness-of-vocational-choice as a criterion of counseling outcome. *Journal of Counseling Psychology,* 1962, **9**, 213–220.

Gottschalk, L. A., Gleser, G., and Hambidge, G., Jr. Verbal behavior analysis. *Archives of Neurology and Psychiatry,* 1957, **77**, 300–311.

Guerney, B. and Stollak, Gay. Problems in living, psychotherapy process research, and an autoanalytic method. *Journal of Counseling Psychology,* 1965, **29**, 581–595.

Guilford, J. *Fundamental statistics in psychology and education,* 4th Edition. New York: McGraw-Hill Book Co., 1965.

Harrison, R. I. Problems in the design and interpretation of research on human relations training, explorations in applied behavioral science, 1967. Washington, D.C.: NTL Institute for Applied Behavioral Science, 1967.

Hobbs, N. Sources of gain in psychotherapy. *American Psychologist,* 1962, **17**, (11), 741–747.

Hopke, W. E. The measurement of counselor attitudes. *Journal of Counseling Psychology,* 1955, **2**, 212–216.

Howe, E. S. and Pope, B. An empirical scale of therapist-verbal activity level in the initial interview. *Journal of Consulting Psychology,* 1961, **25**, 510–520.

Hunt, J. Toward an integrated program of research in psychotherapy. *Journal of Consulting Psychology,* 1952, **16**, 237–246.

Jaffe, J. Dyadic analysis of two psychotherapeutic interviews. In L. A. Gottschalk (Ed.) *Comparative psycholinguistic analysis of two psychotherapeutic interviews.* New York: International Universities Press, 1961, Chapter 5.

Jahoda, M. *Current concepts of positive mental health.* New York: Basic Books, 1958.

Jensen, B. T., Coles, G., and Nestor, Beatrice. The criterion problem in guidance research. *Journal of Counseling Psychology,* 1955, **2**, 58–61.

Kaczkowski, H. R. and Rothney, J. W. M. Discriminant analysis in evaluation of counseling. *Personnel and Guidance Journal,* 1956, **35**, 231–235.

Kagan, N., Krathwohl, D. R., Goldberg, A. D., Schauble, P. G., Greenberg, B. S., Danish, S. J., Resnikoff, A., Bowes, J., and Bondy, S. B. *Studies in human interaction: Interpersonal process recall stimulated by videotape.* East Lansing, Michigan: Educational Publication Services, College of Education, Michigan State University, RR-20, December 1967.

Kaplan, A. *The conduct of inquiry: Methodology for behavioral science.* San Francisco: Chandler Publishing Co., 1964.

Kerlinger, F. N. *Foundations of behavioral research: Educational and psychological inquiry*. New York: Holt, Rinehart and Winston, 1964.

Kerlinger, F. Research in education. In R. Ebel (Ed.), *Encyclopedia of educational research*, 4th Edition, 1969, 1127–1144.

Kiesler, D. J. Some myths of psychotherapy research and the search for a paradigm. *Psychological Bulletin*, 1966, **65**, 110–136.

Kiesler, D. J. Basic methodologic issues implicit in psychotherapy process research. *American Journal of Psychotherapy*, 1967, **10**, 135–155.

Killian, J. D. The law, the counselor, and student records. *Personnel and Guidance Journal*, 1970, **48**, 423–432.

Klee, G. D. Research in psychotherapy: A backward leap into the future. *American Journal of Psychotherapy*, 1968, **22**, (4), 674–683.

Koch, S. Psychological science versus the science-humanism antinomy. *American Psychologist*, 1959, **15**, 629–639.

Krumboltz, J. Parable of the good counselor. *Personnel and Guidance Journal*, 1964, **43**, 118–124.

Krumboltz, J. D. Behavioral goals for counseling. *Journal of Counseling Psychology*, 1966, **13**, (2), 153–159.

Krumboltz, J. Future directions for counseling research. In J. Whiteley (Ed.), *Research in counseling: Evaluation and refocus*. Columbus, Ohio: Charles E. Merrill, 1968, 184–203.

Kuhn, T. S. *Structure of scientific revolution*. Chicago: University of Chicago Press, 1962.

Lacey, J. I. Psychophysiological approaches to the evaluation of psychotherapeutic process and outcome. In E. A. Rubenstein and M. B. Parloff, (Eds.), *Research in psychotherapy*. Washington, D.C: American Psychological Association, National Publishing Co., 1959, 160–208.

Lackenmeyer, C. W. Experimentation – A misunderstood methodology in psychological and social-psychological research. *American Psychologist*, July 1970, **25**, (7), 617–624.

Lennard, H. and Bernstein, A. Dilemma in mental health evaluation. *American Psychologist*, 1971, **26**, 307–310.

Levitt, E. E. Problems of experimental design and methodology in psychopharmacology research. In *Report of the conference on mental health research, French Lick, Indiana*. Indianapolis, Ind.: The Association for the Advancement of Mental Health Research and Education, 1959.

Lister, J. The eclectic counselor: An explorer. *School Counselor*, 1967, **14**, 287–293.

Lorr, M. and McNair, D. M. The interview relationship in therapy. *Journal of Nervous Mental Disorders*, 1964, **139**, 328–331.

Louisell, D. W. The psychologist in today's legal world; Part II: Confidential communication. *Minnesota Law Review*, 1957, **41**, 731–750.

Magoon, T. The assessment of counseling outcomes (Wellman): Discussion. In John M. Whiteley (Ed.), *Research in counseling: Evaluation and refocus*. Columbus, Ohio: Charles E. Merrill, 1968.

Mahl, G. F. Exploring emotional states by content analysis. In I. Pool (Ed.), *Trends in content analysis*. Urbana: University of Illinois Press, 1959, Chapter 3.

Marsden, G. Content analysis studies of therapeutic interviews: 1954–1964. *Psychological Bulletin*, 1965, **63**, 298–321.

Matarazzo, J. D., Saslow, G., and Matarazzo, R. G. The interaction chronograph as an instrument for objective measurement of interaction patterns during interview. *Journal of Psychology*, 1956, **41**, 347–367.

McGowan, J. F. and Schmidt, L. D. Ethical and legal considerations. In J. F. McGowan and L. D. Schmidt (Eds.), *Counseling: Readings in theory and practice*. New York: Holt, Rinehart and Winston, 1962, 583–590.

McNair, D. M. and Lorr, M. An analysis of professed psychotherapeutic techniques. *Journal of Consulting Psychology*, 1964, **28**, 265–271.

Meltzoff, J. and Kornreich, M. *Research in psychotherapy*. New York: Atherton Press, 1970.

Murphy, G. Psychology in the year 2000. *American Psychologist*, 1969, **24**, 523–530.

Murray, E. J. A content-analysis method for studying psychotherapy. *Psychological Monographs*, 1956, **70**, (13), (Whole No. 420).

Myers, R. A. Research in counseling psychology. *Journal of Counseling Psychology*, 1966, **13**, (3), 371–377.

O'Dea, J. D. and Zeran, F. R. Effects of counseling. *Personnel and Guidance Journal*, 1953, **31**, 241–244.

O'Hern, J. S. and Arbuckle, D. S. Sensitivity: A measurable concept? *Personnel and Guidance Journal*, 1964, **42**, 572–576.

Orne, M. On the social psychology of the psychological experiment. *American Psychologist*, 1962, **17**, 776–783.

Panek, D. M. and Martin, B. The relationships between GSR and speech disturbances in psychotherapy. *Journal of Abnormal and Social Psychology*, 1959, **58**, 402–405.

Patterson, C. H. *Counseling and psychotherapy: Theory and practice*. New York: Harper and Row, 1959.

Patterson, C. H. Control, conditioning and counseling. *Personnel and Guidance Journal*, April 1963, **41**, (8).

Patterson, C. H. Counseling. *Annual Review of Psychology*, 1966, **17**, 79–110. a

Patterson, C. H. *Theories of counseling and psychotherapy*. New York: Harper & Row, 1966. b

Patterson, C. H. The selection of counselors. In J. M. Whiteley (Ed.), *Research in counseling: Evaluation and refocus*. Columbus, Ohio: Merrill Publishing Co., 1968.

Paul, G. *Insight versus densitization in psychotherapy: An experiment in anxiety reduction*. Stanford, California: Stanford University Press, 1966.

Paul, G. Strategy of outcome research in psychotherapy *Journal of Consulting Psychology*, 1967, **31**, 109–118.

Pepinsky, H. The selection and use of diagnostic categories in clinical counseling. *Applied Psychology Monographs*, 1948, No. 15.

Perspectives of curriculum evaluation (Tyler, Gagne, and Scriven), *AERA Monograph Series on Curriculum Evaluation*. Chicago: Rand McNally & Co., 1967.

Pittenger, R. E. Linguistic analysis of tone in voice in communication of affect. *Psychiatric Research Reports*, 1958, **8**, 41–54.

Plutchik, R. *Foundations of experimental research*. New York: Harper & Row, 1968.

Polanyi, M. The body-mind relation. In W. R. Coulson and C. R. Rogers, *Man and the science of man*. Columbus, Ohio: Charles E. Merrill, 1968, Chapter 5, 84–130.

Porter, E. H., Jr. *An introduction to therapeutic counseling*. Boston: Houghton Mifflin Co., 1950.

Raimy, V. (Ed.) *Training in clinical psychology*. Englewood Cliffs, N.J.: Prentice-Hall, 1950.

Rank, R. C. Counseling competence and perceptions. *Personnel and Guidance Journal*, 1966, **45**, 359–365.

Robinson, F. P. Modern approaches to counseling diagnosis. *Journal of Counseling Psychology*, 1963, **10**, (4), 325–333.

Rogers, C. R. Persons or sciences? A philosophical question. *American Psychologist*, 1955, **10**, 267–278.

Rogers, C. R. A tentative scale for the measurement of process in psychotherapy. In E. A. Rubenstein and M. B. Parloff (Eds.), *Research in psychotherapy*, Vol. 1. Washington, D.C.: American Psychological Association, 1959, 96–107.

Rogers, C. R. Psychotherapy today: Or where do we go from here? *American Journal of Psychotherapy*, 1963, **17**, 5–16.

Rogers, C. and Dymond, R. F. *Psychotherapy and personality change*. Chicago: University of Chicago Press, 1954.

Rogers, C., Gendlin, E. T., Kiesler, D., and Truax, C. *The therapeutic relationship and its impact: A study of psychotherapy with schizophrenics*. Madison, Wisconsin: University of Wisconsin Press, 1967.

Rychlak, J. F. *A philosophy of science for personality theory*. Boston: Houghton Mifflin, 1968.

Rychlak, J. F. Lockean vs. Kantian theoretical models and the "cause" of therapeutic change. *Psychotherapy: Theory, Research and Practice*, **1969**, **6**, (4), 214–222.

Sanford, N. Will psychologists study human problems? *American Psychologist*, 1965, **20**, (3), 192–202.

Scheflen, A. E. Communication and regulation in psychotherapy. *Psychiatry*, 1963, **26**, 126–136.

Schlien, J. M. Cross theoretical criteria for the evaluation of psychotherapy. *American Journal of Psychotherapy*, 1966, **20**, 125–134.

Schmidt, L. D. Some legal considerations for counseling and clinical psychologists. *Journal of Counseling Psychology*, 1962, **9**, 35–44.

Schmidt, L. D. Some ethical, professional, and legal considerations for school counselors. *Personnel and Guidance Journal*, 1965, **44**, (4), 376–382.

Schmidt, L. Selecting clients for counseling (Sprinthall): Discussion. In J. Whiteley (Ed.), *Research in counseling: Evaluation and refocus*. Columbus, Ohio: Charles E. Merrill, 1968, 51–59.

Schmidt, L. and Pepinsky, H. B. Counseling research in 1963. *Journal of Counseling Psychology*, 1965, **12**, 618–625.

Schwebel, M. Why unethical practice? *Journal of Counseling Psychology*, 1955, **2**, 122–128.

Science Research Associates. Research report: The counselor and ethics; Part I: Problems and responsibilities; Part II: Suggestions on solving ethical problems. Chicago: Science Research Associates, 1965.

Scriven, M. Views of human nature. In T. W. Wann (Ed.), *Behaviorism and phenomonology: Contrasting bases for modern psychology*. Toronto: University of Toronto Press, 1964, 163–183.

Seeman, J. Deception in psychological research. *American Psychologist*. November 1969, **24**, 1025–1028.

Shagass, C. and Malmo, B. Psychodynamic themes and localized muscular tension during psychotherapy. *Psychosomatic Medicine*, 1954, **16**, 295–314.

Shertzer, B. and Stone, S. C. *Fundamentals of counseling*. New York: Houghton Mifflin, 1968.

Shoben, E. J., Jr. Some problems in evaluating criteria of effectiveness. *Personnel and Guidance Journal*, 1953, **31**, 387–394.

Shostrom, E. L. *Personal orientation blank.* San Diego: Education and Industrial Testing Service, 1963.

Shrewsbury, T. B. Legal implications for student personnel workers. In Esther Lloyd-Jones and Margaret Smith (Eds.), *Student personnel work as deeper teaching.* New York: Harpers, 1954, 295–323.

Spielberger, D. and Weitz, H. Improving academic performance of anxious college freshmen: A group counseling approach to the prevention of underachievement. *Psychology Monograph*, 1964, **78**, (13).

Sprinthall, N. Selection of clients for counseling: Are prior conditions limiting or illusions? In J. Whiteley (Ed.), *Research in counseling: Evaluation and refocus.* Columbus, Ohio: Charles E. Merrill, 1968, 36–50.

Standal, S. W. and Corsini, R. J. (Eds.) *Critical incidents in psychotherapy.* New York: Prentice-Hall, 1959.

Stefflre, B. *Theories of counseling.* New York: McGraw-Hill, 1965.

Strupp, H. H. A multidimensional system for analyzing psychotherapeutic techniques. *Psychiatry*, 1957, **20**, 293–306.

Strupp, H. H. The therapist's contribution to the treatment process. In H. H. Strupp and L. Luborsky (Eds.), *Research in psychotherapy*, Vol. II. Washington, D.C.: American Psychological Association, 1962, 25–40.

Strupp, H. H., Chassan, J. B., and Ewing, J. A. Toward the longitudinal study of the psychotherapy process. In L. A. Gottschalk and A. H. Auerbach (Eds.), *Methods of research in psychotherapy.* New York: Appleton-Century-Crofts, 1966, 361–400.

Strupp, H. H. and Luborsky, L. (Eds.) *Research in psychotherapy*, Vol. II. Washington, D.C.: American Psychological Association, 1962.

Sundland, D. M. and Barker, E. N. The orientation of psychotherapists. *Journal of Consulting Psychology*, 1962, **26**, 201–212.

Sutich, A. Toward a professional code of ethics for counseling psychologists. *Journal of Abnormal and Social Psychology*, **39**, 329–350.

Thoresen, C. Relevance and research in counseling. *Review of Educational Research*, 1969, **39**, (2) 264–282. a

Thoresen, C. The systems approach and counselor education: Basic features and implications. *Counselor Education and Supervision*, 1969, **9**, 3–17. b

Thoresen, C. E. (Ed.) Guidance and counseling. *Review of Educational Research*, April 1969, **39**, (2). c

Thorndike, R. L. *Personnel selection: Test and measurement techniques.* New York: Wiley & Sons, 1949.

Tiedeman, D. Comment. *Journal of Counseling Psychology*, 1960, **7**, 90.

Travers, R. M. W. Critical review of techniques for evaluating guidance. *Educational and Psychological Measurement*, 1959, **9**, 211–225.

Travers, R. M. W. *An introduction to educational research*, 2nd Edition. New York: Macmillan, 1964.

Truax, C. Future directions for counseling research (Krumboltz): Discussion. In J. Whiteley (Ed.), *Research in counseling*: *Evaluation and refocus*. Columbus, Ohio: Charles E. Merrill, 1968, 208–214.

Truax, C. and Carkhuff, R. Significant developments in psychotherapy research. In Abt and

Riess (Eds.), *Progress in clinical psychology*, Vol. VI. New York: Grune and Stratton, 1964.

Truax, C. and Carkhuff, R. *Toward effective counseling and psychotherapy: Training and practice*. Chicago: Aldine Publishing Co., 1967.

Tyler, Leona. Theoretical principles underlying the counseling process. *Journal of Counseling Psychotherapy*, 1958, **5**, 3–10.

Underwood, B. J. *Psychological research*. New York: Appleton-Century-Crofts, 1957.

Van Zelst, R. H. Validation evidence on the empathy test. *Educational and Psychological Measurement*, 1953, **13**, 474–477.

Volsky, T., Magoon, T. M., Norman, W. T., and Hoyt, D. *The outcomes of counseling and psychotherapy: Theory and research*. Minneapolis: University of Minnesota Press, 1965.

Voth, H., Modlin, H., and Orth, Margorie. Situational variables and the assessment of psychotherapeutic results. *Bulletin of the Menninger Clinic*, 1962, **26**, 73–81.

Wallach, M. S. and Strupp, H. H. Dimensions of psychotherapists activities. *Journal of Consulting Psychology*, 1964, **28**, 265–271.

Ware, M. L. (Ed.) *The law of guidance and counseling*. Cincinnati, Ohio: W. H. Anderson, 1965.

Warters, J. *Techniques of counseling*. New York: McGraw-Hill, 1954.

Watson, R. I. Psychology, a prescriptive science. *American Psychologist*, 1967, **22**, (6), 435–447.

Wellman, F. E. The assessment of counseling outcomes: A conceptual framework. In J. M. Whiteley (Ed.), *Research in counseling: Evaluation and refocus*. Columbus, Ohio: Charles E. Merrill, 1968, 153–183.

Whiteley, J. M. (Ed.) *Research in counseling: Evaluation and refocus*. Columbus, Ohio: Charles E. Merrill, 1968.

Whiteley, J. and Jakubowski, Patricia. The coached client as a research and training resource in counseling. *Counselor Education and Supervision*, 1969, **9**, 19–29.

Williamson, E. G. and Bordin, E. S. The evaluation of vocational and educational counseling: A critique of the methodology of experiments. *Educational and Psychological Measurement*, 1941, **1**, 5–24.

Wrenn, C. G. The ethics of counseling. *Educational and Psychological Measurement*, 1952, **12**, 161–177.

Wrenn, C. G. *The counselor in a changing world*. Washington, D.C.: APGA, 1962.

Wrenn, C. G. and Parker, C. A. Counseling theory. *Encyclopedia of educational research*, 3rd Edition, 1960, 341–348.

Zax, M. and Klein, A. Measurement of personality and behavior changes following psychotherapy. *Psychological Bulletin*, 1960, **57**, 435–448.

Part II Research Articles and Critiques

Part II represents something of a departure from the usual. As such, it is appropriate to offer several comments which may clarify our purpose and anticipate reader questions or reactions.

The tone of some of the critiques of the following articles may be offensive to some readers. It may appear that we have been unnecessarily intolerant, critical, or naive. Actually, some of the criticisms are deliberately overstressed for emphasis; however, the purpose has been to clearly and forcefully illustrate certain appropriate principles of research. Personal embarrassment or reprimand for the authors is certainly not intended or to be construed.

We certainly want to stress the point that we are well aware of the discrepancy between academic research methodology and the realities of doing counseling research in applied settings. What we have said in the first part of this book, and our own research reports which follow are good examples of this discrepancy. As the counselor-researcher designs and implements research in real settings, he encounters numerous restraints, obstacles, and frustrations between what he knows should be done (the proper and appropriate ways) and what he can, in fact, implement in the setting. Although our critiques of the articles may not reveal our sensitivity to this matter, we would like to emphasize our awareness of these realities to the readers and the research authors.

It should be noted that some of our reactions may be biased. Meltzoff and Kornreich (1970) observed that there are manifold possibilities for bias and error in the preparation and consumption of therapy/counseling research. Besides statistical, sampling, design, and other investigator associated biases, there is reader, editor, and author bias. Hopefully, however, the discipline and detachment of the scientific method may enable all of us involved in the pursuit of knowledge in change producing human relationships to collectively move beyond our idiosyncratic biases. The stimulation of productive thought and enlightened discussion through examples is the central aim of Part II.

We must also remind ourselves that almost all of the reprinted research articles which follow may have been edited or otherwise shortened by the authors themselves to meet publication requirements. The consequence may have been an abbreviated description of the treatment of sample in the original research. Critics of such aspects of the research reports must acknowledge these editorial and publication realities.

As noted earlier, the thirteen articles were not selected for review because of the reputation of the authors or the quality of the research. We identified several simple criteria, and then began to search recent journals for articles that would contribute to a somewhat representative, although arbitrarily defined, collection of current research. The categories and the number of studies in each are:

Category	Number
I. *Type*	
A. Process	2
B. Outcome	6
C. Process-Outcome Combination	5
II. *Theory*	
A. Relationships-Humanistic	7
B. Cognitive-Behavioral	6
III. *Setting*	
A. Elementary School	2
B. Junior-Senior High School	2
C. Junior College-Vocational School	1
D. College-University	3
E. Agency (Rehabilitation, Employment, Hospital) – Private Practice	5
IV. *Design*	
A. Correlational-Descriptive	2
B. Empirical-Case Study	2
C. Control-Experimental	3
D. Own Control	2
E. Multivariate	4

The thirteen articles had been published in eight different journals. These included the *Personnel and Guidance Journal* (3); *Journal of Counseling Psychology* (2); *Journal of Consulting and Clinical Psychology* (2); *Psychotherapy: Theory, Research and Practice* (2); *Journal of College Student Personnel* (1); *Elementary Guidance and Counseling Journal* (1); *Journal of Applied Behavioral Science* (1); and *Journal of Employment Counseling* (1).

The order of presentation of the articles and critiques in Part II follows the outline for the organization of the five types of experimental designs noted in the table above. It should also be noted that the format of each critique follows the topical order of the chapters in Part I.

REFERENCE

Meltzoff, J. and Kornreich, M. *Research in psychotherapy*. New York: Atherton Press, 1970.

PREMARITAL COUNSELING WITH COLLEGE STUDENTS: A PROMISING TRIAD[1]

Mark E. Meadows[2]
Auburn University
and
Jaci F. Taplin
Virginia Commonwealth University

(*Received* February 13, 1970)

A premarital counseling model and its application in a university counseling center are described. Six engaged student couples participated in a series of individual and joint counseling interviews. The results of a postcounseling questionnaire are discussed, revealing a positive response on the part of clients. The premarital counseling triad is recommended as an appropriate and needed service in the college setting.

The present study describes premarital counseling in the Counseling Center at Virginia Commonwealth University. Several factors, including an initial counseling experience with an engaged couple which produced positive results, suggested the desirability of providing premarital counseling. Such a service might respond to a significant problem in college student development and thus, fit well the developmental emphasis of the Counseling Center. Another factor was the increasing number of students who consulted the Center concerning problems arising from conflicts during the premarital period.

A review of the literature offered only minimal assistance in planning a program of premarital counseling. Little attention had been given to the subject. One study (Eastman & Reifler, 1969) described the work of a marital and premarital counselor in a university health service and suggested that this was the only such counselor in a college health service in the United States. Findings of other studies underscored the significance of problems in the area of planning for marriage. These studies have

[1]Meadows, Mark E. and Taplin, Jaci F. Premarital counseling with college students: A promising triad. *Journal of Counseling Psychology*, 1970, **17**, (6), 516–518.

[2]Requests for reprints should be sent to Mark E. Meadows, Department of Counselor Education, Auburn University, Auburn, Alabama 36830.

indicated that (a) nearly one-fourth of all college students marry either before or while in college (Schab, 1966); (b) both male and female college students state that problems of dating and marriage comprise a major source of difficulty (Matthews & Tiedman, 1964; Penney & Buckles, 1966); and (c) students rarely see college deans and counselors as a source of assistance in premarital problems, but rely on "... less informed sources of information—often misinformation [Freeman & Freeman, 1966a]." The conclusion that a university counseling center should provide premarital counseling seems warranted.

DESCRIPTION OF PREMARITAL COUNSELING MODEL

Careful attention was given to the approach that would be taken by the two counselors involved in the program. Two basic approaches to premarital counseling were found in the review of the literature. The techniques advanced by Ellis (1961) seemed to be too far removed from the orientation of both counselors to be useful. An approach suggested by Rutledge (1968) seemed more appropriate and influenced considerably the underlying basis for the counseling utilized.

The counseling model as it was finally conceived was a developmental one and followed somewhat the approach of Rutledge. The approach stressed (a) the need for each partner in the premarital relationship to possess a deep understanding of the personality and emotional life of himself and the intended marriage partner, (b) the importance of the perception held concerning the appropriate marital role of each marriage partner, (c) the importance of communication skills in marital adjustment, and (d) the necessity to develop problem-solving skills in order to resolve the inevitable areas of conflict that arise in both the engagement period and marriage. Values were considered to be especially important dimensions in potential marriage adjustment.

The counseling method was somewhat directive and cognitive. An attempt was made to have each couple confront together certain key issues that have been held to be of importance in marital adjustments. They included such questions as the following: What means of expressing affection do we consider appropriate during the engagement period? How do we feel about the management of financial affairs? How shall we relate to inlaws? How do we feel about the exercise of authority in our married life?

Care was taken not to overemphasize problems, but to focus on how the couple approached problem solving. The counselor did not attempt to offer solutions or advice, but was concerned that the couple honestly face each question. As conflicts developed, the counseling triad attempted to analyze how the couple approached problem solving and to determine the quality of communication achieved in resolving differences.

Each partner was seen individually by the counselor prior to a joint counseling session. Couples were allowed to determine when they wished to see the counselor in the joint counseling interview. As a result, some clients had as many as four individual counseling interviews prior to the joint session; others had only one individual interview. The number of joint sessions for each couple ranged from one to three.

A total of six couples participated in the premarital counseling experience.

RESULTS OF QUESTIONNAIRE

Approximately one month (slightly longer for some) after completion of the premarital counseling, each client was mailed an evaluation form. Eleven of twelve clients completed and returned questionnaires.

Each client was asked to state his marital plans at the time he completed the questionnaire, whether his marital plans had changed, and the role played by counseling in effecting change, if any. Three of the six couples were no longer engaged; two of them attributed their change in status, at

Table 1 Client Responses to Items Related to the Nature of the Counseling Interview.

Question	Response	*n*
Did you consider the individual or joint interviews most productive?	Individual	1
	Joint	9
	No opinion	1
Why did you consider this type interview most productive?[a]	Greater degree of interaction	3
	Opportunity to hear fiancée discuss views	3
	Presence of third party in discussion	2
	No reason given	1
Do you believe all interviews should be joint interviews?	Yes	0
	No	11
Do you believe that group interviews involving three or more couples would be beneficial?	Yes	9
	No	2

Note: $N = 11$.

[a]Includes responses only for those who indicated joint interview was most productive.

least in part, to the premarital counseling experience. Significantly, two of the three couples viewed their broken engagement in a positive way. One client indicated that the engagement was broken in order to "... withdraw and reevaluate our relationship. We are still dating and have relatively the same feeling of warmth."

Nature of counseling interview Four items on the questionnaire related to the nature of the counseling interviews. They are summarized in Table 1. In order to facilitate reporting, highly similar responses are presented in summary form.

Client's evaluation of experience Four items on the questionnaire asked for a qualitative evaluation of the premarital counseling experience. Results of the client responses are presented in Table 2. All four clients

Table 2 Client Responses to Items Related to Clients' Evaluation of Experience.

Item	Response	*n*
I would consider my experience in premarital counseling	Very helpful	4
	Somewhat helpful	7
	Not helpful at all	0
What would you consider the one most helpful aspect of your premarital counseling experience?	The presence of an objective third party	5
	The increased insight obtained with respect to the attitudes and feelings of both fiancée and self	4
	Other responses	1
	No response	1
What changes would you suggest in future premarital counseling offered by the Counseling Center?	More sessions, scheduled closer together	5
	Group sessions	1
	Counselor should be directive with both clients	1
	No response	4
What specific problem areas do your feel need attention in adjusting to the engagement period?[a]	Adjustment to fiancée with respect to emotions, values and interests	8
	Adjustment to families	6
	Communication problems	5
	Sexual adjustments	4
	Financial matters	2

Note: $N = 11$.
[a]Some clients gave multiple responses.

who described the experience as "very helpful" were clients who were not engaged at the time of the survey. Apparently they felt the questions raised in counseling beneficial, even though serious enough to cause the engagement to be broken or postponed. On the other hand, the less positive response on the part of the remaining clients is interesting. It appeared to the writers that the relationship between these couples deepened to the extent that they began to function more as a unified whole. Any forward movement in their relationship would likely be attributed to the new found unity, or oneness, rather than to something extrinsic such as counseling interviews.

DISCUSSION

The positive evaluation of the premarital counseling experience on the part of clients demonstrates a need to provide counseling for engaged college couples. The authors consider that this activity responds to the developmental tasks of the college years as appropriately as vocational counseling, offered routinely in most colleges and universities.

A commitment to provide premarital counseling will require innovations in the operating procedures of most counseling centers. Specifically, services must be available to nonstudent partners since many students are engaged to nonstudents. Efforts will need to be made to extend counseling services to graduate students, a population infrequently served by counseling centers. Also the usual hours when counseling is available may have to be rearranged, since at least one partner frequently will work during the day.

Finally, the development of a theoretical approach to premarital counseling and research to validate its practice is needed.

REFERENCES

Eastman, F., & Reifler, B. Marriage counseling in the student health service. *Journal of the American College Health Association*, 1969, **17**, 289–295.

Ellis, A. A rational approach to premarital counseling. *Psychological Reports*, 1961, **8**, 333–338.

Freeman, A., & Freeman, R. S. Senior college women: Their sexual standards and activity. Part I. To whom does the college woman turn for sex counseling? *Journal of the National Association of Women Deans and Counselors*, 1966, **29**, 59–64. (a)

Freeman, A., & Freeman, R. S. Senior college women: Their sexual standards and activity. Part II. Dating: Petting-coital practices. *Journal of the National Association of Women Deans and Counselors*, 1966, **29**, 136–143. (b)

Glassberg, B. Y. Sexual behavior patterns in contemporary youth culture – implications for later marriage. *Journal of Marriage and the Family*, 1965, **27**, 190–192.

Matthews, E., & Tiedman, V. Attitudes toward career and marriage and the development of life style in young women. *Journal of Counseling Psychology*, 1964, **11**, 375–384.

Penney, F., & Buckles, D. E. Student needs and services on an urban campus. *Journal of College Student Personnel*, 1966, **7**, 180–185.

Rutledge, A. A systematic approach to premarital counseling. In J. C. Heston & W. B. Frick (Eds.), *Counseling for the liberal arts campus*. Yellow Springs, Ohio: The Antioch Press, 1968.

Schab, F. The married college student: A comparison of male undergraduate and graduate student's attitudes and values. *Journal of College Student Personnel*, 1966, **7**, 154–158.

CRITIQUE

1. PHILOSOPHICAL AND THEORETICAL CONSIDERATIONS

The developmental and pragmatic approach used as a counseling model in this study seems to be a sound base for premarital counseling. The goals and objectives are reasonably clear (e.g., the five strategies stressed). Indeed, from a very practical view, it would be important for most young couples to have skills in these five areas.

Because the authors were able to find little in the literature suggesting that premarital counseling is a service in most counseling centers, does not mean, in fact, that counselors ignore or do not deal in this kind of service. Many college counselors do work with these kinds of clients as part of their everyday routine, not really making either theoretical or service distinctions between clients presenting these problems, vocational or other ones.

In reporting or describing their research the authors did not offer any theoretical assumptions underlying this study. Although attention was given to the "approach" used by the two counselors, the conceptual basis for this approach in the total research effort was treated lightly. It would have been helpful to have had some notion of the broad paradigm followed as well as the goals and processes explicit in the assistance process.

With respect to the counselors, can one model fit two counselors? While the common approach was "suggested by Rutledge," the theoretical orientation of Rutledge and any adaptation by the two counselors respectively was not explained. Rather than presenting any clear conceptual elements dealing with diagnostic schemes, processes, or behavioral outcomes, only general characteristics of this model were listed. The reader is shortchanged in understanding what was meant by a "developmental model," which "followed somewhat" the Rutledge approach. Again, what is to be construed from "somewhat directive and cognitive" as a theoretical base?

2. CRITERION

Efforts were made to evaluate this program on the basis of current status, student's feelings about the nature of the counseling interviews, and student's evaluation of the experience. Essentially, these are self-report measures, which were taken immediately after counseling, and are subjective in nature. Interestingly, it appears that the *content* of the counseling emphasized problem-solving, expression of affection, relating to in-laws, management of financial affairs, etc., but the evaluation had to do with feelings about the process of counseling. It would have been more appropriate to assess how the clients were doing in relation to these matters. Yet, it is understood that this was a pilot program, and the primary purpose of the follow-up survey was simply to assess client reactions.

3. RESEARCH DESIGN

The main purpose of this paper was to describe the operation of a premarital counseling program for college students. All variables, e.g., counselors, clients, situation, treatment, were assigned or fixed by the counselor-researchers, and there was no attempt made to provide controls in the study. The post treatment survey simply sought client reactions. The data provided through the survey do not speak to the effectiveness of the program, only the level of client satisfactions. The design of this program development survey was preexperimental, but an appropriate first step in the more complete description and evaluation of a premarital counseling program.

4. SAMPLING SELECTION AND PROCEDURES

There is some question regarding the parameters of the student population which might have been involved in premarital counseling. In the discussion section, the authors hint at some special characteristics of this group, e.g., working, nonstudents, etc. Because the population is undefined, it is unclear whether or not the sample of students involved in this program were representative of anything. The sampling procedure was at best "incidental" (see Chapter 5). At the least, the authors might have better described the students and counselors involved. In general, the sampling procedures employed in the program were haphazard – there is no mention of the way clients were assigned to counselors, or the way either clients or counselors were selected. Poor sampling selection and procedures can be somewhat compensated for by good, clear descriptions of actual procedures used, clients and counselors involved, and so forth. While the program development reported here was only exploratory in nature, it seems clear that a larger or more clearly described sample would have provided better prototype data for evaluation purposes.

5. COUNSELING AND THERAPY TREATMENT

The authors state that they followed a developmental counseling model which was somewhat directive and cognitive. They do a good job of relating those topics and matters which they felt important to emphasize in counseling (i.e., problem-solving, quality of communication, etc.). Because these phenomena are so broad, it is difficult to ascertain whether all couples got nearly equal amounts of each, or whether in some situations one thing was stressed over another because of the individual needs of the clients. This is as it should be, but does not help much in replicating the study. A final question has to do with who did the counseling? It is not clear whether the two authors did it, or whether others did it. Also, their training and experience are not specified for the reader.

6. MEASUREMENT

The criteria which were selected by the author are measured in a very straightforward, simple way. The statistical data stated in percentage terms is descriptive for the eleven clients who responded to the questionnaire, and no attempt is made to generalize to a larger population.

7. ETHICAL, PROFESSIONAL, AND LEGAL CONSIDERATIONS

Several questions must be raised here. The reader is uninformed as to how the clients were chosen and introduced to the research. What choices were given them as to continuation, termination, choice of counselor, or actual involvement in the study? How does the research fit in with the ongoing work of the counseling center?

As a professional research review, several important features are treated lightly or omitted to the extent that replication would be quite difficult. The reader, for example, has no clear notion of the final behavior expected of clients. No reference was made to actual types of process interactions nor to the qualifications of the counselor.

8. RESULTS

The client's evaluation of the premarital counseling seems to be fairly positive, in terms of the preselected questions. But, note that four (almost 1/3) gave no response to the question, "What changes would you suggest in future premarital counseling offered by the Counseling Center?" One's interpretation of this "no response" is important. For example, does it mean "don't make any changes" or "forget the whole project." Over half of the clients felt that the experience was only somewhat helpful.

Clients who are questioned about the counseling they have recently received tend to respond in the affirmative, especially immediately after counseling. The level of satisfaction decreases with time. Hence, the limited evaluation of this study hardly "demonstrates a need to provide counseling for engaged college couples." This result would better be justified at the logical or *a priori* level. In summary, we feel this study could have been strengthened by devoting more time and space to the description of the treatment and subject variables, with the client-satisfaction being reported less forcefully.

NEED FOR APPROVAL AND COUNSELING OUTCOMES[1]

Robert A. MacGuffie,
Gary Q. Jorgensen,
and
Frederick V. Janzen[2]

The intent of this study was to determine the effects of a clients' need for approval on the outcomes of counseling. The expectation that clients who have a high need for approval by others would cooperate more with the counseling process and would more often be successful in the sense of being rehabilitated. The Marlowe-Crowne Social Desirability Scale was administered to 167 applicants at a state rehabilitation agency immediately after the initial interview. It was hypothesized that successfully rehabilitated clients would obtain significantly higher social desirability scores than those clients who were not successful. The results confirmed the hypothesis at the 0.01 level of significance.

According to Riesman (1950), individuals have shifted from an "inner-directed" orientation, where decisions and behaviors stem from internalized standards, to an orientation where standards are based on the approbation of others. The "other-directed" person, they contend, is carefully attuned to signals denoting actions of others toward him. His behavior, then, is partially based upon his interpretation of these signals or cues that he receives, and is similar to what Fromm (1947) refers to as the "marketing orientation." According to Fromm, a person with marketing orientation reacts as though he were a commodity on the market and

[1]MacGuffie, Robert A., Jorgensen, Gary Q., and Janzen, Frederick V. Need for approval and counseling outcomes. *Personnel and Guidance Journal*, 1970, **48**, (8), 653–656.

[2]Robert A. MacGuffie is Assistant Professor of Education and Coordinator of Rehabilitation Counselor Education at Bowling Green State University in Ohio. Gary Q. Jorgensen is Coordinator of the Alcoholic Rehabilitation Clinic and Frederick V. Janzen is Research Director of the Regional VIII Rehabilitation Research Institute, both at the University of Utah in Salt Lake City.

This study was supported in part by Research Grant RD-1437-G from the social and Rehabilitation Service, U.S. Department of Health, Education, and Welfare, Washington, D.C.

must behave in a manner that will enhance his value. Such a person, in approaching others as potential buyers, seems almost to be saying, "What type of person do you want me to be? I will try to be that type." The behavior a person exhibits to increase his market value could be viewed as socially desirable or likely to win the approval of others. The social desirability factor seems to be an important concern in the counseling process because it no doubt affects the type of behavior exhibited by many clients. Thus, the purpose of this study was to determine if clients who were judged to be higher in this trait tended to succeed or fail in the counseling process.

Marlowe and Crowne (1961) define social desirability as the need for social approval and the belief that satisfaction of this need can be attained by means of culturally acceptable and appropriate behavior. They also concur with Goldstein (1960) and Buckholt (1965) who state that there is a predictive relationship between social desirability and conformity. Fordyce (1956) suggests that social desirability is ". . . consensus judgments as to what behaviors, feelings, and attitudes win social approval in American society."

Block (1962) hypothesizes that social desirability and good psychological health must be related. His reasoning was that if a person were psychologically healthy, he would emit behavior which is socially desirable; otherwise, if the behavior exhibited were inappropriate, the feedback from society would seem to destroy the individual's personal equilibrium.

Success in the rehabilitation counseling process culminates with the client's securing gainful employment. To reach this level of success typically requires that the client interact effectively with several people such as counselors, physicians, social workers, and employers. Therefore, it might be assumed that clients who are more responsive to social approval by these key people in the counseling process would have a greater chance of becoming rehabilitated. The hypothesis of this study is that rehabilitants will obtain significantly higher social desirability scores at the point when they apply for jobs than will nonrehabilitants.

METHODOLOGY

The Instrument

The instrument selected to measure social desirability was the Marlowe-Crowne Social Desirability Scale (M-C SD Scale). Horton, Marlowe, and Crowne (1963) reported that individuals scoring high on the M-C SD Scale also tended to be more conforming or other-directed, more responsive to situational demands, and more susceptible to the effects of social reinforcement than those scoring low on the Scale. Crowne and Marlowe (1964) reported an internal consistency coefficient of 0.88 and a test-retest reliability coefficient of 0.88 for the M-C SD Scale. They also reported significant validity coefficients between the M-C SD Scale and both the Minnesota Multiphasic Personality Inventory subscales and the Edwards Social Desirability Scale. It is also suggested by Marlowe and Crowne that the scale has construct validity based on the relationship between a person's score on their instrument and his observable performance on a dull and meaningless spool-packing task.

Subjects

The study was part of a larger research project conducted at the Salt Lake City District Office of the Utah Office of Rehabilitation Services (ORS) from October 1964 through June 1966. The subjects tested were those applicants the counselors thought might return for ORS services after the first interview. The applicants were administered the M-C SD Scale by a member of the research team immediately after the initial interview with their counselors. Of these applicants, 167 were accepted for services and their cases later closed during the period of this study. Of these, 88 subjects were closed as rehabilitated and 79 subjects were closed as nonrehabilitated.

RESULTS

As may be seen from data presented in Table 1, rehabilitants scored significantly higher than did the nonrehabilitants on the M-C SD Scale. Therefore, the hypothesis of the study was accepted.

Table 1 Differences on the Marlowe-Crowne Social Desirability Scale for 88 Rehabilitants and 79 Nonrehabilitants.

	Rehabilitants	Nonrehabilitants	*t*
Mean	19.70	17.38	2.37*
S.E.	0.66	0.74	

*Significant at the 0.01 level.

On the chance that biographical factors might account for the observed differences on the M-C SD Scale, rehabilitants and nonrehabilitants were compared on several biographical variables. There were no significant differences between the two groups on the variables of age, sex, marital status, educational attainment, source of referral, work history, age at disablement, and characteristics of major disabling condition.

DISCUSSION

At first it might seem that the findings of this study are at variance with Crowne and Marlowe's (1964) finding that "high-need approval" psychiatric patients, when compared with "low-need approval" patients, tended to terminate psychotherapy earlier and without improvement. However, this study dealt with a population of state agency rehabilitation clients who could adjust to their environments acceptably enough so as not to be considered psychiatric patients. Also, the goals of counselors would not necessarily be construed as psychotherapy but would involve good counseling techniques as well as adequate use of community resources to assist clients in securing gainful employment. While a high need for approval may be detrimental to successful psychotherapy, it may be an asset for a client's obtaining suitable employment. Perhaps the rehabilitants, having a high need for approval, were better able to respond to the efforts of the typical middle-class counselor and other key people in the counseling process, while for the nonrehabilitants this was not the case. It could be assumed that the client who secured employment would receive the most social approval from the counselor because this was the goal of this counseling encounter. Therefore, it seems reasonable to expect that clients high in the need for social approval would try to earn this approval from the counselor and would respond better to his efforts to help them secure adequate employment.

The unsuccessful clients, who are lower in the need for social approval, may present some special problems for counselors. Perhaps with this type of client the counselor may not be able to use effectively one particular technique of counseling—the use of positive reinforcement for socially desirable behavior leading to the goals of the counseling encounter. The social approval of the counselor may be of no value to this type of client; therefore, he does not respond to the counselor's efforts. It is suggested that counselors consider using other techniques with the client who does not seem to be seeking their social approval, techniques which do not require the client to conform to the wishes of the counselor as a basis for positive rewards. For example, with a rehabilitation population the counselor may have to recognize that for some clients, desirable behavior from their frame of reference is not to work and not to be rehabilitated. In such cases the counselor could not expect the client to respond to his efforts of helping him obtain gainful employment unless the value system of the client was dealt with first. It is our contention that this type of client would be low in the need for social desirability.

A cautionary note for counselors is that they might be selecting clients for services who acquiesce to their demands or who fit their stereotype of a good client. As the findings in this study suggest, a client having a higher need for approval would probably fit this stereotype. Future research should also attempt to study the part played by the desirability needs of counselors as a possible factor in determining the success or failure of their clients.

REFERENCES

Block, J. Some differences between the concepts of social desirability and adjustment. *Journal of Consulting Psychology*, 1962, **26**, 527–530.

Buckholt, R. Need for social approval and dyadic verbal behavior. *Psychological Reports*, 1965, **16**, 1013–1016.

Crowne, D. P., & Marlowe, D. *The approval motive studies in evaluative dependence.* New York: Wiley, 1964.

Fordyce, W. E. Social desirability in the MMPI. *Journal of Consulting Psychology*, 1956, **20**, 171–175.

Fromm, E. *Man for himself.* New York: Holt, Rinehart & Winston, 1947.

Goldstein, M. J. The social desirability variable in attitude research. *Journal of Social Psychology*, 1960, **53**, 103–108.

Horton, D. L., Marlowe, D., & Crowne, D. P. The effect of instructional set and need for social approval on commonality of word association. *Journal of Abnormal and Social Psychology*, 1963, **66**, 67–72.

Marlowe, D., & Crowne, D. P. Social desirability and response to perceived situational demands. *Journal of Consulting Psychology*, 1961, **25**, 109–115.

Riesman, D. *The lonely crowd.* New Haven: Yale University Press, 1950.

CRITIQUE

1. PHILOSOPHICAL AND THEORETICAL CONSIDERATIONS

Although the theoretical rationale for this study is not grounded in formal, comprehensive theories of human development or personality, the authors are quite clear in setting forth the descriptions and assumptions they make about human behavior. It could probably be cast into a trait-factor approach to personality. The important thing is that the authors have surveyed the literature and reviewed some of the empirical findings in a very understandable way. However, one might question whether or not getting a job is quite as simple as being responsive to social approval by key people. Certainly, this may be a part of the more complex behavioral act of getting a job.

It is disappointing to find no firm theoretical basis for relating social desirability to rehabilitated status, an assumption on which this research rests. Likewise, what is the conceptual rationale for linking counseling outcome to social desirability? Nothing precludes examining this relationship, but the basis here seems to be intuition, hunch, or logic rather than theory.

2. CRITERIA

Evidently, the criterion of successful counseling was simply whether or not a client was gainfully employed *during the time of the study*. Presumably, a client who received counseling but only later obtained a job was considered a nonrehabilitant, an unsuccessful client. Also, the stability of gainful employment was not considered. For example, if a client obtained a job, but continued with it for only several weeks, he was still considered a rehabilitant, or a successful client. In an agency such as a rehabilitation office, where presumably all counseling and services are directed toward helping disabled workers obtain employment, getting a job is a legitimate and appropriate criterion of success. It is specific, objective, and external.

3. RESEARCH DESIGN

The authors note at the outset that this study was part of a larger investigation, and this may help explain some of the problems in understanding what was done. Perhaps the phenomenon reported here was one of those incidental findings that only emerged in the analysis of the data from the larger research project.

With a correlational design (Chapter 3), this research must be classified as preexperimental. A *post hoc* analysis of the data by the authors revealed that higher social desirability scores rather than anecdotal characteristics were related to "successful rehabilitation." While this finding tends to support one frequently stated variation as to who is a "good client," causation can only be inferred. The total lack of control makes the findings inconclusive and indefinite. The main contribution of this study is to suggest hypotheses for future research, because the nature of the design alone makes any further significance questionable.

4. COUNSELING TREATMENT

It is assumed that the clients in this study received counseling over a period of twenty months. We do not know who provided the counseling. Nor do we know the training, experience, theoretical orientation, or even the number of counselors involved. We have no idea of the number of sessions each client received. We might speculate that the non-successful, nonrehabilitants received a significantly fewer number of sessions.

Regarding the treatment itself, the only comment is this: "Also, the goals of the counselors would not necessarily be construed as psychotherapy but would involve good counseling techniques as well as adequate use of community resources to assist clients in securing gainful employment." What is considered *good* counseling techniques, and *adequate* use of community resources is left to the reader's interpretation.

With the large *N*, it is assumed that several counselors were involved in the counseling of these clients. If this was true, we are even more unsure that any standard uniform type of counseling was received by the clients.

5. SELECTION AND SAMPLING PROCEDURES

As in most preexperimental designs, there was no plan for selection or sampling. The procedure simply called for the designation of those clients who were probably going to continue in counseling as the sample. It is not reported whether or not any of the people initially interviewed and excluded from the sample actually returned for services. Because of this lack of information, it is impossible to assess the sampling of therapists and therapeutic situations.

The authors do not report how clients were actually assigned to the treatment conditions—counselors, referrals, etc. In fact, it is impossible to say anything about this procedure because the treatment is not described at all.

The external validity of this study (Chapter 5) must be seriously questioned because of the selection and sampling procedures employed. It represents some interesting speculation, but the reader must be wary of seeing more in the results than is really there.

6. MEASUREMENT

Measurement of the criterion in this study is simple and straightforward. If the client secured a job, he was considered a successful client. While this approach certainly has merit, one wonders whether or not some other productive kinds of things might have been obtained from the counseling (i.e., less concerned about his handicap, more positive self-concept, more realistic view of his role in the world of work, etc.). It would have been helpful to have had some measures in these other process areas.

Since the construct of social desirability was operationally defined as the score obtained on the Marlowe-Crowne Social Desirability Scale, no comments are necessary. Did the criterion measure dictate the goals and objectives?

7. ETHICAL, PROFESSIONAL, AND LEGAL CONSIDERATIONS

As the authors seem to have realized in their discussion of the results, the little knowledge generated by these results could be potentially destructive. The client's lack of need for approval could become an excuse for not providing the proper services.

Few ethical or legal issues are raised by this comparative study. Perhaps certain professional assumptions basic to the study should have been made more explicit, however. While rehabilitation counseling is not defined as used in this study the researchers seem to assume that placement is a counseling outcome. One wonders how rehabilitation services, including counseling, are put together. The question thus arises: "Is placement a criterion of counseling or of rehabilitation services, including physical and environmental manipulation?" It may be somewhat academic but the reader could probably use more information from the researchers on their general usage of these concepts and practices.

8. RESULTS

Although the two groups were significantly different (statistically) in amount of social desirability, there does not seem to be much difference between a Mean Score of 19.79 and 17.38. (Certainly the large N would account for much of the significance.)

It was difficult to understand just exactly how this study was implemented. At first reading it appeared that it was planned before it was executed. Yet, closer reading reveals that it might well have been a preexperimental study; that is, the researchers might well have just gone back to the files and uncovered the data. In any event, the comments made above hardly justify using the instrument (Marlowe-Crowne Social Desirability Scale) in any predictive way or really even including it in a battery of tests in working with rehabilitation clients.

THE COUNSELOR-CONSULTANT AND THE EFFEMINATE BOY[1]

Robert D. Myrick[2]

This article presents a case study of an effeminate boy in an elementary school. Rather than counseling the boy directly, the counselor consulted the child's teachers regarding strategies for change. Following experimental procedures, significant changes were recorded in behavior and attitude as measured by pre- and post-experimental measures: playground behavior, lunchroom behavior, physical education activities, class sociogram, and a Semantic Differential. The case demonstrates how deviant children, such as this effeminate boy, can be aided through consultation with teachers and through learning experiences within the regular school program.

All societies have prescribed standards of behavior which are regarded as appropriate for males and females. As American children grow to adulthood they learn attitudes and patterns of responses that are considered suitable for their sex role in this culture. Learning the approved sex role and demonstrating acceptable sex-role behaviors are an important part in the normal social, emotional, and intellectual development of a child.

As early as age three, boys are aware of activities and objects that our culture regards as masculine, and they show an increasing preference for masculine games as they grow older (Brown, 1957; Kagan, 1964; Rabban, 1950). Girls up to 10 years of age, however, have preferences for sex-role activities and objects which are more variable (Brown, 1957; Rosenberg & Sutton-Smith, 1960).

Despite some confusion caused by contemporary styles of dress and personal grooming, sex-role behaviors in American culture can be identified. In general, females are more conforming, nurturant, passive, dependent, and inhibiting of verbal and physical aggression; males are more rebellious, mechanical, independent, and physically active. Several

[1]Myrick, Robert D. The counselor-consultant and the effeminate boy. *Personnel and Guidance Journal*, 1970, **48**, (5), 355–361. Copyright 1970, by the American Personnel and Guidance Association, and reproduced by permission.

[2]Robert D. Myrick is Assistant Professor in the Department of Personnel Services at the University of Florida in Gainesville.

studies show boys to be more aggressive than girls (Bandura, 1962; Bandura, Ross, & Ross, 1961; Sears, 1951; Sears, Maccoby, & Levin, 1957).

THE EFFEMINATE BOY

The effeminate boy is one who has failed to learn attitudes and demonstrate behaviors which are accepted for the male role. For the most part, the effeminate boy is rejected by parents, teachers, and peers as being less than a "real" boy. Because he frequently experiences failure and disappointment when playing with other boys, he often turns to playing games with girls, who are less aggressive and threatening. Playing more exclusively with girls encourages him to imitate and behave like them in speech, gestures, mannerisms, and walk. Increasingly, a pattern is set which leads to social rejection and name-calling.

Effeminacy can be an incapacitating characteristic in a boy's growth and development. Lippman (1956) cautioned that childhood effeminacy is not necessarily or inevitably linked with adult homosexuality. Yet, some clinical evidence has suggested that effeminacy might be an important factor in deviant sexual behavior of adults. For example, in one study a high percentage of homosexual men, in contrast to a control group, were less likely as children to play baseball, participate in competitive group games, or have fights with other boys (Bieber, *et al.,* 1962). Moreover, marked deviance from the masculine sex role can be an antecedent of feelings that one has homosexual tendencies and, consequently, increases the probability of engaging in homosexual behaviors (Chang & Block, 1960).

Excessive anxiety is related to ineffective learning, and the effeminate boy is more prone to anxiety than other boys (Bieber, *et al.*, 1962; Webb, 1963). Failure to develop masculine skills valued by the peer culture frequently results in peer rejection and isolation (Lynn & Sawrey, 1958; Pope, 1953). In one study, effeminacy was linked to the histories of schizophrenic males (Kohn & Clausen, 1956).

Based on limited research, the degree to which an individual regards himself as either masculine or feminine depends upon: (a) inherent biological sex differences; (b) differential identification with parents and significant others who relate to the child; (c) acquisition of attributes or skills that social mores define as masculine or feminine behavior; and (d) a perception that other people regard the individual as possessing appropriate sex-role characteristics (Josselyn, 1967; Kagan, 1964).

Once a sex role has been learned, it is difficult to alter and tends to persist from childhood to adulthood (Holemon & Winokur, 1965; Kagan & Moss, 1962; Mussen, 1961, 1962). Because childhood behaviors from 6 to 10 years of age have been valid predictors of similar responses in adulthood, it appears that this period is a critical stage for modifying the behavior and attitudes of an effeminate boy.

Several years ago, MacDonald (1938) described effeminate behavior as a serious psychological problem which necessitated segregation of the child and individual therapy over an extended period of time. More recently, Brown (1957) has stated that efforts must be made to alter the interpersonal relationships in the effeminate boy's family because parental figures are the primary models for identification and provide the cultural environment in which the child is reared. Lippman (1956) suggested continuous individual and group therapy with both parents and child. He indicated that play process would help a boy work through his complexes, fears, and deep-seated problem of identity. These approaches involve the boy and his family in intensive therapy with a psychotherapist outside the school environment.

How can a teacher or school counselor help an effeminate boy? The following case study is presented as one example of how a counselor-consultant in an elementary school aided teachers in effectively modifying an effeminate boy's behavior and attitudes.

THE PROBLEM

Jerry, a fourth grade boy, age nine years and eight months, was of concern to his classroom teacher. She reported that he was becoming increasingly unhappy with school, despite satisfactory academic success. He did not get along well with boys and spent most of his playing time with girls. During lunch period he was the only boy who sat with the girls, and he consistently chose physical education activities which involved girls more than boys. Some of the boys ridiculed him for being a sissy and at the time of referral he appeared to be adopting effeminate patterns in his speech, gestures, and specified interests. Other teachers noted his tendency toward effeminacy, but they had not considered his problem incapacitating because he was a grade-school child and a reasonably good student. Jerry had an IQ score of 120 on the California Test of Mental Maturity and he was above grade level on standardized achievement tests. The boy lived with his parents and a brother, who was older by six years and constituted a definite source of personal conflict.

EXPERIMENTAL PROCEDURES

The Counselor-consultant's Role

When Jerry's problem came to the attention of the counselor, consultation began with his teachers. The classroom teacher and the physical education (PE) teacher met with the counselor and were encouraged to describe their feelings and ideas regarding effeminacy and the boy. Specific behaviors were defined and identified as those which led to inferences of such a problem. The counselor reviewed available professional literature on effeminate boys and presented it to the teachers. The limited information provided a rationale for the school personnel's intervening in the boy's development with experimental procedures.

The counselor and teachers worked as a team in planning strategies for change and reviewing procedures in behavior modification which could be applied during the regular school day. Experimental procedures were developed which would, if successful, lead to the boy's valuing school more, being more socially accepted by his peers, and demonstrating more appropriate sex behaviors. The counselor outlined a systematic study which allowed for the recording of data that could be used to assess the boy's progress and validate the procedures. The counselor did not counsel the boy; rather, he served as a consultant to the teachers before and during the experimental period, offering support and helping to clarify the procedures discussed below.

The PE Teacher's Role

The woman PE teacher met with Jerry twice a week for 30 minutes of individual tutoring, which occurred prior to her meeting the boy's class for physical education. In the first tutoring session, she explained the rules of touch football, the popular seasonal sport at that time, and coached him in basic fundamentals of passing and catching a ball. During the second session, Jerry learned how to center the ball back between his legs, and he practiced it with the teacher. This skill proved less difficult than a long forward pass and allowed Jerry more opportunity to perform on a team as the "center." In the PE classes which followed the tutoring sessions, the teacher encouraged and praised the boy for his individual efforts with such expressions as, "That's the way, Jerry," "Good job that time, Jerry," and "That's the way to hustle in there, Jerry." She called out his name when encouraging or praising, and did not ask him to perform skills or play team positions for which he was not yet ready.

For example, during the first week while Jerry was learning basic concepts and fundamentals, he was not asked to carry or throw the ball in touch football. Rather, he blocked and rushed opponents. During the five weeks of tutoring, the PE teacher focused on (a) fundamental skills, (b) basic concepts, and (c) successive approximation of skills in class based upon successful practice in individual tutoring.

As Jerry progressed, he was asked to play more difficult team positions during PE and on occasion to demonstrate some basic skills before the class. Once, after practice, he demonstrated to his classmates the proper way to run the school's obstacle course.

The Classroom Teacher's Role

The classroom teacher changed pupil seating arrangements so that Jerry was placed next to the most popular boy in the class, who was also the best athlete. Each day pupils who were seated next to each other worked in pairs on a classroom problem, and they also participated together on class committees – collecting papers and books, carrying materials, and arranging chairs. This pairing provided Jerry more opportunity to identify with a model boy.

During the first week of the experiment, on two separate days the teacher led the class in discussions of (a) friendship and (b) making new friends. The class talked about personal feelings, as well as ideas, which gave Jerry a chance to hear his peers express personal fears, concerns, and specific anxieties related to new experiences. The classroom teacher also followed the approach used by the PE teacher when she conducted the PE class three days a week.

EXPERIMENTAL MEASURES AND RESULTS

There were five pre- and post-experimental measures used in this study: (a) playground behavior; (b) lunchroom behavior; (c) PE activities; (d) a class sociogram; and (e) a Semantic Differential. The study was conducted over a period of seven weeks, with the first and last weeks used for observation and collection of pre- and post-experimental data.

Playground Behavior

Baseline records were obtained consisting of Jerry's playing time on the playground after lunch. Playing time with boys as opposed to girls was gathered by an observer each day for a period of five days prior to the introduction of experimental procedures. Similar observations and records were made during the final week of the study, and these served as post-experimental measures. Figure 1 presents a graphic illustration of the data.

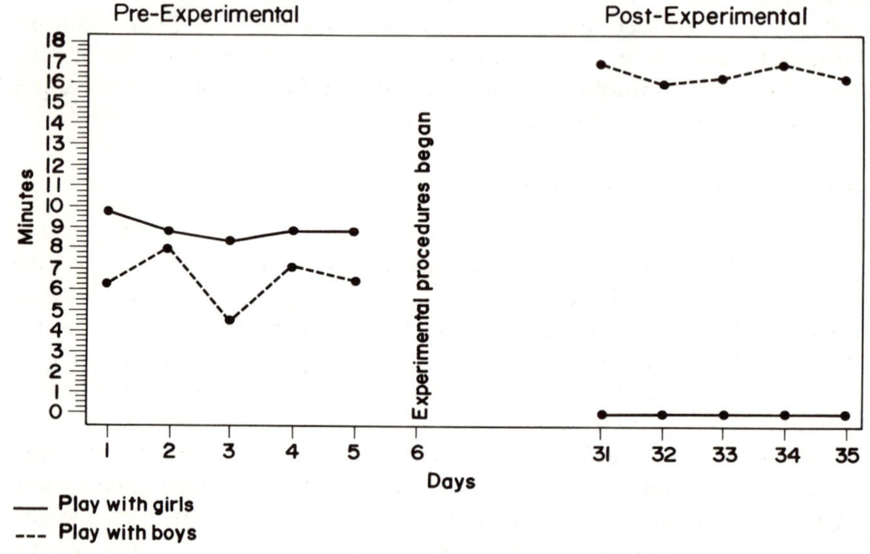

Fig. 1 Playground Behavior.

It can be observed that a marked change occurred in playground playing behavior. Beginning baseline records show that 57 percent of the time on the playground Jerry played with girls rather than boys. After one week of applying the experimental procedures discussed above, the boy made a dramatic change by moving from the girls' to the boys' group. The change was sudden and complete. Each day thereafter Jerry spent all his time playing games with the boys during the play period after lunch.

Lunchroom Behavior

Prior to experimental procedures, Jerry had talked exclusively with girls during lunch and was the only boy who sat at their table. On the following day after he first played football with the boys and thus changed his playground behavior, he also elected to sit at the boys' table during lunch. An observer reported that he was ridiculed at first by a few boys who told him to go sit with the girls. But Jerry remained, and in the five school months that followed, he continued to sit and talk with the boys during lunch period. During that time he went to the girls' table on only two occasions and that was with another boy to tease the girls.

PE Activities

When the classroom teacher conducted the PE class, the pupils chose among various physical education activities. Prior to experimental procedures, Jerry invariably chose those activities which were less aggressive and which involved more girls than boys. A marked change occurred after a week of presenting the experimental procedures. At that time, Jerry chose to play the game of touch football with most of the boys. During the following school months he consistently chose the more aggressive PE activities which were popular with the boys (e.g., basketball, soccer, and softball) as opposed to those games played by girls (e.g., four square, jump rope, and tetherball).

Class Sociogram

A sociogram was administered during the first and last weeks of the study when all pupils were present. Pupils were asked to list in order the names of three classmates whom they would most like to (a) play with, (b) have on a team, and (c) work with on a class committee. Answers to these items would all indicate a positive response. In addition, they also listed three people with whom they would least like to do any of these activities, indicating a negative response. Table 1 presents a summary of the pre- and post-sociogram data.

Prior to the experiment, Jerry was an isolate. Only two children responded positively to him, both girls. He received no negative responses. Post-data showed a definite change in Jerry's social status among classmates.

Table 1 Sociometric Status Before and After.

	Before	After
Number of positive choices received	2	11
Number of negative choices received	0	2
Number of pupils selecting subject	2	9
Median rank among 33 pupils	27th	8th
Median rank among 18 boys	15th	4th

He received positive choices from more people (nine, of which eight were boys), and these choices moved his classroom social status rating (determined by the total number of positive choices minus the negative responses) from 24th to 8th out of a class of 33 pupils. He moved from 14th to 4th in social status among the 18 boys in the class. It is interesting to note that as he became more aggressive in play and had more contact with boys, he also received negative responses from two boys.

Semantic Differential

The Semantic Differential (SD) is a method of measuring the psychological meaning of concepts. A booklet was developed in which 9 concepts were separately presented along with 12 bipolar adjectives on a 7-point scale. The order of presentation was randomly determined. The 12 bipolar adjectives represented the dimensions of evaluation, activity, and potency. Adjectives used were: *pleasant–unpleasant, loud–soft, cold–hot, ugly–beautiful, delicate–rugged, fast–slow, good–bad, weak–strong, dull–sharp, deep–shallow, heavy–light, dark–bright* (Osgood, Suci, & Tannenbaum, 1957).

Table 2 presents a list of the concepts rated and reports the before and after SD data. A difference of six scaled points for each dimension between the before and after SD was considered significant, based upon previous research with grade-school children (DiVesta & Dick, 1966).

It may be observed that Jerry perceived girls in more high esteem than

Table 2 Semantic Differential Scores Before and After.

Concepts	Dimensions											
	Evaluative				Activity				Potency			
	Pre	Post	Dif	Sig	Pre	Post	Dif	Sig	Pre	Post	Dif	Sig
School	19	28	+9	*	17	22	+4		14	16	+2	
Girls	26	28	+2		16	17	+1		18	8	−10	
Principal	18	28	+9	*	22	19	−3		10	25	+15	*
Boys	17	25	+8	*	15	24	+9	*	12	28	+16	*
Teacher	28	28	0		19	19	0		19	27	+8	*
As boys see me	16	7	−9	*	16	9	7	*	16	8	−8	*
As girls see me	16	7	−9	*	16	15	−1		18	8	−8	*
As I see me	20	14	−6	*	15	17	+2		15	12	−3	
As I'd like to be	28	25	−3		19	26	+7	*	19	27	+8	*

*A difference of 6 points was considered significant, either positive or negative in direction.

boys on the earlier SD and also rated them as more potent and active. On the later SD, boys were significantly valued more than girls and were seen as more potent and active. Girls, however were not devalued. This change is interpreted as positive in direction. The later SD also indicated a significant change in how the subject felt other boys and girls perceived him—less valued, less potent, and less active. This may be related to the boy's increased desire to be more active and potent than before. Finally, school was significantly more valued on the second SD.

Overall the SD data suggest that changes in perception of school, boys, girls, and ideal self were significant and in the expected and desired direction.

DISCUSSION

Effeminate boys can be found in almost every school. These children can benefit from additional attention by their teachers and counselors, expecially in the critical elementary school years. The effeminate boy need not be an exclusive client of a counselor or therapist.

This article presented a discussion of effeminate children and a systematic case study in which an effeminate boy learned and demonstrated more appropriate sex behaviors. In this case, as behavior was modified, the child reported he liked school better and his classmates gave him more social status.

While marked changes in behavior occurred in the desired and expected direction, SD data suggest that some psychological conflict was present. For example, the later SD reported a perceived loss of self-esteem (as boys see me, as girls see me, as I see me) and a desire to be more potent. This might be expected when an individual learns new behaviors and participates in a new social group which has been so contrary to previous experience. On the other hand, it may also suggest that behavior modification alone cannot promote the total development and growth of an effeminate boy. Rather, it appears in this case that the boy would benefit from an opportunity to explore and work through his feelings and perceptions of himself, his classmates, his teachers, and new behaviors.

The elementary school counselor-consultant will counsel with children, individually and in groups. He will also work with some parents. But as a counselor-consultant he can help deviant children, such as the effeminate boy, by working closely with teachers and helping them construct special learning experiences for children within the classroom and regular school program.

REFERENCES

Bandura, A. Social learning through imitation. In M. R. Jones (Ed.), *Nebraska symposium on motivation, 1962*. Lincoln: University of Nebraska Press, 1962.

Bandura, A., Ross, D., & Ross, S. A. Transmission of aggression through imitation of aggressive models. *Journal of Abnormal and Social Psychology*, 1961, **63**, 575–582.

Bieber, I., Dain, H. J., Dince, P. R., Drellich, M. G., Grand, H. G., Gundlach, R. H., Kremer, M. W., Rifkin, A. H., Wilbur, C. B., & Bieber, T. B. *Homosexuality*. New York: Basic Books, 1962.

Brown, D. G. Masculinity-femininity development in children. *Journal of Counseling Psychology*, 1957, **21**, 197–202.

Chang, J., & Block, J. A study of identification in male homosexuals. *Journal of Consulting Psychology*, 1960, **24**, 307–310.

DiVesta, F. J., & Dick, W. The test-retest reliability of children's ratings on the Semantic Differential. *Educational and Psychological Measurement*, 1966, **26**, 605–616.

Holemon, R. E., & Winokur, G. Effeminate homosexuality: a disease of childhood. *American Journal of Orthopsychiatry*, 1965, **35**, 48–56.

Josselyn, I. M. Sources of sexual identity. *Child and Family*, 1967, **6**, 38–45.

Kagan, J. Acquisition and significance of sex typing and sex role identity. In M. L. Hoffman and L. W. Hoffman (Eds.), *Review of child development research, vol. 1*. Hartford, Conn.: Russell Sage Foundation, 1964.

Kagan, J., & Moss, H. A. *Birth to maturity*. New York: Wiley, 1962.

Kohn, M. L., & Clausen, J. A. Parental authority behavior and schizophrenia. *American Journal of Orthopsychiatry*, 1956, **26**, 297–313.

Lippman, H. S. *Treatment of the child in emotional conflict*. New York: McGraw-Hill, 1956.

Lynn, D. B., & Sawrey, W. L. The effects of father-absence on Norwegian boys and girls. *Journal of Abnormal and Social Psychology*, 1958, **59**, 258–262.

MacDonald, M. W. Criminally aggressive behavior in passive, effeminate boys. *American Journal of Orthopsychiatry*, 1938, **8**, 70–79.

Mussen, P. H. Some antecedents and consequences of masculine sex-typing in adolescent boys. *Psychological Monographs*, 1961, **75** (Whole No. 2).

Mussen, P. H. Long-term consequences of masculinity of interests in adolescence. *Journal of Consulting Psychology*, 1962, **26**, 435–440.

Osgood, C., Suci, G., & Tannenbaum, P. *The measurement of meaning*. Urbana: University of Illinois Press, 1957.

Pope, B. Socioeconomic contrasts in children's peer culture prestige values. *Genetic Psychology Monographs*, 1953, **48**, 157–220.

Rabban, M. Sex-role identification in young children in two diverse social groups. *Genetic Psychology Monographs*, 1950, **42**, 81–85.

Rosenberg, B. G., & Sutton-Smith, B. A revised conception of masculine-feminine differences in play activities. *Journal of Genetic Psychology*, 1960, **96**, 165–170.

Sears, P. S. Doll play aggression in normal young children: influence of sex, age, sibling status, father's absence. *Psychological Monographs*, 1951, **65** (Whole No. 6).

Sears, R. R., Maccoby, E. E., & Levin, H. *Patterns of child rearing*. New York: Harper & Row, 1957.

Webb, A. P. Sex-role preferences and adjustment in early adolescents. *Child Development*, 1963, **34**, 609–618.

CRITIQUE

1. PHILOSOPHICAL AND THEORETICAL CONSIDERATIONS

The author of this case study has clearly and forcefully developed the rationale for intervening in the life of an effeminate boy in the school situation. He does this primarily by setting forth common sense, his own values, and ample references which all indicate that social situations will be unpleasant and humiliating for a male who manifests overt effeminate characteristics.

The theoretical orientation of the study uses a cognitive approach (tutoring) along with environmental modeling and reinforcement. Implicitly the reader gets the feeling that a lot of attention and facilitative interpersonal relationships were also used by the teachers who intervened in this boy's life.

The goals of treatment were to (1) increase the boy's valuing of school, (2) get the boy to be more socially accepted by his peers, and (3) get him to demonstrate more appropriate sex behaviors. These goals emanate clearly from the rationale established.

On the constructive side, the study would have been strengthened if the reader were given a broader theoretical structure under which the specific approach followed could be identified. What were the researcher's conceptual bases for goals, diagnostic scheme, processes, and outcomes? With several helping agents what commonality in theoretical orientation can be assumed?

It would have been useful too, to have had the author's comment on how this procedure differs from traditional behavior modification. Similarly, what are the reasons for selecting as a conceptual base behavior modification techniques? The assumption that "tutoring" (no detailed description) is a type of behavior modification needs a rationale. The reader would have profited from a statement attempting to explain how much of the helping process was "behavior modification," and how much was "facilitating relationship," in the opinion of the researcher.

2. CRITERIA

The specific criteria set up to check on the above goals were defined as increases in behavior frequency in significant social and school situations and activities, via playground behavior, lunchroom behavior, physical education activities. Also, the more general criterion of how the boy was perceiving himself and his peers was used along with social acceptance.

The first set of criteria (various behaviors) are observable and specific. In order to check on how the boy was perceiving himself and how others were perceiving him, the author used a more general, and in the first instance, a subjective criterion. This is an excellent example of the use of multiple and differential levels of criteria.

3. RESEARCH DESIGN

The functional intensive design employed by Myrick was of the empirical case study variety. A high degree of socioenvironmental control was used and the subject's behavior was observed before and after treatment. Graphs and statistical summaries were utilized to describe the data. The case study reported by Myrick is a dramatic illustration of the power of the intensive design in presenting data about the efficacy of treatment contributions. An advantage of this design is that it can be extended over a longer period of time, which incidentally would have been desirable in this instance. Did the dramatic changes persist? Is it possible that, with all of the attention from the teachers, a kind of Hawthorne effect occurred which would not persist over time?

4. SELECTION AND SAMPLING PROCEDURES

Although this design is characterized by a high degree of control, the lack of selection and sampling restricts the generalizability of the findings. External validity is weakened in the intensive design. Replication of this study with different clients, counselors, teachers, and problems is now highly desirable in order to support the utility of these behavior change procedures. Also, a larger sample of clients and treatment personnel, taken from other areas of the country would be in order. This procedure for confirmation of Myrick's findings would then provide substantial, scientifically based knowledge about counselor-consultants and behavior change of effeminate boys.

5. COUNSELING TREATMENT

Since the author did not actually provide any of the treatment himself, we will deal here with the teachers who were used in this study. Before leaving the author, however, we would like to point out that apparently he did an outstanding job of consultation. His approach to changing the behavior of the teachers (their attitudes and values regarding effeminacy) obviously was one which depended quite heavily on the quality of the relationship with them. Whereas "the counselor did not counsel the boy," we suspect he spent a lot of time establishing counseling-like climates with the teachers.

The PE teacher used a cognitive approach in teaching the boy how to play football, and also used ample amounts of encouragement and verbal reinforcement. She was dealing with a chained-response hierarchy (playing football); hence, it was probably easy for her to know just when to use reinforcement. The reader should compare this behavioral response class (playing football) to the one reported by Alper and Kranzler study in Part II of this book (out-of-seat without permission). Although the contingencies of reinforcement are not described for us, this is a good example of using verbal reinforcement in the applied area.

The classroom teacher in this study attempted to use the phenomenon of modeling in changing the subject's behavior. She did this by rearranging the classroom seating. Also, she manipulated the content of instruction to deal with the psychologically related concerns of the client.

6. MEASUREMENT

There are five measures which followed clearly from the goals. The first three had to do with objective and observable behaviors on the playground, in the lunchroom, and in PE activities. It appears that the client was continuously observed while he was on the playground. However, the temporal segments which were used in recording are not mentioned. Did the observer make a recording each time he played with someone else? What was recorded when the client happened to play with a girl and a boy at the same time?

The measurement for lunchroom behavior was also closely observed. Yet, the observer's recording for this behavior is not specified as clearly as for the playground behavior. Did not some of the boys and girls ever share a table? If so, and if the client sat at this mixed table, how was it recorded? The PE activities represent a good measurement, but they are not as detailed as the other two, particularly the playground behavior.

Since one of the goals of this study had to do with peer acceptance, the use of a class sociogram is an excellent measure. Also, the semantic differential seemed to be quite appropriate to measure how the boy was perceiving himself and others. The last two measures are of the self-report variety.

7. ETHICAL, PROFESSIONAL, AND LEGAL CONSIDERATIONS

One wonders, as an ethical issue, how the client was manipulated, i.e., to what extent was prior approval obtained? The involvement of the subject in the entire process is overlooked. As a corollary, what obligations does the researcher have to the boy's parents for current (and subsequent) support?

Another matter with at least ethical overtones is the question of "labeling." To what extent were labels actually used—and is this professionally justifiable? Could client growth be hampered by this kind of designation if used openly? If this was not the case should research articles use labels which were not applied openly to subjects?

Since one of the stated goals was to demonstrate acceptable sex role behavior one might question the ethics of the researcher's basis for identifying "more appropriate sex behaviors" for Jerry. This is a judgmental matter and might even be at variance with the subject and/or his parents' values. If the researcher took this factor into account, in actuality not too difficult a task, the reader should be so informed.

8. RESULTS

The author has clearly specified the results of this study. Because it is a case study, he has been careful not to over generalize from the results. It should be emphasized that this was no mechanical behavioral modification approach. Several people were concerned with the client, evidently had very facilitative relationships with him, and gave him an abundant amount of time and attention. This is an excellent example of how behavior modification techniques can be applied within the context of professional concern, attention, and productive interpersonal relationships.

TREATMENT OF A PHOBIA BY PARTIAL SELF-DESENSITIZATION: A CASE STUDY[1]

Max W. Rardin[2]

(*Received March* 11, 1968)

The treatment of a disabling case of hemophobia by partial self-desensitization is reported. The client completed the last nine items of a 16-item fear hierarchy by herself at home. Relaxation was self-induced and she presented the desensitization monologue to herself. At a 1-year follow-up she functioned as a student nurse on an obstetrics ward with no indication of recurrence of the phobia. The use of subvocal cues in controlling phobic behavior is discussed. The importance of the discrimination process in phobic reactions is suggested.

This paper presents the treatment of an incapacitating fear of blood and personal injury by a variation of Wolpe's (1966) desensitization technique. The purpose of the report is not to add to the list of exotic fears treated by desensitization but, rather, to illustrate a variation in technique, which to the author's knowledge has not appeared in the literature.

HISTORY AND CLINICAL DATA

The client was an 18-year-old single female in the first year of a nursing program and had been a student in an introductory psychology class taught by the author. At the encouragement of her nursing instructors, she contacted the author about the possibility of controlling her fear of blood. An interview indicated that she had a limited phobia. She reported no dissatisfaction in other areas of her life, was achieving above average grades, and had good relations with family, peers, and faculty.

The following history of the problem was gathered during the first scheduled session. The client indicated that she had been fearful of blood

[1]Rardin, Max W. Treatment of a phobia by partial self-desensitization: A case study. *Journal of Consulting and Clinical Psychology*, 1969, **33**, 125–126.

[2]Requests for reprints should be sent to Max Rardin, Department of Psychology, University of Wyoming, Laramie, Wyoming 82070.

and generally squeamish for several years but her fears had not been a serious concern until she entered nursing—a career goal for her since childhood.

Her reaction to blood and possible physical injury varied from moderate discomfort to dizziness and nausea depending on the topic and circumstances. The immediate concern was her reaction to the films shown in nursing classes which vividly depicted various medical conditions. On a number of occasions, she had to put her head down or leave the room. She felt she would faint or vomit if she continued to observe the film. This reaction was interfering with her performance in the classes in which the films were shown, and the nursing faculty was beginning to question her suitability for the profession. Both *S* and her instructors felt it was imperative that she gain control over her reactions before the start of clinical classes in the hospital or she would not be able to continue in the program.

TREATMENT PROCEDURE

During a latter part of the first session, *S* was given a detailed description of desensitization as it would apply to her situation. The next three sessions were devoted to training in relaxation and construction of a fear hierarchy. The client was capable of deep relaxation and apparently experienced vivid imagery. The 16 items in the fear hierarchy involved increasing amounts of blood due to injury, surgery, and childbirth.

Except for changes in the placement of some items in the hierarchy, desensitization had proceeded routinely through seven items during the next four sessions when the school term ended. The seven items completed were: a scraped elbow; a torn hangnail; squeezing out one drop of blood; a cut in the sole of the foot; compound fracture of the leg; needle in skin for a stitch; and a gash in arm with flowing blood.

The remaining nine items which had not been dealt with were: bleeding from nose and mouth due to internal injury; a sucking chest wound; seeing a blood sample drawn; blood foaming from mouth; waters breaking for childbirth; head emerging and effect on mother; blood flowing after birth; delivery of placenta; and stitching after delivery. At this point, in order to continue treatment, the client was faced with the alternative of commuting 100 miles or attempting an experimental self-desensitization procedure suggested by the author.

The experimental procedures were explained as follows. The relaxation technique and the general style of the monologue accompanying the presentation of each item was reviewed. She was reminded that the goal was to imagine increasingly vivid and personally relevant scenes. The importance of not proceeding if anxiety interrupted her relaxation was stressed. She was given general examples of monologue to accompany the rest of the items. On request, the client was able to produce additional appropriate examples. The possibility of arranging an observation of childbirth at a hospital was discussed. After further assurance that contact with the author would be available if there was difficulty, the client decided to attempt this program.

It was agreed she would work on the hierarchy each night when in bed under the following conditions. She was instructed to retire in her usual fashion, induce relaxation, and to begin with the highest item already completed. Work with the items was to be limited to approximately 1 hour. She was told to omit the procedure if she were sick, unusually tired, or disturbed by other matters. She later reported engaging in self-desensitization 5 or 6 nights a week for 6 weeks.

At the end of the 6 weeks she contacted the author and reported being able to imagine comfortably all of the items on the list and having visited the hospital maternity ward. She was late for the delivery but did see the cord being cut and the delivery of the placenta. At that point she felt mildly faint and left. She requested that she be allowed to use smelling salts at her next birth observation since her dizziness was not accompanied by nausea. Because she attributed this faintness more to excitement than anxiety, she was given permission to use smelling salts with the condition that she not force herself to observe if she felt highly anxious. She observed her next delivery successfully. The last session occurred after her return to school and was primarily a review of events to complete the case history. She reported having observed a complete delivery, successfully taken blood samples, and having her own blood sample taken. One year later she was a student nurse on an obstetrics ward fully assisting in deliveries to the point of dabbing blood between vaginal stitches. Surgical repair after delivery had been the highest item on her hierarchy.

DISCUSSION

The client's progress with self-desensitization was apparently routine with no report of difficulty other than the incident which resulted in the request for smelling salts. At the conclusion of the self-desensitization procedure in a tape recording describing her thoughts on the experience, she revealed a technique she had improvised for maintaining control of her fear when approaching an anxiety-arousing situation. As she neared the situation, she would subvocally repeat to herself phrases abstracted from the desensitization monologue. The phrase "it's not me" was most often used. Her use of this phrase as an aide to discrimination appears similar to that of "it's just a dream" applied in the treatment of a recurrent dream reported by Greer and Silverman (1967). Both studies suggest that perhaps the discrimination process is crucial in controlling phobic reactions.

The need to use such phrases might raise a question about the degree of desensitization. Since she was doing so much of the work on her own, it may well be that desensitization was continuing at the time she reported her impressions. She later reported a decline in the use of the phrases.

This case suggests that self-desensitization may be a useful variation from the usual technique for clinical application. In research it offers a method by which the contribution of the therapist to desensitization might be more precisely defined.

REFERENCES

Greer, J. H., & Silverman, I. Treatment of a recurrent nightmare by behavior modification procedures: A case study. *Journal of Abnormal Psychology*, 1967, **72**, 188–190.

Wolpe, J., & Lazarus, A. *Behavior therapy techniques*. New York: Pergamon Press, 1966.

CRITIQUE

1. PHILOSOPHICAL AND THEORETICAL CONSIDERATIONS

The rationale for treatment in this case is clearly grounded in the writings of Joseph Wolpe, which essentially uses an individually constructed fear hierarchy along with desensitization through relaxation. Although this is not spelled out in this report, appropriate references are provided for the reader not familiar with this therapy technique. In fact, the techniques suggested by Wolpe are rather atheoretical since they deal with specific, observable behaviors.

For the reader some reference to the researcher's personal orientation or theoretical stance would have been helpful. It is difficult to accept the assumption that the application of Wolpe's "desensitization technique" is essentially operational—unrelated to the researcher's beliefs. Is the relationship actually (or theoretically) ignored? Where is the therapist on this question?

2. CRITERION

Implicitly, the criterion in this case study was to increase the client's tolerance for experiencing blood-related situations so that she could pursue her career as a nurse. This criterion has the value of being explicit, fairly specific, observable, and external to the therapy session. By way of constructing the fear hierarchy, the criterion was established.

3. RESEARCH DESIGN

The functional design employed in this study uses the smallest possible *N* in counseling/therapy research—*one*. As an empirical case study it features a high degree of control of environmental variables and a thorough description of the variables involved. Internal validity is very good. As an example of intensive design (Chapter 3), the possibility of extending the data collection over a longer period of time is an option utilized by the author. The follow-up one year later is a strength of the study.

4. SELECTION AND SAMPLING PROCEDURES

Chapter 5 discusses the problems of external validity when inadequate selection and sampling procedures are used. Rardin's report, which is based on no selection procedure or sampling plan, now needs systematic verification with other clients, therapists, and treatment situations sampled in an unbiased way. The chief contribution of case studies, small *N* functional designs, and preexperimental research involves the generation of future hypotheses and the support of theory formulation. The results from one good case study or an *ex post facto* survey of counseling procedures are inadequate bases for unquestioned adoption as treatment methods. But considering that most of what therapists do in treatment sessions is based on even less evidence, intensive designs have both short-term practical and long-term scientific value.

5. THERAPY TREATMENT

The author does not describe in detail the procedures he used to treat this client. However, this is understandable since the procedure has been clearly described in the references, and since journal space is at a premium.

The treatment approach was quite clear and only a couple of comments can be made.

The author reports that the client was capable of deep relaxation, and apparently experienced vivid imagery. We assume the first part—deep relaxation—was assessed in a very clinical, intuitive sort of way, but wonder if there are levels of relaxation. Why wasn't some other more objective manner used to assess this in a continuous way? Also what is it that a client does or says that leads one to infer that they are vividly imagining a certain scene or situation? Is it that they say they are, or is it inferred from emotional reactions they are emitting?

The author is commended on having the client continue self-treatment because of the distance at which the client lived. A more systematic way of having the client report her progress might have been to require her to maintain a daily log of what was happening to her during this time, and to have asked her to submit the log for purposes of therapist monitoring and feedback.

6. MEASUREMENT

Clearly the measurement of the criterion in the case study was whether or not the client did, in fact, come to experience blood-related situations which were arranged in the hierarchy. From a measurement point of view, did she or did she not experience these situations? It is clear that she worked all the way through the hierarchy.

It would be helpful for the counselor-researcher waiting to implement a similar type case treatment to have more objective data on indications or levels of relaxation and imagery. However, this is a tough problem, and with the current state of this kind of behavioral therapy the most relevant data might be subjective clinical acuity.

7. ETHICAL, PROFESSIONAL, AND LEGAL CONSIDERATIONS

The researcher seems to have been aware of his ethical obligations to the client. This is evident by his supervision, his complete instructions, and his availability when necessary. His flexibility in programming to meet the client's needs is commendable.

Perhaps it would have been helpful if the reader could have shared the researcher's more personal relationship with the subject as the schedule for desensitization was worked out. In a similar vein, the author might have pointed out how his variation from typical desensitization procedures might have affected the results and interpretation of his findings. Are there any delimitations to the study, recognized by the researcher?

8. RESULTS

This is a very good example of a case study approach, with the limitations noted above. The author is commended on following-up one year later. The results are helpful for therapy practice, but are limited in their generalizability.

THE EFFECTS OF COUNSELING LOW-ABILITY, HIGH-ASPIRING COLLEGE FRESHMEN[1]

Harman D. Burck
Assistant Professor of Psychology
Temple University
and
Harold F. Cottingham
Professor of Education
Florida State University

(*Received* August 3, 1964)

Forty students who entered the Florida State University in the fall of 1963 who had defined educational aspirations and relatively low academic ability were identified. Thirty-five of these students freely volunteered to participate in the study, and were randomly assigned to an experimental (counseled) group and a control (noncounseled) group. Each subject stated his educational aspiration before and after counseling. This aspiration was rated both times by three counselor-judges on the basis of ability, interest, personality test data, high school transcripts and other personal data. The counseled group received counseling during a three-month period.

Both groups started out with initial pre-counseling educational aspirations that were inappropriate as rated, but the counseled group showed significant increases in appropriateness while the control group did not. The California Test of Personality did not reveal any differences before or after counseling, nor were there any significant differences among the change in scores.

It was concluded that the results of this study (significant increases in appropriateness of educational aspiration) can more closely be attributed to the treatment variable (counseling) since data and information about other important influencing variables were either controlled for, or at least ascertained. Both groups volunteered for the study. The groups did not differ significantly in academic ability as measured by the SCAT. The control group did not receive what could be considered a great amount of outside professional help. And, as measured by the California Test of Personality, both groups were apparently comparable as to personality adjustment.

[1]Burck, Harman D. and Cottingham, Harold F. The effects of counseling low-ability high-aspiring college freshmen. *Journal of College Student Personnel*, 1965, **6**, 270–283.

Special thanks are expressed to Drs. John P. Cummer, John Flanders, and Milton Jones who did the time-consuming task of completing the rating scales.

Study after study through the years has consistently shown that many high school and college students aspire to professional levels. Counselors at the college level have long been concerned about the many students who express unrealistic and inappropriate goals, both in terms of opportunities available and of their aptitudes, abilities, achievements, and interests. About 60 per cent of the advanced college male students in Iffert's (1957) national samples stated that upon entering college they were interested in engineering, science, medicine or law.

It is suspected that many of these students with high aspirations but relatively low academic ability contribute substantially to the turnover, migration, and dropouts of college students. Accordingly, it would appear that early identification and counseling with students who have such inappropriate or unrealistic educational aspirations would insure that more of these students were in courses and majors that were more in keeping with scholastic abilities and interests.

THE PROBLEM

The primary purpose of this study was to evaluate the effects of counseling on the external, immediate criterion of change from relatively inappropriate educational aspirations to aspirations that were more appropriate, that is, more consistent with individual abilities, interests and personality characteristics as rated by counselor-judges. A pre-selected voluntary group of college freshmen served as subjects.

To make use of an internal criterion, an attempt was made to measure changes of personal and social adjustment that would take place between counseled and non-counseled freshman students, using a standardized personality test and attitudinal-type of questionnaires.

While the criterion of appropriateness-inappropriateness is not new (Gonyea, 1962, 1963), this study restricted its use in relation to educational aspiration, rather than global, complex and undifferentiated terms like vocational choice, vocational objective and vocational plans.

The reasons for selecting subjects who had signified an intention to major in one of four pre-professional curricula, viz., pre-medicine, pre-dentistry, pre-law and pre-engineering science, were twofold: (1) These are considered to be *high* aspirations (particularly by college freshmen), curricula for them are fairly well defined and rigid, and because as professional groups more is known about students entering and succeeding in these areas (e.g., required ability for admission, interests, and in some cases, personality characteristics); and (2) because of the above reasons counselor-judges probably could more nearly agree on the appropriateness-inappropriateness level, given certain actuarial information.

PROCEDURE

An examination of the applications of all male freshman students admitted to the Florida State University in the fall of 1963 was made and a list compiled of those who signified an intention of majoring in the four previously mentioned pre-professional majors. From this list those who scored 350 or less total percentile points on the Florida Twelfth Grade Placement Tests (maximum score: 495), or those whose upper limit of the total SCAT band did not exceed the 60th percentile, were identified (N = 40). Generally, students achieving no better than this on either of the above tests are found at the lower end of the freshman curve of academic ability at FSU because of admission standards.

Thirty-five of the 40 students volunteered freely to participate in the study. By random assignment, the experimental (counseled) group contained 18, the control (deferred waiting list – non-counseled) group contained 17 subjects.

Students in both groups completed pre- and postcounseling questionnaires, completed an interest inventory, took the California Test of Personality (form AA, precounseling; form BB, postcounseling), and indicated their educational aspirations on two occasions (initial, precounseling; and postcounseling). In addition, students in the counseled group were administered other tests and received the results as requested on an individual basis.

COUNSELOR-JUDGES AND RATINGS

Three counselor-judges, members of the counseling center staff, rated each aspiration on a six-point scale ranging from Extremely Appropriate (6) to Extremely Inappropriate (1) according to instructions and supplied data about the admission and success of students in the four professional areas. Essentially, the judges used a case-method approach in their ratings since they had a wealth of information for each student (e.g., at least high school grades, parent's occupation, interest inventory results, SCAT scores, personality test scores, and other personal data). The judges did not have access to case notes. Results of the counselor-judges' mean ratings for both pre- and post experimental conditions are presented in Table 1.

Pearson r's for paired judges (pooled preratings) yielded the following:

Table 1 Counselor-Judges' Mean Ratings and Standard Deviations for Pre- and Post Experimental Conditions.

Group	Pre-Counseling Rating	Post-Counseling Rating
Experimental Group	M = 2.22	M = 4.51
(N = 18)	S.D. = 0.83	S.D. = 0.82
Control Group	M = 1.70	M = 1.86
(N =17)	S.D. = 0.47	S.D. = 0.29

0.68, 0.68, 0.52. Conversion to z-transformations and back to a mean r yielded 0.64. Ebel's formula for intra-class reliability produced a coefficient of 0.498 for one judge, and 0.75 for the three judges combined. This reliability was considered sufficient and acceptable considering the following: (1) ratings by the judges were done in a strictly independent fashion (similar studies usually provide for an extra rater in case of disagreement or they have conferences among judges which enhances agreement), (2) homogeneous grouping of high-aspiration, relatively-low-ability subjects is not conducive to high correlation coefficients, (3) a rather small N of 35, and (4) curtailed range of the rating scale which tends to depress the coefficient.

COUNSELING

All counseling was done by the first author, who has had four years counseling experience, the last two being in a university setting. The counseling sessions were largely unstructured, a sincere effort was made to create a permissive atmosphere and the process attempted to follow the postulates of client-centered theory. Care was taken not to covertly or overtly persuade any client that he should change his educational aspiration. The only information about the study which the students had was that certain characteristics of students interested in medicine, dentistry, law and engineering were being investigated. They were not aware of being chosen because of their relatively low ability. A total of 86 counseling sessions were held for a mean of 4.52 sessions per client over a period of about three months.

RESULTS

The counseled group received a pre-counseling mean rating of appropriateness-inappropriateness of 2.22 and a mean postcounseling rating of 4.51 (Table 1). This resulting mean difference of 2.29 was clearly significant at the 0.05 level of significance ($t = 9.27$). Only three of the 18 counseled subjects reported the same educational aspiration as before counseling. There was a noticeable shift to aspirations in business administration (11 such instances). Other reported aspirations at the end of counseling were: military career, art and education (2 cases).

For the noncounseled group, the mean rating on the six-point scale was 1.70; post-counseling mean was 1.86. This difference of 0.16 was not significant at the 0.05 level ($t = 1.35$). Fifteen of this group maintained the same educational aspiration from pre- to post-counseling, which represents 88 per cent of the group. Two subjects changed to other pre-professional goals.

To test the significance of the difference in mean gain of 2.29 (pre- to post-rating, counseled group) and the mean gain of 0.16 (pre- to post-rating, noncounseled group) a t test for uncorrelated means was computed. The resulting t value of 7.74 was highly significant at the 0.05 level, indicating that the counseled group gained a significant amount of appropriateness, whereas the control group did not so gain.

On the post-counseling questionnaire all subjects were asked to state how sure they were of their educational aspiration by checking one of the following: very certain, fairly certain, somewhat uncertain, and completely uncertain. The rating scale was then dichotomized into Appropriate and Inappropriate. Correlating the degree of certainty and the post-counseling mean rating for all subjects produced a biserial r of 0.46. This coefficient was significant at the 0.04 level ($t = 2.35$), indicating a significant positive relationship between each S's post-counseling appropriateness rating and his reported degree of certainty of education aspiration.

To check on the internal criterion of possible personality differences and changes that would obtain as a result of counseling, the California Test of Personality (Secondary Series) was administered to both groups in the following order: form AA was administered before counseling and form BB was administered after counseling. Using total raw scores and the t statistic, no significant differences were noted for the counseled group (difference between pre- and post-test) since $t = 0.74$. Further, no significant difference obtained for the noncounseled group ($t = 0.36$). Nor was there any significant difference between the mean change in total adjustment raw score for the counseled group and the mean change for the control group. Accordingly, in this study, counseling was of no significant help in raising total raw scores on the California Test of Personality, and lack of counseling neither raised nor lowered the total scores for the noncounseled group. Hence, these data suggest that college male freshmen with defined high educational aspirations and relatively low academic ability, as groups, receive "average" total adjustment scores on the California Test of Personality and that counseling or lack of it does not influence the scores significantly.

One of the most outstanding impressions was the overwhelming eagerness, willingness, and cooperativeness of all the students involved. Although the study was completely voluntary (the Ss were reminded of this several times) and a student's time is quite precious under a trimester system of operation, the Ss were quite punctual with appointments and eager to enter counseling.

DISCUSSION

Before interpreting the results of this study in relation to other similar research, the reader should be aware of other important variables concerned with the present study.

1. There was no significant difference between the counseled and the noncounseled group's mean total raw score on the SCAT test (63 and 61 respectively). This difference was not significant ($t = 1.00$). Hence the results of the treatment variable (counseling) cannot be attributed to the counseled Ss having more academic ability as measured by this instrument.
2. It was important to measure the difference on the criterion variable (rated appropriateness-inappropriateness) for the two groups before the treatment variable was administered. Again Table 1 provides these data. It is not surprising that both groups were rated so inappropriate (2.22 and 1.70) because of the selection procedure. The 0.52 difference was not significant at the 0.05 level ($t = 1.30$) suggesting that both groups had approximately the same distance for possible gain in appropriateness of educational aspiration.
3. In order to ascertain the nature and extent of counseling and/or psychotherapy the subjects had received prior to the experiment, each S was asked to give this information on the precounseling questionnaire. No S had seen a psychologist or a psychiatrist for personal reasons. Five of the counseled group and 6 of the experimental group had seen high school counselors for test interpretation and for about the same number of visits. This factor may be ruled out as a strong variable.
4. An important problem in counseling and psychotherapy research is the matter of control groups really being true control groups. Bergin (1963) points this out thusly, "the fact is that we have little knowledge whatsoever as to what goes on in control groups." In this study an attempt was

made to control for this issue in two ways. First, the cooperation of various other units on campus were alerted and supplied a list of the Ss so that outside professional help and influence could be controlled as best possible. These units included the Dean of Men, residence counselors, clinics and academic advisors. The point was not to deny them services but at least ascertain the frequency of such relationships. Second, the post-counseling questionnaire asked if the S had received other help, information or advice with personal or educational problems. Here, off-campus and hometown relationships were sought. Only one S in the control group reporting seeing his dormitory counselor for one counseling interview. Thus, it appears that this outside influence was controlled as best could be done.

The results of this study tend to confirm the findings of Hoyt (1955) who reported that the vocational objectives stated by clients "after counseling were significantly more realistic than those stated by a nonclient control group."

The present study seems to tie in more closely with two recent studies done by Gonyea (1962, 1963). The first study, which did not make use of a control group but which did account for initial precounseling vocational objectives, found that the overall increase in appropriateness of vocational choice was highly significant. Gonyea reported that "the incidence of change in both educational and vocational plans was significantly greater among clients whose precounseling objectives had been rated inappropriate." The results of the present study confirm this (significant change in appropriateness accompanying counseling) and adds credence to it because of the use of a control group. Further, in this study by Gonyea, it was found that after a one-year follow-up the results based on immediate post-counseling plans seemed to "wash out" slightly and even negated what seemed to be evidence for the effectiveness of vocational counseling. Since the present study used an immediate criterion only and did not include a follow-up, this relation cannot be reported.

The second study by Gonyea (1963) had to do with freshmen who stated their vocational objectives initially and then four to six years later. A non-volunteer control group was used. Summarizing, Gonyea reported neither group showed a significant change in appropriateness of vocational choice, and there was no significant difference between the two groups with respect to amount of change. Gonyea interpreted these results to suggest that gains observable immediately after counseling do not endure. The writers find two serious shortcomings of this second study: (1) using a control group who had not requested counseling (this is pointed out in the article), and (2) it is not clear whether or not the control groups did not, in fact, receive some kind of professional attention. Regarding this point, it is only pointed out that the control subjects did not receive vocational counseling at a certain counseling center. It is speculated that at a large university there are many sources from which a student may gain information about himself and about the world of work in both professional counseling and non-professional relationships.

Indeed, one of the major limitations of the present study is the lack of an ultimate criterion. Because of this, the results cannot refute or add anything to the tendency that has already been found, viz., appropriateness of vocational choice is highest immediately after counseling but tends to decline during the following year. It should be pointed out that because of the assumed positive and negative reinforcements students often get from final semester grades, this study was intentionally restricted to this period of time and terminated before issuance of final grades.

It appears that those engaged in counseling research are faced with a paradoxical situation here. On the one hand, there is a plea or even a demand that studies must be of a longitudinal nature so that follow-up observations will include ultimate criteria. Yet, on the other hand, it is indeed difficult, if not impossible at the present time, to control for possible therapeutic relationships in which so-called control subjects may get involved. Perhaps one solution might be to use large numbers of clients and then to simply drop from the study those subjects who have received outside help and attention. This is a problem which must be reckoned with.

REFERENCES

Bergin, A. E. The effects of psychotherapy: Negative results revisited. *J. counsel. Psychol.*, 1963, **10**, 244–249.

Gonyea, G. C. Appropriateness-of-vocational-choice as a criterion of counseling outcome. *J. counsel. Psychol.*, 1962, **9**, 213–219.

Gonyea, G. C. Appropriateness of vocational choice of counseled and un-counseled college students. *J. counsel. Psychol.*, 1963, **10**, 269–275.

Hoyt, D. P. An evaluation of group and individual programs in vocational guidance. *J. appl. Psychol.*, 1955, **39**, 26–30.

Iffert, R. E. *Retention and withdrawal of college students*, U.S. Dept. of Health, Education and Welfare, Office of Education, Bulletin 1958, No. 1. Washington: U.S. Government Printing Office, 1957.

McNemar, Q. *Psychological statistics*. New York: Wiley & Sons, 1955.

Note: Critique of this and the following article appears on page 160.

COUNSELING COLLEGE FRESHMEN: A THREE-YEAR FOLLOW-UP[1]

Harman D. Burck

University of North Carolina, Greensboro
(*Received* October 20, 1967)

The principal service of a university counseling center continues to be educational-vocational in nature (Clark, 1965). The assumption is that students who receive counseling which provides meaningful information, and which sets into motion self-exploration and decision-making processes, will be better off than those who do not receive this service. How true is this? Research findings are inconsistent and inconclusive in supporting this assumption.

This is a three-year follow-up of an original investigation which was concerned with the effects of counseling with comparatively low-ability, high-aspiring college freshmen (Burck and Cottingham, 1965). The first study was an outcome one, using the immediate external criterion of appropriateness of educational-vocational aspiration. That study and this follow-up attempted to control and account for some of the methodological shortcomings of similar counseling research (i.e., using volunteer control group and available precounseling baseline data; and insuring that the control group did not, in fact, receive counseling).

THE ORIGINAL STUDY

Forty male students who entered the Florida State University (FSU) in the fall of 1963 with defined (preprofessional) educational aspirations but comparatively low ability were identified. By letter invitation, 35 freely volunteered for the study and were randomly assigned to an E (counseled) group (N = 18), and a C (noncounseled) group (N = 17). Students in both groups completed the SVIB, the California Test of Personality (form AA and BB), precounseling and postcounseling questionnaires, and indicated their educational aspirations before and after counseling.

All counseling was done by the author on an individual basis. The sessions were unstructured and a sincere effort was made to create a permissive atmosphere in which the processes attempted to follow the postulates

[1]Burck, Harman D. Counseling college freshmen: A three-year follow-up. *Journal of College Student Personnel*, 1969, **10**, 21–26.

of client-centered theory. The S's were not aware of the purpose of the study (other than being told that certain characteristics of students in these preprofessional areas were being investigated) and special care was taken not to persuade any S that he should change his major. The average number of counseling sessions was 4.52 during a three month period. Three counselor-judges, using a case study approach, independently rated each aspiration (pre and post conditions) on a six-point scale ranging from Extremely Inappropriate-1 to Extremely Appropriate-6.

The result indicated that in the E group's postcounseling rating, appropriateness of educational-vocational aspiration was significantly greater than the pre-counseling rating. There was no such significant gain for the C group. These results substantiated Hoyt's (1955) findings that vocational objectives stated by clients "after counseling were significantly more realistic than those stated by a non-client control group," and Gonyea's (1962) findings that the overall increase in appropriateness of vocational choice as a result of counseling was highly significant.

FOLLOW-UP PROCEDURE

A follow-up questionnaire was sent to all S's in the E and C groups seeking pertinent information about their current educational-vocational status, their satisfaction with the counseling received (E S's), and their immediate future goals. Several follow-up letters and one telephone call secured data from all S's (100 percent), by December, 1966. It was found that 10 of the E and nine of the C S's were still enrolled at FSU; eight E and eight C S's were no longer at FSU.

For purpose of a more thorough follow-up, the original two groups were sub-divided into the following subgroups: E, nondropout, (END); E, dropout (ED); C, nondropout (CND); and C, dropout (CD). Dropouts were those who were no longer enrolled at FSU at the time of the follow-up and nondropouts were those who still were enrolled at FSU. Although the main criterion in this study was appropriateness of educational-vocational aspiration, it was considered desirable, in retrospect, to examine some other variables which are often used to evaluate counseling outcomes (e.g., GPA, incidence of withdrawal, satisfaction with counseling, and subsequent counseling). The 0.05 level of confidence was pre-selected to test statistical differences.

The follow-up educational-vocational aspiration of each S in the E and C groups was rated, using the original six-point scale. The judges used essentially a case-method approach as before. No case notes were used by the judges, nor were they able to distinguish between counseled-non-counseled, dropout-nondropout S's.

The follow-up ratings were done by three counselors of the FSU counseling center staff, all of whom were advanced doctoral students. Unfortunately, these were not the judges who did the ratings originally. All ratings were done in a strict independent fashion (no fourth rater or case-conference was used in case of disagreement). Pearson *r's* for paired judges (pooled follow-up ratings) yielded the following: 0.19, 0.34, 0.74. Conversion to z-coefficients and back to a mean *r* yielded 0.40, significant at the 0.05 level. Ebel's formula for intraclass reliability produced a coefficient of 0.45 for one judge, and 0.71 for 3 judges combined. This degree of reliability was considered sufficient in view of the strictly independent fashion in which the raters worked.

RESULTS

This section will report finding for the two groups, E and C, and the four subgroups (END, ED, CDN, CD).

General Findings (E and C groups)

1. GPA: There was no significant difference between the E and C groups' mean GPA (1.88 and 1.93). The counseled S's did not achieve a higher academic grade average than did the noncounseled S's.
2. Degree of satisfaction with counseling: Items on both the post-counseling and follow-up questionnaire were designed to ascertain S's perceived satisfaction with counseling (viz: 1-greatly dissatisfied, 2-dissatisfied, 3-satisfied, and 4-greatly satisfied). These data are, of course, for the experimental S's only (END and ED). They reveal no significant differences ($t = 1.30$) in mean change of degree of satisfaction. Yet, the follow-up mean scores for both groups were in the direction of less satisfaction with the counseling. There was no significant correlation between the reported follow-up degree of satisfaction with counseling and appropriateness of educational aspiration (0.20 for the END group, and 0.17 for the ED group).
3. Subsequent counseling: In the original study care was taken to account for other counseling and professional help received by S's. One item on the follow-up questionnaire sought to ascertain the amount and nature of any subsequent counseling and therapy that either the E and C S's had received. Only one control S and none in

the E group returned to the FSU counseling center for services! This one student returned for one interview for test interpretation. Yet, at the conclusion of the study in 1963, all control S's were invited by letter to come to the center for test interpretation and counseling. In addition, none of the S's reported having received any counseling or therapy of any nature from any source during this three year period.

Dropouts (ED and CD subgroups)

The ED group was employed thus: 2 junior college, 2 military, 1 state trooper, 1 finance collector, 1 TV technician and 1 enrolled at a different university. The CD group was employed thus: 2 junior college, 4 military, 1 unemployed, and 1 enrolled at a different university. The 4 in junior colleges were enrolled in terminal programs.

1. GPA: There was no significant difference between the cumulative mean GPA (1.37 and 1.66) of these two subgroups ($t = 1.52$) indicating that during their stay at FSU the counseled group did no better academically than did their controls.
2. Incidence of dropout: Eight S's from the E group and eight from the C group dropped out of FSU. Hence, counseling had no greater influence on college retention than did no counseling.
3. Appropriateness of Educational-Vocational Aspiration: Table 1 contains the mean ratings, standard deviations and *t* values for all

Table 1 Means, Standard Deviations, and *t*-Values for Three Rating Conditions.

Group	A Precounseling	BC Postcounseling	Follow-up	*t*		
				AB	AC	BC
END (N = 10)						
Mean	2.22	4.36	3.79	7.13*	3.82*	1.35
SD	0.92	0.98	0.80			
CND (N = 9)						
Mean	1.73	1.99	4.06	1.30	8.03*	7.93*
SD	0 38	0.37	0.58			
ED (N = 8)						
Mean	2 22	4.70	4.60	9.27*	4 63*	1.10
SD	0.73	0.89	0.63			
CD (N = 8)						
Mean	1.66	1.70	4.70	1.26	9.70*	8.95*
SD	0 26	0.39	0.76			

*Significant at the 0.01 level of confidence.

conditions. Among the students who had dropped out of FSU at the time of the follow-up, the rated appropriateness of educational and vocational aspirations had increased in the counseled group during the period of counseling but had remained essentially the same in the noncounseled group during the same period. The ratings of the two groups had been comparable before counseling and were again substantially the same at the time of the three-year follow-up. The gain in appropriateness seen in the counseled group during the period of counseling was matched by the noncounseled dropouts by the time of the follow-up.

Nondropouts (END and CND subgroups)

1. GPA: The END group accumulated 731 trimester hours and the CND group accumulated 760 hours (no significant difference $t = 1.10$). No statistical significance occurred between the mean GPA (2.29 and 2.18) of these subgroups ($t = 0.55$), signifying that the counseled S's did not achieve a higher grade average than the noncounseled.
2. Appropriateness of Educational-Vocational Aspiration: Table 1 reveals that among the students still enrolled at FSU at the time of the follow-up, the rated appropriateness of educational and vocational aspirations had increased in the counseled group during the period of counseling but had remained essentially constant in the noncounseled group during the same period. The ratings of the two groups had been comparable before counseling and were again substantially the same at the time of the follow-up three years later. The gain in appropriateness seen in the counseled group during the period of counseling was matched in the noncounseled group by the time of the follow-up.

In summary, three years following counseling, the counseled dropouts and nondropouts maintained about the same degree of rated appropriateness (the difference in change not being significant). Yet, the noncounseled dropouts and nondropouts did significantly increase in rated appropriateness.

DISCUSSION

This section will interpret the findings of this study within the context of findings of similar studies having to do with the effects of counseling.

Appropriateness/Realism of Vocational Choice

The most obvious finding is that the significant gains in rated appropriateness of educational-vocational aspirations of nondropouts noted immediately after counseling did not endure for two years. These results substantiate an earlier finding of Gonyea (1962): "It was also noted that the pre- to post-counseling trend was rarely continued in the follow-up period and in many cases even reversed, and that results based on immediate post-counseling plans seemed to wash out slightly when follow-up objectives were considered."

The results support another finding by Gonyea (1963), "on the basis of the results of the present study it was concluded that these apparent gains, measurable soon after counseling, are in fact not very enduring." It appears that the use of a volunteer control group and attempts to correct other methodological shortcomings in this study add credence to Gonyea's conclusions.

Another finding, the fact the noncounseled S's (CDN, CD) gained significantly in appropriateness, hints at the old issue of spontaneous remission suggested earlier by Eysenck (1961). The results here seem to suggest that college freshmen with initial inappropriate educational aspirations will change to more appropriate aspirations with time and the usual influences found in the college environment, but without having received professional counseling. An equally important finding is that counseling accelerated the change from inappropriate to more appropriate aspirations.

This study relates also to a recent seven- to eight-year follow-up by Hewer (1966) which reported data for a group of marginal students receiving individual and group counseling. Hewer concludes, "Realism of vocational choice is a meaningful goal for vocational counseling and suitable criterion for judging its effectiveness." This conclusion is tenuous since use of a control group was not made, and, had there been one, it may have been found that those not receiving either form of counseling may have been just as realistic in earlier vocational choices.

Grade Point Average

Although GPA was not a concern in the original study, it was examined in retrospect because of its continued frequent use as a criterion in college counseling. The results here tend to confirm Gonyea's (1962) finding "that changes in appropriateness of vocational choice were not reflected by changes in academic performance."

The present study found no significant differences in GPA between the two groups of E and C S's, and no significant GPA differences between nondropouts and dropouts. These results, in general, support the findings of Hill and Grieneeks (1966a), "the unfortunate truth seems to be that counseling just does not markedly influence grades," and the same authors' later findings (1966b), "if academic counseling is positively affecting performance it is not being reflected when the criterion measure chosen is grade point average." Again, Hill and Grieneeks' results should be considered quite tentative since both studies lacked a volunteer control group, and the nature of counseling (who counseled and for how long) was not specified. This finding also supports negative findings of other studies concerned with GPA as a criterion (Goodstein and Crites, 1961; Richardson, 1960, 1964; Winborn, 1962; Searles, 1962, and Volsky, Magoon, Norman & Hoyt, 1965, p. 163).

Satisfaction with Counseling

Although reported satisfaction of counseling has been a disputed criterion in counseling research (Patterson, 1958; Goodstein and Grigg, 1959) there is some consensus that it is an important factor in a total evaluation effort. The results here showed no significant difference in mean change of satisfaction and no significant relationship between satisfaction and appropriateness. Since the counseling received was of a client-centered nature, this substantiates a finding of Forgy and Black's (1954), "these same clients no longer had these feelings (reported greater satisfaction with client-centered counseling) in a three-year follow-up; indeed, the reverse was then true although the differences were not statistically significant." It might be speculated that S's initially reported satisfaction with counseling is a transient phenomenon and largely the result of a halo-effect.

Subsequent Counseling

Since this study made use of a volunteer control group another factor appears relevant. As reported earlier, only one S in the original C group returned for one counseling interview. None of these S's requested nor received professional help elsewhere during the follow-up period. This interesting fact supports a similar finding by Volsky *et al.* (1965, p. 160): "Continuing follow-ups of these controls revealed that none sought formal counseling during the remainder of the time they spent at the university!" Frank (1958) points out that clients put on waiting lists show a low rate of return. The shift in appropriateness of the control group during the three year interval tends to support the hypothesis that students who seek help, but are temporarily denied it, find other ways and other sources of information which eventually lead to aspirations that are just as appropriate as those receiving more immediate help. For those interested in the problem of waiting lists, a possible remedy is suggested by Sinnett and Danskin (1966).

Incidence of Dropout

The fact that eight S's in each original group dropped out supports the finding of Gonyea (1963), "clearly there were no significant differences between clients and non-clients with respect to incidence of withdrawal from the university.

IMPLICATIONS

This study again raises the question of the vocational realism/appropriateness criterion being a valid measure of stable, meaningful effects of college counseling. If we accept the results of this study as well as Gonyea's finding then we should begin to take hard looks at our goals and objectives, procedures, and expectations of counseling at the college level, since educational-vocational counseling accounts for the great bulk of our efforts. Certainly, an intensive search for more sensitive criteria is in order. The suggestions of Krumboltz (1966) and others (Volsky, p. 178; Tiedeman, 1960), which argue for individualizing goals and objectives for the client should seriously be considered.

The effects of vocational counseling in college centers using the criterion of appropriateness or realism of vocational choice are still not demonstrated. Magoon's (1962) question remains unanswered, "Counselor judgement of appropriateness of vocational choice should be valid criterion measures. If they are not, then why aren't they?"

REFERENCES

Burck, H. D., & Cottingham, H. F. The effects of counseling low-ability high-aspiring college freshmen. *Journal of College Student Personnel*, 1965, **6**, 279–283 .

Clark, D. D. Current emphasis and characteristics of counseling centers in universities of over 10,000 enrollment. Unpublished manuscript. Lubbock: Texas Technological College, July, 1965.

Eysenck, H. J. The effects of psychotherapy. In H. J. Eysenck (Ed.), *Handbook of Abnormal Psychology*. New York: Basic Books, 1961, 697–725.

Forgy, E. W., & Black, J. D. A follow-up after three years of clients counseled by two methods. *Journal of Counseling Psychology*, 1954, **1**, 1–8.

Frank, J. D. Problems of controls in psychotherapy as exemplified by the psychotherapy research project of the Phipps psychiatric clinic. In E. A. Rubinstein, & M. B. Parloff (Eds.), *Research in Psychotherapy*. Washington, D.C.: American Psychological Association, 1958, 11–24.

Gonyea, G. C. Appropriateness of vocational choice as a criterion of counseling outcome. *Journal of Counseling Psychology*, 1962, **9**, 213–219.

Gonyea, G. C. Appropriateness of vocational choice of counseled and uncounseled college students. *Journal of Counseling Psychology*, 1963, **10**, 269–275.

Goodstein, L. D., & Grigg, A. E. Client satisfaction, counselors, and the counseling process. *Personnel and Guidance Journal*, 1959, **38**, 19–24.

Goodstein, L. D., & Crites, J. D. Brief counseling with poor college risks. *Journal of Counseling Psychology*, 1961, **8**, 318–321.

Hewer, V. H. Evaluation of a criterion: Realism of vocational choice. *Journal of Counseling Psychology*, 1966, **13**, 289–294.

Hill, A. H., & Grieneeks, L. Criteria in the Evaluation of educational and vocational counseling in college. *Journal of Counseling Psychology*, 1966, **13**, 198–201. (a)

Hill, A. H., & Grieneeks, L. An evaluation of academic counseling of under- and over-achievers. *Journal of Counseling Psychology*, 1966, **13**, 325–328. (b)

Hoyt, D. P. An evaluation of group and individual programs in vocational guidance. *Journal of Applied Psychology*, 1955, **39**, 26–30.

Krumboltz, J. D. Behavioral goals for counseling. *Journal of Counseling Psychology*, Summer, 1966, **13**, 153–159.

Magoon, T. Comment. *Journal of Counseling Psychology*, 1962, **9**, 220.

Patterson, C. H. Client expectations and social conditioning. *Personnel and Guidance Journal*, 1958, **37**, 136–138.

Patterson, C. H. The evaluation of guidance and personnel services. *Review of Education Research*, 1963, **33**, 214–222.

Richardson, L. H. Counseling the ambitious mediocre student. *Journal of Counseling Psychology*, 1960, **7**, 265–268.

Searles, A., Jr. The effectiveness of limited counseling in improving the academic achievement of superior college freshmen. *Personnel and Guidance Journal*, 1962, **40**, 630–633.

Sinnett, E. R., & Danskin, D. G. Intake and walk-in procedures in a college counseling setting. *Personnel and Guidance Journal*, 1967, **45**, 445–451.

Tiedeman, D. Comment. *Journal of Counseling Psychology*, 1960, **7**, 90.

Volsky, T., Jr., Magoon, T. M., Norman, W. T., & Hoyt, D. P. The outcomes of counseling and psychotherapy: theory and research. Minneapolis: University of Minnesota Press, 1965.

Winborn, B., & Schmidt, L. G. The effectiveness of short-term group counseling upon academic achievement of potentiality superior but under-achieving college freshmen. *Journal of Educational Research*, 1962, **55**, 169–173.

CRITIQUE

1. PHILOSOPHICAL AND THEORETICAL CONSIDERATIONS

The counseling approach in the original and follow-up study is reported to follow the postulates of client-centered theory. The authors report this to be the provision of sessions which were largely unstructured containing a permissive atmosphere. Yet, the primary purpose is "to evaluate the effects of counseling on the external, immediate criterion of change from relatively inappropriate educational aspirations, ... to aspirations that were more appropriate. ..." Since we have stated that theoretical models should generate the goals and objectives of counseling (Chapters 2 and 3), we find the above quite inappropriate. For example, why should one *expect* a person to have more appropriate educational aspirations as a result of *x* sessions of client-centered counseling? In fact, he may have more inappropriate aspirations as judged by certain kinds of counselor-judges. Concisely, it does not follow that a college freshman's educational (or vocational) aspirations would be any more appropriate after having received a few sessions of so-called client-centered, permissive, unstructured counseling. Perhaps a more direct and logical way to change one's educational aspirations would have been to follow a more cognitive (i.e., providing information about who gets into professional schools), informational approach.

The authors fail to offer any broad theoretical outline as a framework for their study. They could have included to advantage conceptual material on aspects of the interaction, such as goals, processes, and outcomes, in much greater detail.

There is insufficient evidence that the orientation designated as "client-centered" is clearly justified. The authors should provide data that support this theoretical assumption. It would have been helpful to have had a clearer delineation of the therapist and his behavior as independent variables as well as dependent variables of the experiencing type.

2. THE CRITERIA

These comments will be divided into two sections to correspond to (a) the original study and (b) the follow-up.

a. Three criteria were used in the original study: (1) appropriateness/inappropriateness of educational objectives, (2) degree of certainty of the educational aspirations, and (3) change in group mean scores on the California Test of Personality. The first one is immediate, somewhat objective and external. The last two are immediate but of the self-report variety. The criterion of appropriateness/inappropriateness seems to follow clearly from the goals and objectives as stated by the authors, but does not necessarily follow very closely from the theoretical rationale of client-centered counseling. Regarding the last two criteria, several things might be said: Why should a student be more certain about his aspirations as a result of unstructured counseling? One might well speculate that he would be much less certain, but not yet decided and that this uncertainty might be a psychologically healthy phenomenon. Why would a student be expected to respond more like norm groups *vis-à-vis* personality items as a result of this undefined treatment? No wonder there were no significant differences between the two groups on this criterion measure.

b. In the three-year follow-up, the author used GPA, satisfaction with counseling, incidence of dropout, and appropriateness of educational aspiration. The author states that it was "considered desirable, in retrospect to examine some other variables which are often used to evaluate counseling outcomes." This is very interesting, but the criterion of GPA seems like an artifact of the original study. Logically, why would one expect a student's GPA to increase or be high because of a couple of sessions of undefined client-centered counseling (which, incidentally, was supposed to increase his appropriateness of educational aspirations)? Incidence of dropout and GPA are, however, external, objective measures. Degree of satisfaction with counseling is a subjective criterion, and the finding here substantiates other findings—clients generally respond in a very satisfied way immediately after counseling. Yet, on follow-up there is a tendency to report less satisfaction.

3. RESEARCH DESIGN

The matter of control is of paramount importance when the design of a counseling research study is assessed. In general, this study (including the follow-up) is well designed. Examination of the control problems noted in Chapter 3 and the methods employed by the authors to handle those problems supports the quality of the experimental design.

The design employed by the counselor-researchers was of a classical experimental variety, a pre-post control group design. The control group was composed of delayed treatment clients, and the authors may be judged from their comments to have been sensitive to the manifold problems of wait control groups. The purpose of the study was to compare counseled and noncounseled subjects, and the design employed was appropriate for that purpose.

4. SELECTION AND SAMPLING PROCEDURES

The population in this study was composed of low-ability, college freshmen males, planning majors in several preprofessional areas. In effect this population became the sample. The arbitrary definition of the sample may be questioned. Why were females, physics majors, or those scoring above the 350 total percentile excluded? The sample, then, was purposively drawn. Unfortunately, no sampling was possible regarding the counselor because only one was used—the counselor-researcher himself.

Assignment to experimental or control groups was done randomly, and this procedure adequately controls for several kinds of bias (See Chapter 5). However, the exact randomization procedure should have been reported.

The number of subjects used in the study is small, but adequate. There are especially noticeable difficulties in the follow-up, because only seven or eight people are included in the dropout-non-dropout categories for E and C groups. The fact that the findings are cautiously generalized and related to other research tempers the problem of the small *N*.

In general, the main problem in this area relates to the possible experimenter-bias effect, and the lack of any adequate sampling procedure for the counselor treatment variable. This study could have been improved if several counselors and proportionally more clients had been involved, but this would have drastically increased the work involved for the counselor-researcher. The continuing question is whether or not the added control is worth the price.

5. COUNSELING AND THERAPY TREATMENT

The only description of what the treatment actually involved is that reported by the counselor-researcher, who also did the counseling. The report that the sessions were largely unstructured, permissive, and attempted to follow the postulates of client-centered theory, is really not very helpful. This is a very serious limitation of this study. This would have been a good study to use some of the process rating scales which attempt to measure the degrees of empathy, warmth, genuineness, etc. It would have been simple to have tape-recorded some of the sessions in a random way, and to have had other counselors rate the sessions on important process dimensions.

Of course, there is a concern that the author both designed and executed the study. In fact, he was the counselor for all treatments. This may have introduced experimenter bias in the study in an unknown quantity or direction. For example, realizing he was counselor and researcher he may have been unduly cautious not to influence the client; conversely, being human, the counselor may not have been able to control his natural biases. Generally, the counselor/therapist should not be researcher/designer.

6. MEASUREMENT

The central criterion in this study was the appropriateness of educational aspirations. While the authors restricted this to the educational objective, rather than vocational or career objectives, the concept of appropriateness is still quite vague and global. Who determines what is appropriate for a college student to major in? Whereas ability, interests, and personality characteristics are related to appropriateness, it seems that the main element is a value loaded one. In a complex and rapidly changing world of work, at a time when the college student could pick a job from a multitude of opportunities, who can say when an educational aspiration is appropriate for one student, and not for another. Yet, the authors are wrestling with a real problem, and, in this situation, measured the criterion in the best way they could (a case method approach and rating scales). One way of handling this would have been to have several actual case demonstrations of appropriate and inappropriate educational aspirations. This would have helped to objectify the concept of appropriateness.

Although the reported reliabilities of ratings seemed to be low (even though they are statistically significant) the raters did do the rating in a very strict independent fashion. The authors could have increased the reliability by using a judge or referee to smooth out extreme differences between judges. Our preference is for the independent ratings, even if they do not yield as high a coefficient.

7. ETHICAL, PROFESSIONAL, AND LEGAL CONSIDERATIONS

Each student evidently had a clear choice as to whether or not to participate in this study. None of the students are identified by name. The study seems to have been handled in an ethical and professional manner.

As a research study, little if any recognition is given to any counselor bias that may be present in the dual role of researcher and change agent. It is regrettable that this point is not even mentioned. Could any subtleties be at work here?

In another area, the reader finds no awareness of the possible interferences with the on-going services of the counseling center due to the time and energy needed for this research. Was additional time, out of office, used for research without any loss of services to regular clients? Some cognizance of the problems here might have been included.

8. RESULTS

Essentially, the results of this study show the following: (1) Students who are judged to have inappropriate educational aspirations, and who receive a few sessions of counseling will change their educational objectives to ones which are more appropriate. (2) Students, as described above, who do not receive such counseling, finally choose more appropriate aspirations, but it takes them much longer (in this situation, three years or less). So, counseling, here described, accelerated more realistic and appropriate educational decision-making. (3) This kind of counseling does not increase GPA, incidence of dropout, or amount of subsequent counseling sought or received. (4) There is a tendency for clients to become less satisfied with counseling over time. Yet, because of the nature of the sample, generalizations are confined to college students.

EFFECT OF FEEDBACK ON INTERPERSONAL SENSITIVITY IN LABORATORY TRAINING GROUPS[1]

Gail E. Myers, Michele T. Myers, Alvin Goldberg, and Charles E. Welch[2]

The sixty-nine participants in the 1966 Rocky Mountain Workshop in Group Development, sponsored by the Adult Education Council of Metropolitan Denver, served as subjects in the present investigation. The study was designed to determine whether an instrumented feedback procedure based on sociometric ratings would help the members of laboratory training groups increase their sensitivity to others. It was found that subjects in experimental groups who filled out sociometric questionnaires and received feedback on their mutual ratings showed a significantly greater increase in sensitivity during a three-day period than control subjects who were not exposed to the sociometric procedure. Subjects in #1 and #2 control groups who rated one another but who did not receive feedback did not show a significant increase in sensitivity between the beginning and the end of the workshop, regardless of a time control in the administration of the questionnaire.

INTRODUCTION

The last twenty-five years have seen the development of a new human relations training methodology generally called laboratory training, sensitivity training, or T-Group training. Expansion of the methodology into industrial, community, educational, and military settings has been rapid and is still accelerating (Ferguson, 1959). Laboratory training is designed to provide individuals with an opportunity to learn about themselves, obtain insight into the behavior of others, and gain an understanding of group processes. By interacting with others in unstructured group situations in which openness and emotional frankness are encouraged, it is claimed that individuals can become aware of behavioral inadequacies and perhaps modify their feelings, attitudes, and values (Bradford, Gibb, &

[1]Reproduced by special permission from the *Journal of Applied Behavioral Science*, April/May/June 1969, **5**, (2), 175–185.

[2]Gail E. Myers is president, Monticello College, Godfrey, Illinois. Michele T. Myers is assistant professor of sociology, Social Science Department, Monticello College. Alvin Goldberg is professor of speech, Speech Department, University of Denver. Charles E. Welch is assistant professor, Radio and TV Department, University of Denver.

Benne, 1964; Schein & Bennis, 1965; Tannenbaum, Weschler, & Massarik, 1961).

There is no substantial scientific proof that laboratory training has an overall lasting effect. Some research evidence, however, indicates that the methodology does bring about change in people. For example, in a study of the effectiveness of a laboratory for school principals, Miles (1960) found that the participants improved significantly more than a control group in sensitivity, diagnostic ability, and action skills. Burke and Bennis (1961) discovered that the way people see themselves and the way in which they are seen become more similar over time as a result of a laboratory experience. Roberts, Schopler, Smith, and Gibb (in an unpublished paper cited by Dorothy Stock in Bradford, *et al.*, 1964) found that a T-Group experience is effective in reducing feelings of defensiveness and in increasing task efficiency.

One of the specific goals of laboratory training is to make T-Group members more sensitive to the interpersonal relationships which develop as their group matures. According to Miles (1960, p. 303), sensitivity is "... the ability to perceive what is actually going on in a social situation (including both behavioral events and inferred feelings of other persons)." This definition of sensitivity implies that interpersonal relationships can be studied along two dimensions: the behavioral and the perceptual. Tagiuri (1952, p. 91) has suggested: "At a broad level of generality, understanding of an interpersonal relationship depends upon the availability of information regarding two of its aspects: The first of these is the nature of the response of each person to the other. The second aspect consists of the *perception* that each person has of the other person's response toward him." Tagiuri believes that the evaluation of others' perception of self is an important dimension of social interaction.

Traditional sociometric methods focus primarily on the nature of the mutual responses of people in a group and not on the perceptual aspect of those responses. Standard sociometric procedures provide simultaneously two types of data about any member of a group: (a) data about his affective response to the other members and (b) data about the others' affective responses to him. To get at the perceptual dimension of interpersonal relations, Tagiuri (1952) developed a method by which data on the subject's perception of the situation can be gathered along with the information usually yielded by traditional sociometric approaches. The main feature of the method is the addition of "a 'guessing' or perceptual procedure"(Tagiuri, 1952, p. 92). Subjects are required to guess who will choose and reject them. This procedure is somewhat similar to Dymond's

Empathic or Rating Test (1949), where, in addition to rating members of his group on six personality scales, each subject is asked to predict how each group member will rate him. Since each rating is made on a five-point scale, the Dymond test can be scored in terms of the total number of points an individual is in error in his predicting. This is called the *Deviation Score*. Another method of scoring consists of counting the number of predictions which actually coincide with the ratings. This is called the *Right Score*.

Welch (unpublished instrument, University of Denver, 1966) developed an instrument designed to provide information about the degree of accuracy of a member's evaluation of other' perception of him. To complete the Welch instrument, each participant is required to rate every other member of his group on five-point scales. Comparisons can be made between ratings received by any member of a group and ratings each member anticipated from all the other members. The number of correct and incorrect guesses as well as the number of total points missed can be computed for each individual member. The direction of the error can be established (whether members under- or overrated themselves). Finally, a discrepancy percentage can be computed. This is the ratio between the total number of points actually missed by a member and the total number of points he might possibly have missed by, had he missed every guess maximally. Since the discrepancy percentage represents an index of a member's ability to "read" correctly how other members perceive him, it might be called a *sensitivity* index under Miles's terminology.

One of the goals of laboratory training is to increase the degree of accuracy of members' evaluation of how they are perceived—their sensitivity. One of the premises on which laboratory training is based is that in the accepting climate of the T-Group, members will feel freer to give honest feedback to one another. It is assumed that by receiving feedback on their behavior, members of the T-Group will learn how they affect others, a first step in the direction of change (Benne, Bradford, & Lippitt in Bradford, *et al.*, 1964, pp. 15–44).

The influence of feedback was investigated by Jenkins (1948), who found that giving feedback on interaction and on members' abilities was an important factor which led to increased group efficiency. Roberts, Schopler, Smith, and Gibb (cited by Stock in Bradford, *et al.*, 1964) found that there was a significant relationship among positive feedback, reduction of feelings of defensiveness, and task efficiency. Bass (1965, pp. 222–223) stated that members of a problem-solving group will feel dissatisfied if "feedback is not provided indicating the success with which a group is carrying out its assignments." Bass added: "Performance of individual members working as a group improves the most when they receive constructive information about their individual effort. . . . Equally useful is personal feedback of one member to another in improving problem-solving efficiency of all."

In an exploratory study, Myers, Tolela, and Welch (unpublished study, University of Denver, 1966) investigated the effect of feedback on interpersonal sensitivity. They found that groups of students enrolled in one section of the University of Denver Laboratory in Interpersonal Communication who regularly received the information derived from the Welch instrument significantly improved their sensitivity and interpersonal awareness. Students in a control section of the laboratory who did not receive systematic feedback improved significantly less in reducing their discrepancy between anticipated and received sociometric ratings.

THE STUDY

The present investigation was concerned with the following general question: Will a regular instrumented feedback procedure based on sociometric ratings help participants in a laboratory training group increase their sensitivity to interpersonal phenomena occurring in a group? Sensitivity was operationally defined as *the degree of discrepancy between ratings received and anticipated*. It was felt that an increase in sensitivity would be reflected in a reduction of the discrepancy percentage.

Hypotheses

More specifically, the study was designed to test the following hypotheses:

1. T-Group members who regularly provide and receive sociometric feedback will show a greater increase in sensitivity than T-Group members who do not systematically provide or receive such data.
2. T-Group members who regularly provide and receive sociometric feedback will show a greater increase in sensitivity than T-Group members who systematically provide but do not receive such data.

Subjects and Setting

The subjects for this study were the sixty-nine participants in the 16th Annual Summer Workshop of the Rocky Mountain Workshop in Group

Development, sponsored by the Adult Education Council of Metropolitan Denver. The three-day workshop took place at Glen Isle Lodge, Bailey, Colorado, June 16–19, 1966. Thirty-two subjects were male and 37 were female. All participants lived at the lodge for the three-day period.

Six T Groups were formed at the outset of the workshop. All of the groups met individually for a total of eight sessions. The sessions ranged from one hour and a half to two hours in length. Two staff members (trainer and assistant trainer) were present in each group for each meeting. In addition to the T-Group training sessions, lectures, discussions, and demonstrations on theoretical material were regularly scheduled throughout the workshop and were presented by the training consultant[3] and by some members of the training staff. The lectures and demonstrations dealt primarily with the conditions that foster individual and group growth. Periods of free time during the day and after the last session of the evening provided the participants with an opportunity for informal social interaction.

METHOD

At the beginning of the workshop the participants were divided into six T Groups. While an attempt was made to maintain a balance between the number of men and women in each group, the six training teams were assigned to groups on a random basis. Each T Group was randomly assigned to an experimental or to one of two control conditions. Since there were six groups, two T Groups were placed in each of the following conditions:

Experimental Condition

The members of the two experimental groups (ten men, thirteen women) were asked at the end of each of the eight group meetings to fill out a sociometric questionnaire designed to provide information on ratings given and received by each member as well as ratings anticipated by each member from all the other members of his group. Ratings were made on a five-point scale. In the seven remaining sessions a feedback form was distributed to each member before he filled out the sociometric questionnaire. The feedback form provided each subject with information about

[3]William G. Dyer, Professor of Sociology at Brigham Young University, Provo, Utah. Dr. Dyer is a Fellow of the NTL Institute for Applied Behavioral Science, associated with the NEA.

his own behavior and the behavior of all the other members of his group on the following items: (a) mean of the ratings given to all other members, (b) mean of the ratings received from all other members, (c) mean of the ratings anticipated from all other members, (d) number of correct guesses, (e) number of incorrect guesses, (f) total number of points missed in the incorrect direction, and (g) discrepancy percentage.

Control Condition #1

The members of the two # 1 control groups (eleven men, twelve women) filled out—at the end of each of the eight group meetings—the same Welch questionnaire administered in the experimental groups. The #1 control groups did not receive any feedback on their mutual ratings.

Control Condition #2

The members of the two #2 control groups (eleven men, twelve women) filled out—at the end of the first and the last sessions only—the Welch questionnaire administered in the other two conditions. The #2 control groups did not receive any feedback on their mutual ratings.

Tape-recorded instructions explaining how to fill out the sociometric questionnaire were played at the first meeting of every group in the three conditions. Tape-recorded instructions on how to read and interpret the feedback form were given at the second meeting of the two experimental groups.

RESULTS

To test the hypotheses of this study, the discrepancy score data collected during the first (pre) and last (post) sessions were analyzed.

An analysis of variance (summarized in Table 1) revealed no significant differences among the three conditions in their pretest discrepancy scores.[4]

Table 1 Analysis of Variance of the Pretest Discrepancy Scores of the Experimental, #1, and #2 Control Groups.

Source	Sum of Squares	*df*	Mean Squares	*F*	*p*
Between	455.4	2	227.7	2.77	NS
Within	5004.4	61	82.0		
Total	5459.8	63			

[4]A Hartley test was computed for the pretest data. The F max obtained was 1.13 (df = 1, 22; NS), indicating homogeneity of variance.

An analysis of variance (summarized in Table 2) indicated that there were significant differences among the three conditions in their posttest discrepancy scores. The Scheffe Nonsequential Comparison Between

Table 2 Analysis of Variance of the Pottest Discrepancy Scores of the Experimental, #1, and #2 Control Groups.

Source	Sum of Squares	*df*	Mean Squares	*F*	*p*
Between	756.5	2	382.7	5.47	0.01
Within	4266.2	61	69.9		
Total	5031.7	63			

Means was utilized to ascertain the specific location of the variances contributing to the significant *F* obtained by the analysis of variance. Table 3 contains the results of these group comparisons. The difference of 8.08

Table 3 Scheffe Nonsequential Comparisons Between Means.

Comparisons	Means	*p*
Experimental – #2 Control Groups	8.08 > 6.15	0.05
Experimental – #1 Control Groups	3.12 < 6.15	NS
#1 Control – #2 Control Groups	4.96 < 6.15	NS

between the means of the experimental and the #2 control groups was significant at the 0.05 level. The postsession discrepancy scores of experimental and #1 control groups and of #1 and #2 control groups did not differ significantly.

It was hypothesized that T-Group members who regularly provided and received sociometric feedback would show a greater increase in sensitivity than T-Group members not providing or receiving such data. The pre and post discrepancy score data confirmed this hypothesis.

A second hypothesis which stated that T-Group members who regularly provided and received sociometric feedback would show a greater increase in sensitivity than T-Group members providing but not receiving such data was not statistically supported by the findings, although the results obtained were in the predicted direction.

In a further analysis, *t* tests were computed between the pre and post means for each group to determine whether the experimental and control subjects improved significantly in their discrepancy scores from the beginning to the end of their T-Group experience. Results of this analysis are presented in Table 4. The *t* tests indicated that a significant reduction of the discrepancy scores occurred between the pre- and posttests for the experimental groups only.

Table 4 Mean of Differences Between Pre- and Posttests for Experimental, #1 Control, and #2 Control Groups.

Conditions	Mean Diff.	SD of Mean Diff.	*t*	*df*	*v*
Experimental Groups	10.21	2.83	3.60	22	0.005
#1 Control Groups	2.73	2.18	1.25	18	NS
#2 Control Groups	3.73	2.53	1.47	22	NS

DISCUSSION OF RESULTS

The prediction that the sensitivity to interpersonal phenomena of subjects who are given insight into the reactions of others to their behavior by means of a sociometric questionnaire and an instrumented feedback procedure would significantly increase was confirmed by the findings. The findings also indicated that a sociometric procedure without feedback did not result in a significant increase in sensitivity between the beginning and the end of a three-day workshop.

In the light of T-Group theory, the present results seem to give strong support to the assumption that by receiving feedback on their behavior, members of a T Group will become more sensitive to interpersonal relationships and social interaction. This investigation lends support to the view that the openness fostered by the feedback procedure leads to more satisfactory and more honest human relations than are ordinarily experienced in laboratory training.

From a methodological point of view, the feedback procedure may have served to encourage inquiry by the members into their behavior and the behavior of others. Trainers in the experimental conditions reported that the subjects used the feedback form with a spirit of honest search. Behaviors exhibited in the preceding meetings were carefully analyzed to determine the effect they had on the group as a whole and on individual members. The experimental group trainers unanimously felt that the feedback procedure fostered open discussions of feelings and close observation of individual and group behavior. It also seemed to accelerate the development of an accepting climate in the T Group.

Nevertheless, the findings of this investigation could be interpreted in a different manner. Since every subject in the experimental condition had an opportunity to see the ratings of every other group member, it is conceivable that the significant reduction of the experimental groups' discrepancy scores was due to conformity on the part of the subjects to group norms and not to a growing sensitivity to interpersonal responses within the group. Conceivably, members of the experimental groups simply began giving one another the ratings they had received earlier. Over time, this would cause the ratings to converge and thus reduce the discrepancy scores.

CONCLUSION

The results can be interpreted as supporting the assumption that members of a T Group who received feedback from others in their group will become more sensitive to interpersonal relationships and social interaction. However, the significant reduction of the discrepancy scores of the experimental subjects may be interpreted as a desire to conform to group norms. Further research is needed to determine whether sociometric feedback increases the interpersonal sensitivity of T-Group members or merely encourages group conformity. Such feedback could, of course, have a multiple effect. If the feedback procedure results in increased sensitivity, then experimental subjects should be expected to carry over their increased awareness to new membership groups.

REFERENCES

Bass, B. *Organizational psychology*. Boston: Allyn & Bacon, 1965.

Bradford, L., Gibb, J., & Benne, K. (Eds.) *T-group theory and laboratory method: Innovation in re-education*. New York: Wiley, 1964.

Burke, R., & Bennis, W. Changes in perception of self and others during human relations training. *Hum. Relat.*, 1961, **2**, 165–182.

Dymond, Rosalynd F. A scale for the measurement of empathic ability. *J. consult. Psychol.*, 1949, **13**, 127–133.

Ferguson, C. Management development in "unstructured groups." *Calif. Mgmt Rev.*, 1959, **1** (3), 66–72.

Jenkins, D. H. Feedback and group evaluation. *J. soc. Issues*, 1948, **4** (2), 50–60.

Miles, M. Human relations training: Processes and outcomes. *J. counsel. Psychol.*, 1960, **7**, 301–306.

Schein, E., & Bennis, W. *Personal and organizational change through group methods: The laboratory approach*. New York: Wiley, 1965.

Tagiuri, R. Relational analysis: An extension of sociometric method with emphasis upon social perception. *Sociometry*, 1952, **15** (1–2), 91–104.

Tannenbaum, R., Weschler, I., & Massarik, F. *Leadership and organization: Behavioral science approach*. New York: McGraw-Hill, 1961.

Walker, Helen M., & Lev, J. *Statistical inference*. New York: Holt, Rinehart & Winston, 1953.

Wiener, B. G. *Statistical principles in experimental design*. New York: McGraw-Hill, 1962.

CRITIQUE

---

1. PHILOSOPHICAL AND THEORETICAL CONSIDERATIONS

The authors of this study have very adequately discussed the philosophical rationale and cited appropriate and ample references. The theoretical underpinnings of laboratory training and the various techniques and exercises used have been documented and reported.

The goal of this study, concisely stated, was to see if regular instrumented feedback based on sociometric ratings would help the participants increase their sensitivity to interpersonal phenomena occurring in the group.

2. CRITERION

The criterion was, simply, sensitivity. This was operationally defined as the degree of discrepancy between instrumented feedback rating received and anticipated, by each member. This follows clearly from the goal set forth above. This is an immediate, subjective, internal criterion, and seems quite appropriate. Although the concept of sensitivity should certainly include how one thinks others see him, and how others actually do see him, there certainly is more to it than that. For example, it should include how, in fact, he relates to people in his real world, including specific behavioral deeds and acts (i.e., a good listener, an empathizer, and other behavioral cues) which manifest being in tune with others. More specifically, we feel that a person might be able to be quite accurate in predicting how people see him, and yet not be considered a sensitive person.

It might also be noted that out of group behavior, the generalization of increased sensitivity to other groups or individuals, group member reactions to the workshop T-group experience and procedures were not assessed. Only one criterion measure was employed.

3. RESEARCH DESIGN

A strong, multiple treatment-control group design was used in this study. The authors utilized two control procedures to control for both feedback and the use of the questionnaire. The latter was necessary in order to account for possible increases in sensitivity as a result of simply completing the Welch Scale. Analysis of variance, a robust statistical test, was then used to test statistical significance of the findings.

The study was designed in such a way that significant control over experimental variance was accomplished. In this regard it is also possible to suggest that three treatment groups were compared, rather than one treatment and two controls. All groups received some treatment or training—there was no "non-counseled" control group. Experimental controls were accomplished through multiple treatments.

A follow-up measure of some kind after the three-day treatment would have been useful to assess the time dimension of the effects. The members of the other groups may have become more "sensitive" in subsequent group meetings or after formal treatment was terminated.

4. SELECTION AND SAMPLING PROCEDURES

The workshop participants were gathered according to an incidental sampling plan. The authors should have described the sample in terms of some variables which might have been considered most relevant to sensitivity training. For example, had members had prior experience in groups? Did they volunteer or were they selected for the workshop? The therapists or trainees were also sampled in an unspecified way, and their skills and backgrounds were not disclosed.

The researchers assigned members to groups in a random way. The six groups were also assigned to the three treatment conditions in a random way. This is an excellent technique, and is usually the most desirable way to control a variety of biases. However, the exact randomization techniques should be reported. It is also not clear how the trainer and assistant trainer were paired.

In view of the possibility of a non-representative sample, the authors have wisely and carefully generalized and summarized the results of their research.

5. COUNSELING TREATMENT

The only notion of what went on in these training groups is that the same trainer and assistant trainer were present in each group meeting for each and all treatment groups. Although we are aware that (1) NTL trainers have undergone a certain amount of group experiences themselves and are certified (and this is laudable), and (2) the techniques and exercises have been published, we would still like to know the experience, education, and personal style of these leaders and their assistants. How did they see their role, and were they aware of this investigation? NTL approaches are not standardized and uniform as any participant can testify. Also groups differ widely on a host of dimensions, and sensitive leaders usually adjust their strategies and styles to meet the group needs. It is hard to believe that each of the groups proceeded in similar fashions (process and content-wise). Obviously, the level of openness and emotional frankness obtained in each group might well have influenced the results. A few statements on these topics, along with some report of what indeed was happening would have helped very much.

Other very significant activities were going on concurrently with the specific treatment provided. The same participants were attending lectures, discussions, and demonstrations which were to foster individual and group growth. One would hope that these activities would increase the sensitivity of the participants differently. By chance, it might have been that those in the experimental groups got more out of these activities than those in the control groups. To be more fair, one would expect these impacts to have been randomly dispersed among all participants. Yet, it makes it more difficult to attribute the results to the training groups only. The treatment effects might also have been confounded in another way. While the no-feedback groups did complete the scales, they were probably aware that some other participants were discussing the Welch results. One wonders how the "control" leaders reacted when participants wanted to know about their results on the questionnaire or wanted systematic feedback?

6. MEASUREMENT

The criterion was measured with an unpublished instrument by Welch in which information is provided about the degree of accuracy of a participant's evaluation of others' perception of him. Comparisons are made between anticipated and actual ratings by others. Unfortunately, little is known about the reliability and validity of this instrument, and the problem of reactivity (effect it has on a subject in a cumulative sort of way). Regarding this point one could speculate that the subjects learned how to fake their responses in terms of the task assigned.

As suggested above, it would have been important to have had some external measure of sensitivity for the subjects. As an example, this might have been done by having expert-raters (or all other participants in all groups), who had a clear knowledge of the phenomenon of sensitivity, rate brief five-minute videotapes of each participant interacting with another person.

7. ETHICAL, PROFESSIONAL, AND LEGAL CONSIDERATIONS

Ethical principles in general seem to have been followed in this research. Even so, one or two considerations were not accounted for in the authors' review of their work. We do not know, for example, whether the participants volunteered for the study. Likewise we are not told how the research endeavor was related to the Group Development Workshop objectives. Was it implicit or injected? The degree of communication or information exchange regarding the research, among groups and individual members, is not mentioned.

8. RESULTS

The authors handled the results of their interpretations in an extremely fair way. Their interpretation that the significant reduction in discrepancy scores for the experimental groups might have been due to conformity to group norms is very valid. Briefly, this was a very well executed piece of research, and the authors did an excellent job of writing up and interpreting the results.

AN ENCOUNTER GROUP AND CHANGES IN COUNSELOR'S VALUES[1,2]

Robert C. Reardon
Assistant Professor
and
Harman D. Burck
Associate Professor
Florida State University
Tallahassee, Florida

The purpose of this study was to assess the effect of encounter group treatment on the values and value systems of 24 employment service counselors. A time series own-control design was used. Treatment consisted of 27 hours in encounter groups over a three-week period. Thirty-six value rankings were obtained before and after treatment, and again six months later. There was greater change in instrumental than terminal values during and after treatment. Contrary to expectation, personal and conservative values became more important than social and liberal values after treatment. Most value changes during treatment did not persist six months later.

There is one currently unmistakable similarity between individual and group counseling: there is little scientific substantiation of outcome effectiveness. Yet, group work, under various names and banners and sponsored by schools, colleges, churches, hospitals, businesses, neighborhood centers, and governments, is proliferating at a startling rate. Comprehensive reviews of group research reveal the same kinds of methodological shortcomings as found in individual counseling and therapy research (Anderson, 1969; Campbell and Dunnette, 1968; Gazda and Larsen, 1968).

The changing of values is usually implicitly or explicitly implied in most of the goals which have been postulated for group counseling or encounter groups. Whether the goals are the relief of symptoms, release of feelings, strengthening self-esteem, resolving target problems,

[1]The authors express thanks to Dr. Robert S. Lushene for assistance in the analysis of the data.

[2]This paper was also published in *The Journal of Employment Counseling*, 1972, in press.

improving interpersonal relationships, living the good life, or changing life-styles, all imply changing the values of the participants. More specifically, Rokeach (1968a, 1968b) has written about the organization and change of value systems, and suggests that value is a dynamic concept which has a strong motivational component as well as cognitive, affective, and behavioral components. Briefly, an individual has a basic motivation for consistency, and the way to bring about value changes involves (1) trying to get a person to engage in inconsistent behaviors, (2) providing an individual with new inconsistent information by a significant other, and (3) with new information, pointing out the inconsistencies already within the person's own value system.

This paper is a report of an experimental study in which the attempt was made to engage group members in the above ways, and then analyze the concomitant changes in their values and the stability of these changes.

METHOD

Subjects

The 24 *S*'s were counselors with the Florida State Employment Service. Through a process of self-selection and nomination by others, several counselors from each district in the state were identified as having good counseling skills and likely to benefit from a group counseling workshop. From this population, the state supervisor of counseling invited 24 persons to attend the workshop. Their amount of employment service experience ranged from 1 to 12 years. The age range of the 15 men and 9 women was from 22 to 59, with a mean age of 37 years. All *S*'s had a minimum of a BA degree and there were wide varieties of previous vocational experience. There were seven black counselors in the sample.

Treatment

The *S*'s attending the group counseling workshop were alternately (alphabetically) assigned to one of three encounter treatment groups. One of the three group leaders had a doctorate degree in counseling with five years of counseling experience; the other two leaders were advanced doctoral students with almost three years of counseling experience. The group leaders met several times for planning purposes, and also met weekly during the three-week workshop. During these meetings the goals and objectives of the groups were discussed. The consensus of the three leaders was that the overall objective of the encounter groups was to encourage each *S* to explore, reveal, and evaluate his own and others' feelings, attitudes, and values. The leader sought to keep the group discussion at the affective level, and to concentrate on the here and now. Group members were encouraged to question one another about values which related to their work and to themselves as human beings. Confrontation, openness, honesty, and candor in verbal expression were constantly encouraged by each leader. No use was made of the more pronounced nonverbal techniques, e.g., dance, body contact, music.

About one third of the formal workshop time was devoted to encounter groups. Each *S* met for three hours per day, three days per week, or about 27 hours in formalized encounter. The other workshop time was spent in didactic and demonstration sessions on groups.

Instrument

The criterion measure in this study was Rokeach's Value Survey, Form D (1968a). The Survey is composed of two parts consisting of 18 terminal and 18 instrumental values. Rokeach (1968b) has observed that instrumental values have to do with modes of conduct, while terminal values refer to end states of existence. An instrumental value is defined as a single belief which always takes the following form: "I believe that a mode of conduct (e.g., honesty, courage) is personally and socially preferable in all situations with respect to all objects." A terminal value takes a comparable form: "I believe that an end-state of existence (e.g., salvation, world peace) is personally and socially worth striving for." On both Parts I and II *S* is asked to rearrange the values or items "in order of their importance to you, as guiding principles in your life." Test-retest median reliabilities for different college student samples ranged from 0.78 to 0.80 for the terminal value scale and 0.70 to 0.72 for the instrumental value scale.

Design and Analysis

A repeated measures, own-control design was used in this study. Rankings of terminal and instrumental values for each *S* were obtained on three different occasions: (1) prior to the encounter group treatment period (pre-test); (2) after the three-week intensive treatment period (post-test); and (3) six months after the end of treatment (delayed post-test).

This design provided for the exploration of several research questions:

(1) How are terminal and instrumental values ranked by employment service counselors? (2) Were terminal and instrumental values equally susceptible to change? (3) Was there evidence of value change immediately following the three-week treatment period? (4) Did changes in values following treatment persist six months later?

RESULTS

Regarding question one, the mean ranks for terminal and instrumental values for the three measurement periods are presented in Table 1. Values that are from most to least important to employment service counselors prior to the treatment are arranged from top to bottom in column one.

Regarding question two, a repeated measures analysis of variance procedure revealed little change in the 18 terminal values over the three measurement periods (Table 1). F-values were statistically significant at 0.10 or less for only two values: equality and wisdom. In comparison to the few changes in terminal values, significant F-ratios were found for 9 of the 18 instrumental values: ambitious, capable, courageous, forgiving, helpful, independent, intellectual, logical, and polite.

Regarding questions three and four, F-values were obtained for those 11 sets of mean differences identified by the ANOVA. The significant F-values are reported in Table 2 for the three possible mean comparisons. It should be noted that the F-tests reported in Table 2 are equivalent to the t-test for comparison of means between 2 groups, and are available on a standard computer program used for testing statistical significance of differences between group means.

DISCUSSION

The following discussion proceeds according to the order of the basic research questions noted earlier.

Ranking of Terminal and Instrumental Values

Inspection of Table 1 shows the arrangement of the 18 terminal and 18 instrumental values from most to least important for employment service counselors (ESC). The terminal value salvation (saved, eternal life) is consistently ranked lowest of the 18 values. According to Rokeach (1970) it may be inferred that ESC have little in common on this value with religious professionals or individuals with a strong religious orientation. This

Table 1 Means, Standard Deviations, and *F*-Values for Differences of Three Rankings of Terminal and Instrumental Values.

	I		II		III		
Terminal Values	$\bar{x}$	SD	$\bar{x}$	SD	$\bar{x}$	SD	*F*
Self-respect	4.79	4.38	4.96	4.08	4.13	3.26	1.04
Freedom	5.04	3.29	5.00	3.82	5.54	3.75	0.28
Wisdom	5.29	4.50	3.13	2.29	4.21	3.40	3.36**
Accomplishment	6.83	4.71	6.63	3.87	7.63	4.68	0.50
Inner Harmony	6.96	4.47	5.96	4.36	6.38	4.75	0.60
Mature Love	7.21	3.59	7.67	4.34	7.63	4.80	0.22
Equality	7.50	9.95	9.17	4.74	8.92	4.56	2.44*
Family Security	7.88	4.00	9.42	3.79	8.46	4.03	2.28
Friendship	8.75	3.07	8.83	3.58	8.92	3.74	0.03
Happiness	8.92	4.55	9.00	4.66	8.67	3.60	0.07
World Peace	9.92	4.93	10.33	3.66	10.29	4.47	0.15
Exciting Life	10.46	4.09	9.54	4.03	9.54	3.70	1.11
Beauty	10.63	4.51	9.33	3.95	10.71	4.65	2.21
Pleasure	13.04	3.74	13.13	2.97	13.71	4.03	1.06
Comfortable Life	13.33	3.42	13.38	3.56	13.17	3.16	0.60
Social Recognition	13.71	3.56	14.17	3.42	12.67	4.10	2.06
National Security	14.96	2.40	15.33	3.00	14.88	4.03	0.21
Salvation	15.97	3.58	16.04	3.64	15.58	4.30	0.31
Instrumental Values							
Honest	4.58	4.24	4.17	3.49	5.00	4.18	0.47
Broadminded	5.50	4.16	5.50	3.74	6.50	4.69	1.53
Responsible	6.67	4.36	7.92	4.28	7.33	3.96	1.59
Helpful	6.88	4.06	6.46	4.72	8.04	4.47	2.62*
Independent	7.33	4.59	8.08	5.03	6.17	4.38	3.19**
Capable	7.67	4.35	9.63	3.67	8.17	4.13	4.05**
Loving	7.92	4.26	6.08	3.79	7.50	4.58	2.30
Intellectual	8.08	4.72	9.58	4.41	7.21	3.67	4.83**
Imaginative	8.08	4.62	7.29	4.23	7.88	4.48	0.64
Courageous	9.21	4.36	7.29	4.59	8.00	4.92	3.48**
Self-controlled	9.75	5.12	9.38	4.96	9.75	4.56	0.18
Forgiving	10.50	3.76	8.71	3.67	10.58	3.28	3.93**
Cheerful	10.75	3.96	10.75	3.39	11.08	3.74	0.11
Logical	10.83	4.36	9.04	3.75	8.00	3.68	4.39**
Ambitious	11.08	4.71	13.08	3.17	12.58	4.75	3.20**
Polite	14.21	3.35	15.58	2.19	15.04	2.49	2.73*
Clean	15.33	2.53	16.17	2.74	15.42	3.93	0.36
Obedient	16.63	2.81	16.29	3.07	16.75	2.64	1.33

*$p < 0.10$, **$p < 0.05$.

Table 2 *F*-Values for Three Paired Comparisons of Rankings of Selected Values.

Values	I–II	II–III	I–III
Wisdom	5.85**	1.88	1.75
Equality	2.90*	0.12	3.82*
Helpful	0.30	5.87**	2.54
Independent	1.10	7.75***	1.78
Capable	5.80**	3.76*	0.81
Intellectual	5.75**	6.75**	1.35
Courageous	8.18***	0.93	2.30
Forgiving	5.24**	6.54**	0.01
Logical	3.74*	1.27	7.35**
Ambitious	7.46**	0.48	2.31
Polite	3.35**	1.25	2.71

*$p < 0.10$, **$p < 0.05$, ***$p < 0.01$.

suggests that ESC are not preoccupied with saving their own souls to the extent that they are without social compassion. On the other hand, the mean rank of equality relative to freedom indicates that ESC have more in common with college students sympathetic toward, but not participating in, civil rights demonstrations than either those who are opposed to demonstrations or who have participated in them (Rokeach, 1968b). Because freedom is ranked considerably higher than equality, it may be inferred that ESC have more in common on those two values with policemen than with unemployed blacks, who would reverse the relative position of those values. In general these counselor's values and value systems are more easily labeled liberal, than middle-of-the-road or conservative (Rokeach, 1968–1969).

Other terminal values in the personal areas (self-respect, freedom, wisdom, sense of accomplishment) are more strongly held than social values (national security, a world of peace, a world of beauty, or equality).

Inspection of Table 1 shows that honesty (sincere, truthful), a value important in the encounter group treatment, remained consistently the most important value over the three measurement periods. Rokeach (1970) views this as part of the typical American value pattern.

Inspection of Table 1 also shows that *F*-values associated with those values least strongly held (not ranked at the extremes) tended to change most over the three measurement periods. However, some values initially ranked in the middle of the distribution also changed very little.

Comparative Change in Terminal and Instrumental Values

At the 0.10 level, 9 instrumental values changed over the three measurement periods in comparison to only two terminal value changes. This is consistent with Rokeach's distinction between instrumental values as modes of behavior and terminal values as end states of existence. The impact of treatment on value change is much greater on the instrumental values than the terminal values – more on the present and short-term than the long-term values. The impact of the encounter group treatment focused more on means kinds of values (an imperative to action) than ends values (a standard to guide actions).

Value Changes Following Treatment and Six Months Later

Inspection of Table 2 shows when the 11 value changes identified in Table 1 actually occurred. Of the two terminal values that changed, wisdom (a mature understanding of life), a personal value, became dramatically more important to ESC following treatment. Perhaps these counselors who were exposed to deeper levels of interpersonal relationships became more aware of the need for a truly integrating philosophy of life. Wisdom, which was already important to ESC, became easily the most important value following treatment, but this value change did not persist six months later.

Equality (brotherhood, equal opportunity for all), a social value, became significantly less important to ESC following treatment and remained so six months later, while the rank of freedom remained constant. ESC apparently became more conservative in social/political values following encounter group treatment (Rokeach, 1968a). Thus the changed freedom-equality relationship in values following treatment places these ESC more in common with those college students who do not support civil rights activities than those who are sympathetic to such activities.

Inspection of Table 2 reveals that seven instrumental values changed following treatment, but three values, capable (competent, effective), intellectual (intelligent, reflective), and forgiving (willing to pardon others) returned to virtually the same position as the pretest. Three other values (polite, ambitious, and courageous) did not return to the same pretest mean during the six-month interval after treatment, although the means moved in that direction. Only one value, logical (consistent, rational), continued in the same direction following treatment and was even more important six months later. Two values, helpful (working for the welfare of others) and independent (self-reliant and self-sufficient), did not change during treatment, but changed dramatically during the six-month period following treatment. Helpful became less important (a drop from fourth to ninth place in the hierarchy) and independent became more important (moved up from eighth to second place). While it is difficult to speculate about the reasons for this delayed shift away from a helpful orientation to others following the encounter treatment period, it is a disturbing finding in light of the personal growth goals of the treatment.

CONCLUSION

It is apparent that the encounter group treatment did have a significant impact on the values and the value system of the employment service counselors. This is particularly true of instrumental or means type values as opposed to terminal or end state type values. Given the values that did change, it is not altogether reassuring to look at the implications of those value changes. For example, of the two terminal values that did change as a result of encounter groups, there was an increase in importance of personal as opposed to social values. Wisdom, a personal value, became much more important than equality, a social value. The implication is that these ESC became less socially oriented in terms of political/economic values. Given the lack of change in other terminal values it appears that the counselors became more conservative and rigid in their social philosophy.

Regarding changes in instrumental values it is clear that many changes following the three-week treatment period did not maintain themselves six months later. In fact, it is clear that productive and achievement oriented values, e.g., capable, ambitious, and intellectual, became much less important as a result of the encounter group treatment. Social/humanistic values, such as forgiving, did not maintain a higher position six months after the treatment. More alarming is the fact that the changes in helpful and independent indicate that the ESC were less oriented to helping others as opposed to caring for themselves six months after the encounter group treatment.

Several delimitations of the study should be noted. First, the sample was small and selected in a nonrandom way. Second, the group workshop milieu included a variety of activities in addition to the encounter groups. One must assume the changes in values stemmed from encounter groups rather than lectures, class discussions, etc. Finally, the own control design employed in this study did not provide for a "no treatment" control group.

However, the results of this study would suggest the analysis of value changes in particular values or in value systems is a productive avenue for future research in the effectiveness of counseling treatments. It also suggests that an encounter group experience may serve to promote those values which are the antithesis of values generally considered important in a helping relationship. Rokeach[3] has surmised: "It may well be that from what you have found out that encounter groups serve to make people too preoccupied with their own personal happiness and as a result less sympathetic with the plight of others." It is apparent that simply being in an encounter group is not a panacea and does not in any way guarantee that people, in this case counselors, are going to hold values that make them more humane, tolerant, or wise.

REFERENCES

Anderson, A. Group counseling. *Review of Educational Research*, 1969, **39**, 209–226.

Campbell, J. and Dunnette, M. Effectiveness of T group experiences in managerial training and development. *Psychological Bulletin*, 1968, **79**, 73–104.

Gazda, G. and Larsen, Mary. A comprehensive appraisal of group and multiple counseling research. *Journal of Research and Development in Education*, 1968, **1**, 57–132.

Rokeach, M. *Beliefs, attitudes, and values*. San Francisco: Jossey-Bass, 1968. a

Rokeach, M. A theory of organization and change in value-attitude systems. *Journal of Social Issues*, 1968, **24**, 13–33. b

Rokeach, M. The role of values in public opinion research. *Public Opinion Quarterly*, 1968–1969, **32**, 547–559.

Rokeach, M. Faith, hope, and bigotry. *Psychology Today*, 1970, **3**, 33–37, 58.

CRITIQUE

1. PHILOSOPHICAL AND THEORETICAL CONSIDERATIONS

The authors do not present a very clear theoretical orientation for this study. Group work is discussed as some kind of uniform standardized routine, and no relevant theories of personality, learning, or counseling/therapy are mentioned. They do, though, present their concern (e.g., values) and indicate that, indeed, this hypothetical construct is basic to most counseling approaches. In this regard, the notion of values is held up as a central dimension of personality and behavior change, and the recent theorizing of Milton Rokeach is cited. We must agree that the popularity

[3]Milton Rokeach, personal communication. July 12, 1971.

of groups and values are certainly topical in today's psychological literature and practice.

However, the authors gave little explanation of the overall purposes of the workshop, or of the primary goals of the encounter groups. For example, was the focus theoretically and practically on personal growth, group process, insight, or value change?

Regrettably the authors did not offer any postulated theory of value change which could be documented in their research. Nor did they relate value change in conceptual terms to encounter group process, except in broad language. One must also ask what interpretations were followed, or theoretical positions taken on "revealing and exploring of attitudes" as distinct from "values." Are they treated synonymously? Why was the Rokeach used if group process outcomes embrace other than values?

2. CRITERION

The criterion of personal values was used in this study. This is a self-report, internal criterion. An important question which should be raised is: What is the difference between the values a person says he holds and his behavior in value-related situations? Stated differently, do the values a person reports as of essence to him, manifest themselves in his behavior? Any counselor or therapist realizes that it is exactly this discrepancy which brings many people to therapy. Values do surface as behavioral acts and this fact is not properly dealt with in this study. This is regrettable.

3. RESEARCH DESIGN

An own-control design was used, in that each subject was compared only with himself. Repeated measures were taken on each subject (pre, post and follow-up). The external validity of the study could have been greatly increased if a control group, or even a regular academic-discussion oriented graduate class in guidance had been used. As it is, it is not possible to generalize to any other group from this study.

One good feature of this design is that a six-month follow-up was incorporated into the study. Own-control designs are solid and worthwhile in counseling research, especially if one can assume there is no treatment effect from the repeated measurements. It would appear that this assumption was met satisfactorily by the researchers. One other advantage of the own-control design is that it can utilize the powerful repeated measures analysis of variance test in statistical analysis.

4. SELECTION AND SAMPLING PROCEDURES

No sampling plan, controlled by the counselor-researchers, was used in this research. The State Employment Service selected the counselor/participants and it is assumed that the workshop director selected the group leaders. The sample, then, of both counselors and clients must be described as incidental or purposive and is probably not representative. As noted earlier, this weakens the external validity.

All 24 subjects were involved in every part of the program and data collection. This is somewhat unusual because it is frequently very difficult to get data from all subjects involved in a long-term research project.

5. COUNSELING TREATMENT

As is usually the case, this is the most serious limitation of the study. The authors make an attempt to tell us about who the counselors were, their experience, education, and stated personal counseling orientations. It is helpful that attempts were made to establish similar goals and strategies for each counselor, and weekly meetings of the counselors was a valiant attempt to keep leaders on target.

Yet several questions must be raised: What did, in fact, occur in these group meetings? (Did each counselor focus content and process on value-laden material?) This could have been better controlled by having some kind of process measure. What was the natural inclination or preference in counseling theory for each counselor? (What were his personal theoretical approaches?) This could have been handled by having the counselor state this beforehand (i.e., the Therapist Orientation Inventory). How much experience had the leaders actually had in leading encounter groups? Counseling experience and encounter group experience might well be two entirely different phenomena. Were there other experiences in the three-week workshop besides the encounter group which might have brought about changes in values? (This is obvious since the institute topically had to do with group work and counseling, and this included discussions, lectures, demonstrations, rap sessions, etc.) Finally, were the counselor-leaders male, female, or were both sexes used? This might have made a difference.

6. MEASUREMENT

The criterion measure in this study was Rokeach's *Value Survey*. This follows clearly enough from the goals and criterion, but it is most regrettable, that even a subjective statement by participants as to the meaning of the group experience was not included. This would have at least provided additional data about the value changes and even the processes of the encounter groups. Yet, the follow-up provides vital information about how the participants viewed their values, out of the institute and encounter group situation.

Analyses of variance were used in the analysis of the ranked data from the *Value Survey*. What assumptions did the authors have to make about their data in order to use parametric rather than nonparametric statistical procedures?

The authors also saw fit to report significant values at the 0.10 level. One must wonder if the exploratory nature of the study, the importance of the problem, and the absence of a control group warrant reporting of findings at that level.

7. ETHICAL, PROFESSIONAL, AND LEGAL CONSIDERATIONS

The basic question revolves around the right and authority to change values. Who says that employment service counselors with certain kinds of value hierarchies make the most effective counselors? Indeed, what rationale is used in implying that being in an encounter group has any bearing at all on one's counseling skills or techniques? And did the counselors know that value change was one of the goals of the encounter groups?

One must ask also whether the goal of value change was the primary task or one of several purposes. This ambiguity of the researchers may not be unethical although it is disturbing. In the same vein the question arises: "Can we assume that value change is an automatic outcome of group process?" Were the subjects considered in designing research around this question? Were they aware of the purpose, if indeed, it was value change?

8. RESULTS

The authors apparently went fishing for some data about value changes, and its persistence following a three-week encounter group experience. And they apparently found something—but we cannot be very sure exactly what. They do not say which specific values they did or did not want to change by encounter treatment. The failure to hypothesize about particular values leaves the authors merely describing what did happen in the results and conclusion.

It is notable that the authors did not attempt to generalize beyond their sample, but only pointed to differences which emerged in their data.

TEACHING INTERNALIZATION BEHAVIOR TO CLIENTS[1]

Richard M. Pierce
Michigan State University
and
Paul G. Schauble
University of Florida
and
Andrea Farkas
Children's Hospital, Boston

INTRODUCTION

Internalization vs. externalization (I-E) (Farkas, 1969; Kirtner and Cartwright, 1958; Perry, 1969; Pierce and Schauble, 1969) (Gendlin 1969); and (Gendlin & Tavris, 1970), concerns the manner in which a client approaches his problem in therapy. More specifically, it is concerned with whether he sees his problems stemming from his own acts, feelings, and contributions to his problems (internalization) or whether he sees his problems as situational and himself as a victim of environment or circumstance (externalization). The research to date indicates that: clients who begin therapy as internalizers are more likely to be judged as having a successful therapy experience than are externalizers (Farkas, 1969; Kirtner and Cartwright, 1958; Perry, 1969). Clients who accomplish successful or satisfactory change during therapy show increased internalization behavior, while non-successful clients do not (Pierce and Schauble, 1969). If internalizing behavior is related to successful progress in therapy, and if successful or effective therapy results in increased internalization for the client, could internalizing behavior be systematically taught to clients in the early stages of therapy, thereby accelerating client progress? The main purpose of this study was to evaluate whether or not the client's behavior in approaching his problems could be changed using a direct,

[1]First printed in *Psychotherapy: Theory, Research and Practice*. Pierce, Richard M., Schauble, Paul G., and Farkas, Andrea. Teaching internalization behavior to clients, 1970, **7**, (4), 217–220.

straightforward learning technique. A secondary purpose was to assess various ways of predicting internalizing behavior.

The four instruments used were: the *Rotter* "Internalization-Externalization Scale" (Rotter, 1966), the "Learning Strategies Questionnaire" (Kagan, Krathwhol, Goldberg, Campbell, Schauble, Greenberg, Resnikoff, Danish, Bondy, and Bowles, 1967), a modification of a behavior rating scale developed by Kirtner and Cartwright (1958), and a therapist-report rating scale.

1. The Rotter is designed to assess the degree to which a person sees the world as being shaped by him, i.e., the degree to which he sees a causal relationship between his behavior and his life situation.

2. The Learning Strategies Questionnaire (LSQ) samples behavior in academic situations, designed to assess whether a person learns by "focusing" or "scanning" behavior. A person who scans, looks for the major principles or "total picture" in an attempt to integrate and relate information. A person who focuses attempts to collect details and specific bits of information without attempting to integrate them into a conceptional whole. There is evidence to indicate that scanning behavior is related to more effective learning, as measured by grade point average and instruments predictive of academic success in college (Kagan, Krathwhol, Goldberg, Campbell, Schauble, Greenberg, Resnikoff, Danish, Bondy, Bowles, 1967).

3. Assessment of in-therapy I-E behavior was accomplished through use of the Kirtner-Cartwright Typology which originally contained five discrete categories. For the present study, the typology was modified into a five-point continuous scale with level one as the lowest possible rating (indicative of extreme externalizing behavior) and level five as the highest possible rating (or extreme internalization). At level one the client simply describes attributes of people and situations with very little awareness of self responsibility or control. At level five he immediately deals with an awareness of how he acts and feels, and recognizes the effects and impact of his behavior.

4. The therapist rating instrument required each therapist to evaluate his client's behavior on a five-point semantic differential system, with 1.0 being externalizing and 5.0 being internalizing.

Previous research has shown that therapist level of functioning on the dimensions of empathy, regard, genuineness and concreteness influences client process behavior (Carkhuff and Berenson, 1967). Therefore, validated rating scales of these dimensions were used to assess therapist functioning (Carkhuff and Berenson, 1967).

METHOD

The subjects were seven female and eight male undergraduate college students who sought help at the University Counseling Center, and after meeting once with their therapist, agreed to participate in the research.

The therapists were two experienced counselors who were known from previous research to offer high levels of empathy, regard, genuineness and concreteness (above 3.0 on the five-point scale). Therapist I counseled seven client subjects and therapist II counseled eight.

The raters were two Ph.D. counselors and one advanced doctoral candidate in clinical psychology. Raters I and II rated the behavior of seven clients and raters II and III rated eight. A Pearson *r* revealed the inter-rater reliability for raters I and II to be 0.87 and raters II and III 0.92.

Training Procedure

The research was described as an attempt to help the clients conceptualize their own behavior and they were requested to complete the Rotter and the LSQ before their next interview. During the next interview the subject was allowed to talk about his problem in any way he saw fit for the first twenty minutes, i.e., the session was run in a "traditional" manner wherein the therapist primarily engaged in interchangeable reflections. During the second twenty minutes, the therapist stopped the client, explained very straightforwardly what I-E was about, and that it was thought to be a very helpful way of looking at problems. The session then proceeded for twenty minutes while the therapist very directly made the client aware of when he was internalizing or externalizing and offered positive verbal reinforcement ("that's good," etc.) for internalizing behavior. During the last twenty minutes of the session the therapist resumed his more traditional behavior, again engaging primarily in interchangeable reflection, and the client was allowed to explore his problem as he wished.

From the *first* and *last* twenty minutes of the recorded sessions, two three-minute excerpts were extracted for purposes of rating. These excerpts were then presented in randomized order to the judges and rated on I-E as well as the therapist dimensions of empathy, regard, genuineness and concreteness.

RESULTS

Assessment of therapist ratings indicated that both therapists functioned slightly above 3.0 on all therapist dimensions. In the early period (first twenty minutes) they averaged 3.17 across dimensions and in the late period (last twenty minutes) they averaged 3.08.

A Wilcoxon matched pairs rank test was used to assess the significance of change in the objective ratings of I-E from the early to the late period. This test revealed a positive change in ratings significant at the 0.01 level.

Spearman rank order correlations were also performed between the early I-E ratings and the therapist ratings of I-E, the Rotter, and the LSQ (see Table 1). The therapist ratings correlated +0.80 with the initial

Table 1 Rank Order Correlations Between the I-E Scale and Therapist Ratings, the Rotter, and the LSQ.

	Therapist ratings of client	Learning strategies questionnaire	Rotter scale
I-E ratings	0.80	0.68	0.57

objective measure ($p < 0.02$). Of the predictive instruments, the LSQ correlated +0.68 with the initial I-E measure ($p < 0.02$), while the Rotter correlated +0.57 ($p < 0.10$) with the initial ratings.

In an attempt to determine change trends, a Spearman rank order correlations performed between the early and late measures indicated a +0.63 correlation ($p < 0.05$). In addition, initial rank on I-E and amount of change on I-E correlated −0.75 ($p < 0.02$). Thus, those clients who had a lower level of internalizing behavior at the onset of therapy gained most from the interaction, but tended still to remain below clients who were initially at higher levels.

DISCUSSION

Previous research has shown that success in therapy is related to client internalization behavior. The major implication of the present study is that client behavior on the dimension of I-E can be positively changed with brief, straightforward intervention. The clients at the lower end of the I-E continuum benefited most from this concrete approach but still tended to fall short of clients who initially demonstrated a higher degree of internalization. This is consistent with earlier research indicating that the client's initial level of internalizing behavior is a good predictor of eventual success in therapy (Farkas, 1969: Kirtner and Cartwright, 1958).

The results also indicate that therapists familiar with the internalization-externalization concept (and functioning at relatively high levels of facilitative behavior) can judge the degree to which their clients internalize. It would follow that, if the therapist can differentiate level of client internalization/externalization (at least in the extreme), he should be able to decide when a direct approach to teaching more appropriate client behavior (i.e., internalizing) is called for. The generalization of this result beyond the population of the study should be viewed with caution, since the data exists which indicates that across therapists with a wide range of functioning, it is difficult to arrive at consistent discriminations. In other words, perhaps only therapists capable of offering high levels of facilitative conditions and who are familiar with the concept of I-E will be able to accurately evaluate client internalizing behavior.

In regard to prediction of internalization, the LSQ was found to correlate significantly with I-E behavior, while the Rotter showed a positive but non-significant correlation. Earlier research using the Rotter also failed to find correlations with initial I-E behavior. (Farkas, 1969). Thus only the LSQ was found to offer potential as a pre-contact index of the level of client I-E behavior. Since the LSQ is basically an instrument sampling academic or learning behavior, it is interesting to speculate about the relationship between adequate coping behavior in an academic setting and adequate coping behavior in the therapy process. Research in behavior therapies indicate they are instrumental in changing behaviors; it may be that effective interpersonal problem-solving or coping behavior could be acquired through direct teaching methods.

If clients can learn to understand and alter their behavior through brief intervention by their therapists, does this in fact have a positive influence on the overall therapy process? While outcome criteria would provide a better base for making this conclusion, the purpose of the study was simply to determine if such intervention could lead to increased internalization behavior, since internalization has been consistently related to therapy success in previous research.

While the permanence of the intervention impact varied across clients there was frequent evidence of self-regulation of externalizing behavior, as illustrated in the following excerpt (from the tape of a sixth therapy session):

Cl: I guess I am excited about leaving, but I thought maybe it would help if you could write a letter telling them not to push me too hard . . . if they leave me alone I can do it myself.

Th: You want *me* to stop *them* from making it hard on you.
Cl: Well . . . no . . . oh wow, I'm putting it all out there again, huh . . . It's me that's scared about blowing it . . . and I'm saying it's my folks.
Th: Or me?
Cl: Yeah . . . I guess . . . I suppose I can tell them myself.

Furthermore, once the client had acquired the I-E conceptualization, it was a simple matter for the therapist to point out to the client when he lapsed back into externalizing behavior, (e.g., "It sounds like you're externalizing again John, can you look at it so that it's clear what *you're* contributing to the problem and what your reaction is?"). Thus it would seem that the intervention training resulted in a twofold benefit for subsequent therapy. First, the client could evaluate and regulate his own behavior within the conceptualization of internalization. Second, the therapist could help the client maintain the new "set" through appropriate and direct reminders.

The data shows that externalizers gained more than internalizers (−0.75 correlation between pre ratings and amount of change). One explanation for this is that the externalizers had more room for growth, i.e., a "ceiling" that was further away. Another possible explanation might be that the externalizers are simply continuing their pattern of responding to situational variables, i.e., doing what their therapist *tells* them to do. In either case, the externalizers *did* acquire internalizing behavior, and if this was initially due to the therapists' direction, the results have direct implication for therapist behavior. In the case of an obese client with a negative self-image, a therapist might proceed to deal with the underlying dynamics of the patient's obesity while *at the same time* supporting (if not directing) the client's efforts to lose weight. The process of losing weight, while due in great part to therapist intervention, can have a direct effect on the client's successful exploration of underlying dynamics and resultant behavior change. In the same way, if an externalizer having difficulty coping with his environment can be taught the more productive behavior of internalization (even if he has to be *told* to do so), he is better able to use this new behavior to arrive at an understanding of how his externalization behavior developed, leading to desired behavior change.

REFERENCES

Cannon, J. R. & Carkhuff, R. R. Effects of rater level of functioning and experience upon the dimensions of facilitative conditions. *Journal of Consulting and Clinical Psychology*, 1969, **33**, 189–194.

Carkhuff, R. R. & Berenson, B. G. *Beyond Counseling and Therapy*. New York: Holt, Rinehart and Winston, 1967.

Farkas, Andrea. The internal-external dimension of experience in relation to the process and outcome of psychotherapy. Unpublished Master's Thesis, Michigan State University, 1969.

Gendlin, Eugene T. Focusing. *Psychotherapy, Theory, Research and Practice*, Vol. 6 #1. 1969.

Gendlin, Eugene T. A small, still voice. *Psychology Today*, with Tavris, Carol. June, 1970.

Kagan, H., Krathwhol, D., Goldberg, A., Campbell, R., Schauble, P., Greenberg, B., Resnikoff, A., Danish, S. J., Bondy, S., & Bowles, J. Studies in human interaction: stimulated recall by videotape. Michigan State University, College of Education Publications, 1967.

Kirtner, W. L. & Cartwright, D. S. Success and failure in client centered therapy as a function of initial in-therapy behavior. *Journal of Consulting Psychology*, 1958, **22**, 329–335.

Perry, Cereta. Client internalization-externalization and therapy outcome. Unpublished doctoral dissertation, Michigan State University, 1969.

Pierce, R. M. & Schauble, P. G. Client behavior in therapy: A therapist guide to progress. Manuscript in process, Michigan State University, 1969.

Rotter, J. B. Generalized expectancies for internal versus external control of reinforcement. *Psychological Monographs*, 1966, **80**, 1–28.

CRITIQUE

1. PHILOSOPHICAL AND THEORETICAL CONSIDERATIONS

In this study the authors have built their hypotheses from some earlier empirical findings of therapy research. The basic question is whether or not the hypothetical construct of internalization can be taught to clients in therapy. This construct is derived from psychodynamic models of personality and therapy; more specifically from Rotter's learning theory approach.

The theoretical orientation of the therapists was assumed to follow the postulates of client-centered therapy. Here, high levels of empathy, regard, genuineness, and concreteness are seen to be crucial for successful outcomes. The technique of verbal reinforcement was used to teach the client a different way of conceptualizing and talking about his problem.

The research would have been more valuable had the researchers sought to offer a paradigm of behavior change within which their study could be located. No complete conceptual foundation is given; instead the investigation seems to rest more on a single construct, supported by designated instruments. It is somewhat difficult to find any clear reference between theoretical bases for the study and the language and tools used to collect observational data. For example, "interchangeable reflections" are named but are not defined, described, nor given any construct meaning. Likewise, are "teaching internalization" and "therapist" actions viewed synonymously? Ideally the reader could profit from a stronger section on internalization/externalization as a theoretical basis for the study. In any case, a conceptual or operational definition of internalization would be helpful.

2. CRITERION

The criterion in this study was the change in objective ratings of internalization/externalization during a second therapy interview. This follows clearly and logically from the goal set by the researchers. The construct of internalization/externalization is a specific one. Whereas it is a subjective state, it was measured in an objective (judges) way. The fact that the authors used a single criterion (rather than multiple ones as recommended in Chapter 3) seems appropriate in this situation.

3. RESEARCH DESIGN

As noted, this is essentially a process study which is highly compatible with the functional type design. Each client was in effect his own control, and three measures were taken on each client during the treatment interview. Pre and post treatment measures were then compared for each client. In this type of design, it is not unusual for a few subjects to be used and for group statistics to be avoided in lieu of graphs, charts, etc. to present the data. The use of this design seems quite appropriate in reference to the goals of the research, and the authors are appropriately cautious in the interpretation of the results.

4. SELECTION AND SAMPLING PROCEDURES

The authors do not explain how the 15 subjects were drawn or describe the client population. We can assume that an incidental sampling procedure from the pool of potential clients seeking personal/social counseling was used. Generalization and external validity are seriously compromised with this process. The authors correctly allude to the lack of adequate sampling of counselors, and suggest the need for caution in generalizing the research results.

There is one other omission that involves the method of assignment of clients to the two therapists. The authors fail to mention how this was carried out, e.g., randomization, matching, combination.

5. THERAPY AND TREATMENT

Of all the studies critiqued in Part II, these researchers have done an outstanding job of explicating the treatment process. Perhaps it would have been helpful to have known how much experience the therapists had, their sex, and how the clients were assigned to them.

The authors did an excellent job of objectifying the levels of therapist functions *vis-à-vis* the client-centered constructs of empathy, regard, genuineness, and concreteness. Only when the reader comes across the statement that the first twenty minutes of the interview was run in a traditional manner of interchangeable reflections, does the process become less clear. The second twenty-minute period of the interview is tighter, although one would like to see the response class of internalizing behavior, and the frequency of reinforcement dealt with more explicitly. In other words, since it appears there might have been wide subject variation between client talk during the second twenty minutes, and since some talk (content) fits the internalization-externalization dimension more closely, some subjects would have received much more reinforcement. How much reinforcement the different clients received is not known.

The researchers did an excellent job of demonstrating objectively the significant change which took place during the interview, by obtaining both therapists and judges' ratings of internalization/externalization taking place.

6. MEASUREMENT

The goal of this study was to determine if the construct of internalization could be taught to clients in a single interview session. The researchers made use of a self-report instrument designed especially for this purpose (The Rotter), an assessment of in-therapy, I-E behavior (a five-point rating scale) which defined how a client talks about things at each end of the scale, a therapist's rating instrument (a semantic differential) for the I-E behavior, and judges' ratings of counseling phenomena (empathy, genuineness, etc.) to establish changes in client verbal behavior. In addition, the training procedure was measured quite adequately, except with the few minor limitations noted above. The authors have done an excellent job of measuring the concepts and constructs under investigation.

A final comment should be made. This study was primarily a process one. Although the authors cite evidence that internalizing behavior is related to successful and effective therapy results, the reader is not sure just what this means.

He would have to refer to the documented sources to discern what those authors defined as successful or effective therapy, and this might not be easy because the authors cite several unpublished studies. From these results we can infer that internalization can be taught in therapy. The logical next step would be to define successful therapy and define appropriate and relevant criteria, and to see what effects internalization would have on those criteria.

7. ETHICAL, PROFESSIONAL, AND LEGAL CONSIDERATIONS

It is assumed that the clients in this study who sought help at this Counseling Center were followed through with professional services.

Professional and ethical concerns are of interest in the selection of subjects. No data is given on whether they were completely voluntary. Could some have been "drafted" and subsequently given less help than otherwise? One can't help but think that research vs. client growth may be an ethical question here. Approaches to clients for research purposes carry strong professional obligations.

As a research report this article could have been more adequate if definitions of such terms as "traditional manner," "experienced counselors," and "internalizing behavior" had been included. Also the researchers could have examined the question: "What difference this research might make in the behavior of the practicing counselor?"

8. RESULTS

The results are quite clear in this study—internalization as a psychological process can be taught to clients.

We feel that this is an example of an excellent study. The counselor-researchers selected a very specific phenomenon to be investigated and clearly established the goals and criterion. Great care was taken to explicate the treatment according to the theoretical orientation. The authors do not over generalize from the data, and point out clearly the implications for therapy practice.

EMOTIONALITY IN MARATHON AND TRADITIONAL PSYCHOTHERAPY GROUPS[1]

Howard L. Myerhoff,[2] Alfred Jacobs,[3] and Frederick Stoller[4]

Marathon groups may meet for a continuous 8–12 hour period one day, or for such periods on several consecutive days, or continuously and throughout the night for several days. George Bach has called such groups "Pressure Cooker" or "Marathon" groups (1967), and Frederick Stoller has called them "Accelerated Interaction" groups (1966). Therapists who have had experience with Marathon groups report a heightened intensity of emotionality beyond that which occurs in ordinary therapy groups. Not only is emotionality more intense, it is also more variable. The present study attempts to demonstrate that more intense emotionality and greater variability would be observed in the Marathon group as compared to a traditional group.

A second hypothesis, also derived from clinical impressions, proposed that group cohesion would be greater in the Marathon than the conventional group. The operations for measuring group cohesion were to be based on attendance rates as well as the desire of group members to continue treatment.

METHOD

Subjects

The subjects were selected by canvassing a large segment of the hospital population, and offering them: "the opportunity to receive treatment in a more intense kind of group which has had outstanding success in helping people to get to know themselves better, and in helping them become more able to help themselves. However, this treatment is not effective for people who feel that they have 'been put away' here, and who feel that their behavior has nothing to do with why they are here."

Patients were required to meet the following criteria for selection:

[1]First printed in *Psychotherapy: Theory, Research and Practice*. Myerhoff, Howard L., Jacobs, Alfred, and Stoller, Frederick. Emotionality in marathon and traditional psychotherapy groups. 1970, **7**, (1), 33–36.

[2]Southern California Permanente Medical Group. Formerly at Camarillo State Hospital.

[3]Department of Psychology, University of West Virginia.

[4]University of Southern California, Youth Studies Center. Formerly at Camarillo State Hospital.

1. Be willing to remain in hospital for three weeks. 2. Be able and willing to fill out the Jacobs Adjective Check List (JACL) (Jacobs, Meehan, Dale, 1966). 3. Be between the ages of twenty and sixty-five. 4. Be able to communicate verbally in a group, and be able to control hallucinations, or other disordered thinking enough to participate in verbal interchange.

All patients were offered the option of continuing in treatment with the same therapist, the same group, but on a reduced schedule (two times per week) after the experimental period. No patient was excluded on the basis of diagnosis, though several who volunteered were excluded because they were too confused to participate. Volunteers were assigned at random to the E and C groups. Of thirteen *S*s originally selected for the control group, four withdrew after the first two sessions, and nine completed the nine sessions. Of nine *S*s originally assigned to the E group, eight completed the three six hour sessions.

PROCEDURE

The independent variable is the *arrangement* of time. Based on pilot studies it was decided that eighteen hours of treatment for both the experimental and control groups would be adequate to test the main effects. The administration of the criterion, an adjective checklist designed to measure affective responses, (the JACL) occurred after each two hour interval of psychotherapy in each group. The Experimental (E) group received its eighteen hours of treatment in three days, six hours each day. The Control (C) group received its eighteen hours of treatment in three weeks, three two hour sessions each week. Therefore, the C group completed a JACL at the conclusion of each of the nine two hour sessions. The E group filled out a JACL after two and four hours each day and at the end of the six hour session. Each administration of the JACL is called a trial. Emotionality was defined as the total number of adjectives checked by a *S* on each trial.

*S*s in each group were asked at the conclusion of the eighteen hours of therapy if they wanted to continue meeting (though on a somewhat reduced schedule) with the same therapist. Group cohesion was measured by the number of patients electing to continue and by their attendance record for six subsequent group sessions.

The therapist was the same for both groups to control for therapist differences. Non-participating observers in each group used a Hill Interaction Matrix G (HIM-G) (1965) to provide evaluations of therapist as well as group interactions. This procedure allowed an assessment of the possibility that differences in therapist belief or enthusiasm for one treatment method may have resulted in differences in his behavior in the E and C groups. Ratings of therapist interactions (both for "sponsoring" behavior and for "participating" behavior) were made every two hours for both the E and C groups. The correlations between measures of therapist behavior in the E and C group, taken over nine observations for each group, yield a Spearman Rho of 0.754 (including correction for ties), which is significant well beyond the 0.01 level. Considerable consistency of therapist behavior in both E and C groups is thereby demonstrated on the dimensions of interaction measured by the HIM-G.

Instruments

The Jacobs Adjective Checklist (JACL) was revised for hospitalized patients and used for assessment of affective states. It consists of twenty-six dimensions of affective responses derived from two factor analyses. Six clusters of emotional factors Anger, Fear, Depression, Weakness, Activity, and Well-Being were generated on the basis of the intercorrelations between scores on the twenty-six scales. A pilot administration to a sample of hospital patients revealed that the items most frequently chosen as descriptive of "how you feel right now" were in fact those items which previous factor analyses had demonstrated to be those loaded most heavily on the six emotion clusters or factors. Therefore, the fifteen items in each of the six emotionality factors which a) loaded most heavily on that factor, and/or b) were most frequently chosen as descriptive of momentary feelings by hospital patients, were cast into the current JACL. This form demands that each of the ninety items be checked either Y (yes, that item describes how I feel right now) or N (no, that item doesn't describe how I feel right now).

RESULTS

The distribution of the scores obtained was extremely bimodal, precluding a meaningful variance analysis. Most *S*s checked very few negative items (anger, fear, depression, weakness) and very many positive items (activity, well-being), whereas a few *S*s checked very many negative and very few positive items. Therefore, the scores for each *S* on all negative scales were combined into one negative emotion score, and scores on positive scales were treated in a similar manner in order to obtain analyzable distributions. The total number of items checked was used as an overall emotionality score.

The mean number of adjectives checked by *S*s over all nine trials was 255.6. The control group checked 178.6 items for each subject. The mean number of Positive and Negative adjectives checked in the Marathon group were 130.7 and 124.9, and in the Traditional group 124.3 and 53.7.

The phenomena most clearly demonstrated in Fig. 1. are the rapid and rather regular decrease in frequency of elicited negative emotional responses in the C group as contrasted with the saw-toothed and markedly higher rate of endorsement of negative items in the E group. The data on which Fig. 1 is based were evaluated by the analysis of variance in Lindquist Case IV (1963).

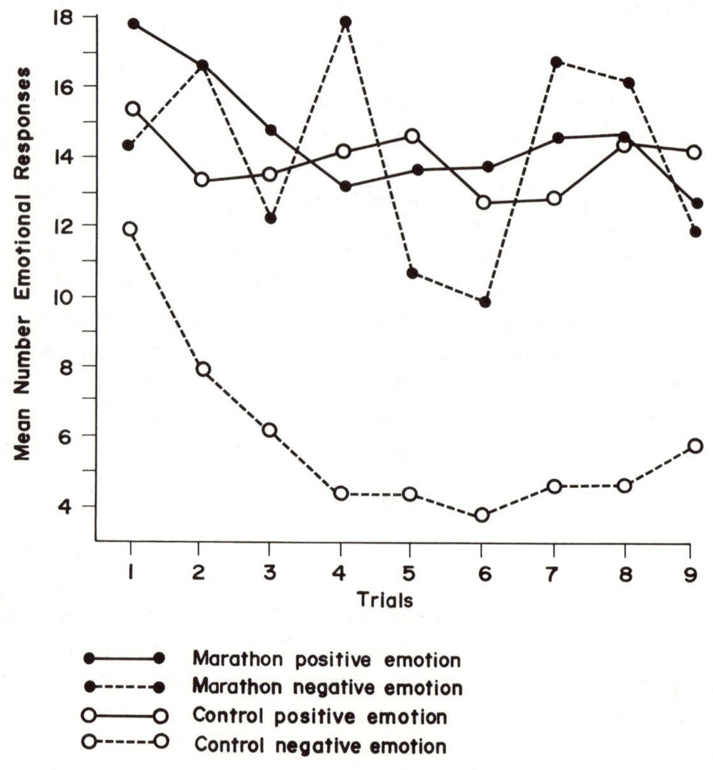

Figure 1 Mean number of Positive and Negative Adjectives checked by Marathon and Traditional psychotherapy group patients at each two hour testing period.

Table 1 Analysis of Variance of Emotional Responses in Marathon and Traditional Therapy.

Source	af	MS	F
Between Subjects	16	538.3	
Groups (G)	1	1,418	3.0
Error (b)	15	480	
Within Subjects	289	63.7	
Emotions (E)	1	1,424.0	2.3
Trials (T)	8	68	4.3**
E×T	8	15	
E×G	1	988	
T×G	8	27	
E×T×G	8	61	2.4*
Error (W)	255	57.6	
Error 1 (WE)	15	629.0	
Error 2 (WT)	120	15.7	
Error 3 (WE×T)	120	25.6	
Total	305		

**$p < 0.01$, *$p < 0.025$

Table 2 High and Low Cohesion Scores in Marathon and Traditional Groups.

	Low Cohesion Index 0–3	High Cohesion Index 4–7	*n*
Marathon	2	6	8
Traditional	7	2	9
	9	8	17

It may be observed from Table 1 that significant differences in scores exist between trials ($p < 0.025$), and that the Emotions × Trials by Group interaction is also significant ($p < 0.01$).

The analysis suggests that it is not the overall greater emotionality that differentiates the Marathon from the Traditional group, but that the differences emerge from the style of expression of negative emotional states. The sustained high level of negative emotional response peaking at one trial during each session of the Marathon group is in contrast with the regular smooth decrease in the expression of negative emotion by the Traditional group. There is a regular steady expression of positive emotional responses in both groups.

To derive a score for cohesion, one point was given for voting "YES" to the question about continuing the group, and one point for each of the 6 sessions attended.

Fisher's exact probability test yields a $p = 0.05$ for this distribution which shows more Marathon than Traditional Groups *S*s with high cohesiveness scores. It should be noted that four of the *S*s left the hospital on convalescent leaves or discharges before the three week "cohesion period" was over.

Three additional sets of analyses tested whether the differences between the Marathon and Traditional treatments could be attributable to differences in responsiveness of *S*s, or to differences in diagnostic composition of groups, or to differences in length of hospitalization of *S*s within groups. The Emotionality scores of high and low item checkers divided at the median, of diagnosed schizophrenic and nonschizophrenic patients, and those patients hospitalized more or less than two years were treated without reference to experimental conditions by the Lindquist Case VI Analysis of Variance. In no instance did the Groups × Trials × Emotions interaction approach significance. Neither were Fisher tests significant for Cohesion Indexes. The analyses based on length of hospitalization were particularly crucial because the self selection process resulting from patients dropping out of therapy had resulted in the accumulation in the traditional therapy condition of significantly greater number of patients who had been hospitalized for over two years.

DISCUSSION

The more intense or heightened emotional involvement supposedly characteristic of Marathon therapy is represented in the present study by a generally higher rate of occurrence and variability in the expression of negative feelings.

Marathon therapists have speculated that the maintenance of psychological defense systems which inhibit the awareness and expression of responses which are unacceptable in many ordinary social contexts is an energy consuming process. In the longer uninterrupted period in the Marathon group there is a greater probability that the defense system will deteriorate or break down.

A variation of the preceding explanation might be the "too tired to be polite" phenomena. Increased fatigue or increased drive level is often associated with irritability, frustration, and impatience, and has often been observed to lower the threshold for the occurrence of behavior which is ordinarily considered less socially acceptable.

The augmented length of session of Marathon and/or the more frequent elicitation of intense emotional response may also initiate a cumulative process in which warm up, modeling or other therapeutic learning variables as well as inhibitory or fatigue like variables may be discovered to develop at a different rate than in shorter time periods. One may also speculate that newness and dramatic form of a Marathon treatment, as has been observed in the history of the introduction of other treatment innovations, plays some role in the more intense patient response apparently elicited.

However, the evaluation of Marathon therapy reported here is based on only one of the many possible variations in Marathon duration. The generality of conclusions is further limited by the nature of the subject population which consisted of an in-patient mental hospital sample, half of whom had been diagnosed schizophrenic. It is the subjective impression of the authors that, perhaps typical of traditional group psychotherapy in such populations, the systematic decrease in negative emotions reported here represented more patient comfort as therapy progressed, and a decrease in the propensity to express more personally meaningful but also more anxiety-provoking content.

Marathon groups composed of differently diagnosed patients or of normals, it is the impression of the authors, respond in various patterns of emotional expression. Normal *S*s for example, often express a high level of negative emotion towards the middle of a Marathon period, and ordinarily a high level of positive emotion before the conclusion. The increase in cohesion may thus ordinarily be plausibly attributed to an increase in intimacy which may develop from the positive quality of the shared experience as well as a consequence of the expression of negative affect.

The major impact of this research is the demonstration that hard data may be gathered on clinical material. This hard data corresponds quite clearly to the clinical impressions of the therapist and the observers of the groups.

REFERENCES

Bach, George R. Marathon Group Dynamics: II Dimensions of Helpfulness: Therapeutic Aggression. *Psychological Reports*, 1967, **20**, (3, PT2), 1147–1158.

Bach, George R. Marathon Group Dynamics: III Disjunctive contacts. *Psychological Reports*, 1967, **20** (3PT2) 1163–1172.

Hill, W. *Hill Interaction Matrix*. Los Angeles: Youth Studies Center, University of Southern California, 1965.

Jacobs, A., Meehan, J. P., & Dale, T. Subjective dimensions of emotion. Paper presented at Western Psychological Association Meetings, 1962.

Lindquist, E. F. *Design and Analysis of experiments in psychology and education.* Boston: Houghton Mifflin, 1953.

Stoller, F. H., Robinson, Margot, & Myerhoff, H. L. Effects of video-tape feedback on student participants in a two day marathon group. Unpublished manuscript, 1966.

CRITIQUE

1. PHILOSOPHICAL AND THEORETICAL CONSIDERATIONS

It is difficult to ascertain just what theoretical rationale was used by the therapist in this study. The goal as described to the subjects was to get to know themselves better, and to help them become more able to help themselves. Yet, because this study is more properly described as a process one, the goals were to see which arrangement of time (marathon or traditional) produced more intense and variable emotionality, and to ascertain which approach produced more cohesion. There is certainly no reference to any theory of personality which might orient the research goals or therapeutic intentions.

With respect to any underlying theory, this research fails to present a recognizable conceptual scheme which might suggest differences in traditional and marathon group processes. Similarly the justification, in theory language, for focusing on the intensity and variability of emotion is not offered. Such an assumption was given but not rooted in theory. Likewise there is no strong linkage, theoretically, between the emotionality (particularly intensity) being examined and the dependent variables used.

2. CRITERIA

The criteria used to check on the above goals were (1) intensity and variability of emotionality, and (2) group cohesion.

The construct of emotionality was operationally defined as the total number of positive and negative affective responses checked on an adjective checklist. This is a subjective, internal kind of criterion. Although the researchers operationally defined the criterion, we wonder if emotionality might not have been better defined according to certain theories of personality.

The criterion of group cohesion generally refers to how close the members feel toward one another in a unity sort of way. This too is a subjective, internal criterion.

3. RESEARCH DESIGN

A multiple treatment design was used in this research. All subjects received treatment which simply varied in kind. In the strict sense, there was no "control" group, even though the effects of the marathon were controlled. As a factorial design, the analysis of variance is the primary test used to assess differences in the adjective criterion measure. The strength of this design enabled the counselor-researchers to examine important interaction effects, which adds an important dimension to the value of the study.

4. SELECTION AND SAMPLING PROCEDURES

The authors report that subjects were randomly assigned to treatment groups, although the procedure is not explained. Subjects were initially involved in the research on a self-selection basis. As is frequently the case in counseling-therapy research, the investigators were troubled by patient retention problems, particularly in the "control" group. As noted in Chapter 5, there are clearly stated bases reported in the literature for "dropping" subjects from samples. Why and how were the five subjects dropped? Did attrition have some relation to treatment or not?

In the discussion, the investigators are careful not to generalize the results. They note the demonstration of certain measurement techniques as being the primary contribution of their research. Considering the lack of representativeness of therapist, client and situational variables, the hesitancy to generalize to even other hospitalized populations is appropriate.

5. THERAPY TREATMENT

We know very little about what actually happened in these groups. The rationale for the use of the same therapist for each treatment group is noteworthy and sound. Who was the therapist? What was his training, education, experience with groups, and his personal orientation about fostering emotionality and cohesion in groups and its relative importance in treatment? More importantly, was the therapist one of the authors or was he aware of the nature of the study? The authors tried to control for these questions by using the Hill Interaction Matrix. This is insufficient because this only points out that the therapist was consistent and tells us little about his personal beliefs about the nature of emotionality in behavioral change, or the importance of cohesion for therapy outcomes. It would have been interesting for the authors to include more on how the therapist did check out on the HIM, that is, the specific kinds of therapist behavior he was inclined to use. This would have certainly helped to make the treatment process more explicit.

6. MEASUREMENT

The criterion of emotionality was measured by the use of a revised adjectival checklist. This form used a dichotomized format in which the client checked either *yes* or *no*, that is, "how I am feeling right now." This is interesting in light of the earlier emphasis on intensity of emotionality. Our point is that people generally do not feel either intensely angered or not—they might just be annoyed about something. The authors are to be commended for using a repeated measures approach, in which they systematically (each two hours) and consistently obtained the emotionality of the clients.

The second criterion of group cohesion was measured by asking whether or not the client wanted to continue with the group, and by attendance at subsequent sessions. We feel that this is not a very exact measure of group cohesion as we understand it. Certainly, whether or not a person wants to continue, and whether or not he does, in fact, attend meetings, are *related* to the phenomenon of cohesion, but group cohesion is more than that. A client might have felt very close to the group, but did not want to jeopardize his chance of being discharged from the hospital by saying yes. Perhaps, the way of handling this might have been to define, describe, and demonstrate (via videotape) to the clients what high and low cohesion is, and then to obtain consistent measures from them on how they perceived cohesion in their group. Anecdotal reports or some sociometric device could have been constructed for this purpose.

The use of observers in the group using the Hill Interaction Matrix is sound. Yet, several questions occur here: Was there only one, or were there more than one in each group session; if the latter, what was their reliability of ratings? Had they been trained to use the HIM? Finally, a Spearman Rho of 0.754 while statistically significant, is not really very high.

7. ETHICAL, PROFESSIONAL, AND LEGAL CONSIDERATIONS

No information was given on the specific manner in which clients were obtained for the study, so any ethical issues are clouded. The element of explanation or interpretation to "volunteer" is not too clear. Replication would be aided if the authors had critically evaluated their study. There appears to be some discrepancy between the primary hypothesis posited and the conclusions discussed. Instead of "emotionality" (undefined), the results dealt mostly with "variability in expression of negative feelings."

8. RESULTS

We feel that the authors have posed an interesting process question. They have done a good study, except for a few methodological concerns noted above, and did not stray too far from their data in their interpretations. We do not agree that the major impact of the study was the demonstration that hard data can be gathered on clinical material. But to put it another way, the data could have been much harder. The next step in such research should be to include some outcome criteria to see what effect emotionality has on behavior change.

A TEST OF GROUP COUNSELING[1]

Marilyn Bates
Assistant Professor of Education, California State College at Fullerton

High school students were counseled in groups designed around either a "traditional" or an "accelerated interaction" format. The efficiency of each approach in achieving the goals of guidance in education was studied. Group counseling appeared to be a useful counseling tool if organized on a weekly basis.

Group counseling may have slipped into the public schools analogically by way of the reasoning that if the principles of individual therapy apply to the principles of individual counseling, then the principles of group therapy could be adapted to group counseling. Counselors seem to have assumed that, since the techniques borrowed from individual therapy and applied to individual counseling have worked out rather well in the school setting, the dynamics of group interactions pioneered in psychiatry and in social work could also be used appropriately in educational institutions.

No one would quarrel with the concept that the counselor's general obligation in the school setting is to deal as effectively as possible with the overwhelming variety of student problems, but his specific professional responsibility of being certain that his procedures are consonant with his ethical commitment to the educational philosophy of the school is given less emphasis. The responsibility to evaluate group counseling in terms of acceptable educational goals is particularly incumbent on the school counselor who works with a "captive" counselee and who works with time requisitioned from the classroom teacher. It seems unethical for counselors to continue to use their own and their counselee's time to engage in a process concerning which past research has been inconclusive as to benefits and vague as to goals. If the technique of group counseling is to continue to be a routine counseling procedure, the counselor ought to know which of the goals of guidance in education can be achieved through this process.

[1]Bates, Marilyn. A test of group counseling. *Personnel and Guidance Journal*, 1968, **46**, 749–753.

THE DESIGN OF THE STUDY

In an effort to determine whether or not group counseling did indeed belong in the public schools, a study of the effectiveness of group counseling in meeting goals of guidance in education was conducted by the writer during the school year 1965–66 at Western High School, Anaheim Union High School District in California. Two contrasting group counseling formats were used during the 13-week experimental period. The "traditional" format involved weekly class period meetings, while the "accelerated interaction" format involved an equal amount of group counseling time, but with the time being concentrated into a two-day continuous session held during school hours. Thirty-six boys and girls were assigned to each group, which, in turn, was broken into three subgroups containing equal numbers of tenth, eleventh, and twelfth graders. Students were matched on the basis of sex, grade level, academic potential, socioeconomic level, and academic achievement, then randomly assigned to groups. Each experimental group was paralleled by a control group, and evaluation was made by means of a matched-pairs t formula, using the pre-test–post-test gains scores. Instrumentation involved the Bills' Index of Adjustment and Values (IAV), the Tyler Vocational Choice Cards, the Rotter Incomplete Sentences Blank, academic grades, effort grades, citizenship grades, and attendance patterns. These measures were taken both pre and post, the week prior to the initial group sessions and the week immediately following the final group sessions. Thus for the traditional groups and their controls the pre–post test intervals were 15 weeks, while the pre–post test intervals for the accelerated interaction groups and

Table 1 Summary of Statistical Findings.

Measuring Instrument	Traditional vs. Controls		Accelerated vs. Controls	
	t	Level of Significance*	t	Level of Significance*
GPA	2.72	0.01	1.41	NS
Attendance	2.10	0.05	0.06	NS
Effort Grades	2.54	0.01	−1.50	NS
Citizenship Grades	2.42	0.05	−1.17	NS
Vocational Choice Cards	2.42	0.05	1.32	NS
Rotter Incomplete Sentences Blank	3.85	0.001	4.27	0.001
Bills IAV – Self Scores	1.75	0.05	0.81	NS
Bills IAV – Other Scores	2.86	0.01	1.62	NS

*One-tailed test.

their controls were three weeks. A summary of the statistical findings is presented in Table 1.

The goals of group counseling were related to the goals of guidance, then analyses were made to determine if these goals could be implemented through counseling with groups. Although a complete reporting of the results of the study would go beyond space limitations, a brief overview, presenting the goals, the findings, and the implications, may be of interest.

THE GOAL OF COGNITIVE KNOWLEDGE

According to the findings of the study, which was concerned with middle class adolescents, either of the group counseling formats—traditional or accelerated interaction—might be used in the school setting to make the student more receptive to the learning process through a reduction of tensions and hostilities. The Rotter Incomplete Sentences Blank provided the data for the statistics which were significant for both groups at the 0.001 level. Apparently the process of group discussion, which involves venting feelings in the safety of the group counseling situation, is an effective means of providing release from internal pressures. Presumably the students are then better able to attend to classroom instruction, thereby gaining in cognitive knowledge. Whether or not this is sufficient reason to include group counseling in routine procedures is open to conjecture. If a reduction of adolescent tensions, however, is considered sufficient justification, either the traditional format or the accelerated interaction format could be used with equal effectiveness. When additional purposes, cognitive or otherwise, are involved, the interchangeability of the two contrasting formats ends.

For example, in the second measure of cognitive change—grade-point average (GPA)—the comparison of the pre-test–post-test gains scores indicated that the traditional model was effective in assisting counselees to sustain their GPA's, while the GPA's of the traditional controls, and the accelerated interaction counselees and their controls, deteriorated. Perhaps in the traditional group counseling finding of enabling the student to sustain rather than to improve his grade-point average can be found a clue to the typically disappointing results obtained by workers who have tried to break the underachievement syndrome through group counseling. According to the results of this study, what can be done for the group counselee is to help him to *maintain* a grade-point average that would otherwise have deteriorated, rather than to effect an improvement in GPA.

THE GOAL OF BEHAVIORAL CHANGE

The group counseling and guidance goal of positive behavioral change was measured in several ways and only the traditionally counseled groups demonstrated a statistically significant improvement. When citizenship grades were analyzed, it was found that apparently the process of meeting on a weekly basis over a period of time was necessary for students to demonstrate behavioral changes in the classroom. It will be noted that, while the traditional *t* score was significant at the 0.05 level, the accelerated interaction score was not significant. The limited reinforcement of "good intentions" experienced by the accelerated interaction group may have resulted in a "letting down" once the two days' intensive interaction was terminated. In the accelerated interaction group there was no ongoing opportunity to share "improvement victories" with other group members; thus motivation to change may have been diminished.

The same pattern can be discerned in the analysis of the effort grades, in which the traditional group showed a significant difference at the 0.01 level of confidence while the accelerated interaction group did not. Apparently the accelerated interaction group members were not able to sustain any effect that the group counseling process may have had on them, at least when translated into the amount of effort that the teacher saw demonstrated in the classroom. On the other hand, the traditional group members, who were periodically reinforced through weekly interaction, seemed able to sustain their efforts to improve behavior to a degree that was obvious to the teacher.

The goal of behavioral change was measured also by attendance patterns. The usual expectancy of attendance pattern seems to be for an increase in absenteeism as the school year progresses. Students tend to stay out of school more days toward the end of the year than at the beginning of the year, and this expected pattern was followed by the accelerated interaction group and by both control groups. In the case of the traditional group, there was no great reduction in the number of days absent but this group continued to show the same pattern of attendance late in the year after group counseling as they had evidenced early in the year before group counseling. They showed a significant difference from their controls at the 0.05 level of confidence. Apparently the group counseling process is effective in "holding" the students in school if the groups meet on a weekly basis rather than on an intensive basis.

There seem to be some implications in these findings for attendance counselors, who might find the group process useful in assisting with truancy problems. It is possible that meeting with peers weekly in an unstructured group counseling situation would give the adolescent something in the school setting that he particularly enjoyed, and thus he might become more regular in his attendance.

According to the findings concerning behavioral changes, the group counseling process, if organized on a weekly basis, can be used to help the counselees demonstrate better behavior in the classroom, both in general attitudes and in manifested effort. It is important to point out, however, that this statement is based on the findings of group data. If a counselor were to assure teachers that the nonconformity of every counselee might be corrected through the group counseling process, some unfortunate repercussions might occur. Also, although the results which used teachers' marks as criteria were statistically significant at the 0.05 level or above, it is doubtful if these counselees were models of decorum as a result of group counseling. It is important to keep in mind that one of the tasks we have in counseling is to determine what we *cannot* do, as well as to determine what we can do, and this general attitude is vital when applied to group counseling. To promise results beyond those that can realistically be achieved will only lead to disillusionment and disappointment, and subsequently to the abandonment of group counseling as an appropriate and useful educational tool.

THE GOAL OF VOCATIONAL EXPLORATION

A rather unexpected finding of this study was concerned with vocational exploration. When group counseling was conducted on a weekly basis the occupational horizons of the group counselees were significantly expanded. According to the results of the Tyler Vocational Choice Cards, the students who met in weekly group sessions were able to project themselves into more occupations—and these chosen occupations were more realistic when assessed against the student's tested academic potential. Just how the group counseling process was instrumental in increasing the realism of vocational choices by the traditionally counseled group is unknown, as no direct "teaching" concerning occupations was attempted. Both groups—traditional and accelerated interaction—did, however, voluntarily discuss some aspects of the world of work. Perhaps the main contributing factor for the significant difference (0.05) demonstrated by the traditional group was the additional knowledge of and positive feelings toward self that were gained as a result of the group experiences. It is possible that a common characteristic of students typically recommended for group counseling is the possession of a rigid perceptual field with limited occupational boundaries, and that, as these students expanded their perceptions of others through the group process, they also projected themselves into more occupational roles.

THE GOAL OF CONATIVE KNOWLEDGE: INDIVIDUATION

The goal of conative knowledge is often seen as the *sine qua non* of group counseling since the affective domain is so deeply involved in self-acceptance and since acceptance of self is so inextricably bound up in the search for identity, a basic developmental task of the adolescent (Erikson, 1959). That the traditional format of group counseling could facilitate the individuation process was demonstrated by the findings of this study which used the "Self" score of the IAV for instrumentation of this area. Students who worked in a group that met weekly came to place more value on themselves, became more aware of themselves as unique persons, and become more self-accepting, while students who participated in the accelerated interaction group demonstrated no significant gain in conative knowledge.

THE GOAL OF ACCULTURATION

The traditional group also came to place a great deal more value on others, thus moving in a positive direction toward the group counseling and guidance goal of socialization. Over and over the students expressed relief that other peer members were experiencing the same problems as they. Somehow, they commented, this made their lives seen less lonely and easier to endure. And as they saw that others shared their experiences, they became more accepting of their peers. A counselor can only hope that this feeling will generalize to include all "others" in the life space of each counselee, perhaps even the adults! At any rate, there was a clear trend on the IAV "Others" score of the traditional group away from a negative view of self and toward a positive view of others. Even if a student placed little value on himself, he still tended to place more value on others in relation to himself, if he were in the traditional group. It seems to the writer that an increased valuing of others would justify the use of school time for group work, even if it were the only achievable goal. Since one of the major struggles of adolescence is to adjust successfully to the world about one, the apparent success of traditional group counseling in enlarging a student's awareness of others recommends its inclusion as an acceptable procedure in a guidance program.

The accelerated interaction groups did not experience this shift in perceiving others in a more favorable light. Perhaps the accelerated pace of the intensive interaction did not allow for the "settling in" of any changes this group may have had in their ideas concerning the universality of human problems. It is also possible that the rapidity of the verbal interchanges did not allow the counselees to digest the import of the comments and to internalize a "new" view of their peers. Our long accepted tenet that more counseling takes place between sessions than during sessions seems supported by the results of this study.

REFERENCES

Bates, M. A study of the effectiveness of group counseling in achieving the goals of guidance in education, using two contrasting formats. Unpublished doctoral dissertation, University of Southern California, 1967.

Bills, R. E. *Manual for the High School Form, Index of Adjustment and Values*. School of Education, University of Alabama, undated.

Erikson, E. H. Identity and life cycle. *Psychological Issues*, 1959, **1**, (1), 88–94.

Rotter, J. B., & Rafferty, J. E. *Manual: Rotter Incomplete Sentences Blank*. New York: Psychological Corp., 1950.

Tyler, L. E. & Sundberg, N. D. *Factors affecting career choices of adolescents*. Cooperative Research Project No. 2455, U.S. Office of Education. Eugene, Ore.: University of Oregon, 1964.

CRITIQUE

1. PHILOSOPHICAL AND THEORETICAL CONSIDERATIONS

Philosophically the researcher in this study has attempted to tie the goals and objectives of group counseling in with the goals of guidance in education. Although the goals are specifically stated, it is not clear where they came from. Even less clear is the theoretical orientation used as a base for the group counseling provided in this study. It is assumed that the educational philosophy of the school should generate the goals of group counseling. While the goals of education are set forth, they are not necessarily logically related to the goals of group counseling, either in this study or in general. Theoretically, the counseling rationale seems to borrow from client-centered theory (safety of the group counseling situation, positive feelings toward self, self-acceptance, rigid perceptual field, acceptance of others, etc.), neo-analytic theories (reduction of tensions and hostilities), and cognitive-behavioral (positive behavioral change, limited reinforcement of "good intentions," reducing absenteeism, etc.).

Because the philosophical and theoretical bases are not too clear, the goals and objectives are broad and vague. The goals of cognitive knowledge, behavioral change, vocational exploration, conative knowledge and acculturation, are certainly laudatory; yet, one wonders how close one could get to meeting all these goals in a study which lasted for only thirteen weeks. Any one of these goals would have been enough to tackle in a short period of time. These goals are too broad and comprehensive to be undertaken in a single study. Indeed, the title itself promises more than can be delivered, while at the same time fails to convey important facts about the content of the paper, e.g., setting.

2. CRITERIA

Several criteria were used:

a. Gains in Cognitive Knowledge

The criterion performance used to measure this goal was the Rotter Incomplete Sentences Blank and change in grade point average. Evidently, the first instrument was used to measure release from internal pressure. Although this was significantly reduced there was no significant increase in GPA. There is no logical reason to believe that such would occur. The two measures obviously are getting at two different intrapersonal phenomena. The first criterion measure is of the self-report variety (subjective), whereas the second one is an objective, external one.

b. Positive Behavioral Changes

This was measured by use of citizenship grades, effort grades, and attendance patterns. Grading practices vary greatly from teacher to teacher, especially on such vague and undefined dimensions as citizenship and effort. We do not know what grading scale was used. (Was it the usual A, B, C, or something else?) Perhaps a more exact procedure would have been to provide the teachers assigning the grades with an observation schedule along with examples of what kinds of behavior constitute good citizenship or improved effort.

The use of attendance patterns is quite good. This is an objective, external behavioral referrant, and one in which the researcher might logically expect improvement.

c. Expansion of Occupational Horizons

This is a simple, yet significant, expectation from most high school group counseling programs. The use of the Tyler Vocational Choice Cards seems very appropriate in measuring the ways in which students have expanded the vocational range from which they are considering choosing their vocation.

d. Gains in Conative Knowledge

As stated by the author, the goal of greater affective self-understanding is implicit in most group counseling theories. While values seem to be at the heart of individual emotionality, it can be inferred from many other constructs, e.g., attitudes, feelings, opinions, etc. A more relevant measure might have been the use of a self/ideal-self Q-sort.

e. Acculturation

An increasing valuing of others is just one part of a greater socialization. One can hardly justify saying that the students in the traditional group became more acculturated or socialized simply because on a self-report index they appeared to value others more. This criterion might more appropriately have been labeled, valuing others.

3. RESEARCH DESIGN

Although the author includes a section on design in the report, it is quite unclear just what the nature of the design actually was. Apparently two treatment and two corresponding control conditions were used, but the actual number of experimental or control groups, group leaders, students in groups, etc. are not detailed. Among the control problems (Chapter 3) not dealt with in the report are: (1) the nature of the "noncounseled" control subjects; (2) counselor or group leader cooperation; (3) situational variables; and (4) the topical format for the treatment groups.

Although the author does not identify it as such, the design employed is of a multiple treatment-control group variety. It is unclear what kind of control groups were used—no treatment, delayed treatment, etc.

4. SELECTION AND SAMPLING PROCEDURES

The author does not describe how counselees were selected for the program or how they were assigned to treatment-control groups. Equal numbers of males and females, and tenth-, eleventh-, and twelfth-grade students were assigned by some means to various treatment-control conditions. Assuming more than one counselor or group leader was involved the reader cannot know how they were selected because the author has failed to include any details about this important matter. In general, the method section of this report is not clearly written, and the design and sampling procedures are presented so unsystematically that the value of the entire study is jeopardized.

5. COUNSELING TREATMENT

The clients in this study received group counseling. This statement is as about as accurate as can be made, according to the report. We do not know who did the counseling (the author, classroom teachers, or who). We do not know anything about their education, counseling training, years experience, counseling orientation and strategies, or more importantly, their personal expectations from the study. When we look at the treatment variables, we simply do not know what happened in these groups. Was the 13-week counseling really similar to the two-day "accelerated interaction" counseling? Does a "traditional" format imply that those groups met once a week? For how long—20 minutes or sixty? Did the no treatment-control group really not receive anything? We might speculate that the control groups were with a very warm and facilitative teacher during the time the experimental groups were receiving group counseling. In short, it would be impossible to replicate this study.

6. MEASUREMENT

As noted in the section on Criteria, the phenomena which the researcher attempted to measure is not presented in as clear and specific language as would be desirable. Hence, it was necessary to make an awkward leap from the stated goals to the measuring instruments. For example, gains in cognitive knowledge is a worthwhile goal, but many would agree that the GPA alone is not sensitive enough to tap it. Citizenship and effort, grades, and attendance patterns are certainly indices of positive behavioral changes, but they are also limited. There might have been significant gains in conative knowledge and in socialization, but perhaps the IAV is not comprehensive or sensitive enough to capture these gains.

One final comment regarding measurement is the time dimension. The traditional group had much more time (i.e., 15 weeks) to show changes, whereas the accelerated interaction group only had 3 weeks to show change. Although adolescents probably change faster than older age groups, expecting very much change on these dimensions in a period of three weeks is probably not realistic. Finally, there is some limited research which indicates that counseling and therapy sets into motion many potential changes, and that these changes surface only after a period of time (incubation effect). It would have been quite interesting to have a follow-up report of this study. One could speculate that the gains showed by the traditional group might not have endured, or that the accelerated interaction groups might have later showed equally significant gains on the measures.

7. ETHICAL, PROFESSIONAL, AND LEGAL CONSIDERATIONS

The only comment to be made here concerns the ethical practice of providing counseling services to some clientele and not to others. It cannot be discerned whether or not the subjects in this study did or did not volunteer for the study. In either event, the control subjects should have been provided the group counseling or some professional help, on a volunteer basis, at a later time.

While not so much a question of ethics, the wide scope of this research in terms of examining the role of "guidance in education" must be seriously questioned. This is especially true when this expression was not defined. Some conceptual justification for using the dependent variables as measures of "guidance in education" would have been welcomed.

In the reporting process, this research suffers, although the study itself has weaknesses. As a professional accounting of research efforts, however, several questions must be raised. It appears that perhaps the study is over titled, i.e., it does not produce the evidence the title would indicate. In the discussion of the outcomes some inferences were drawn which seemed to go a bit beyond the data. This is particularly true in the material about "conative knowledge" and "vocational exploration." One senses here a tendency to introject editorial comments not always directly inferred from the findings.

8. RESULTS

Because of the limitations above, it cannot be determined from this study alone whether or not group counseling does indeed belong in the public schools. Perhaps, this question should not even have been asked here. Yet, the author is complemented for tackling a very serious and contemporary concern; namely, the use of group counseling in the high schools.

EFFECTS OF VICARIOUS THERAPY PRETRAINING AND ALTERNATE SESSIONS ON OUTCOME IN GROUP PSYCHOTHERAPY WITH OUTPATIENTS[1,2]

Charles B. Truax[3]
University of Florida
and
Donald G. Wargo
Arkansas Rehabilitation Research and Training Center, University of Arkansas

(*Received* August 5, 1968)

The present study investigated the effects of therapist-absent alternate sessions and a vicarious therapy pretraining experience on group psychotherapy outcome with outpatients. It also related patient self-exploration to outcome. The alternate sessions regimen and high levels of self-exploration both led to slightly better outcome. Vicarious therapy pretraining was found to be highly facilitative, having its greatest effect on neurotic symptomatology.

The use of alternate sessions in group psychotherapy has led to some controversy regarding its efficacy. By alternate sessions is meant the use of group therapy sessions in which the therapist is absent, alternating with sessions in which both patients and therapist are present. Their use has been recommended by Wolf (1961), Wolf and Schwartz (1962), and Truax (1962a, 1962b). On the other hand, Slavson (1963) and Ginott[4]

[1]Truax, Charles B. and Wargo, Donald G. Effects of vicarious therapy pretraining and alternate sessions on outcome in group psychotherapy with outpatients. *Journal of Consulting and Clinical Psychology*, 1969, **33**, (4), 440–447. Copyright 1969, by the American Psychological Association, and reproduced by permission.

[2]This research was supported by Rehabilitation Services Administration Grant RD-906 and Social and Rehabilitation Services Grant RT-13.

[3]Requests for reprints should be sent to Charles B. Truax, College of Education, University of Florida, Gainesville, Florida 32601.

[4]H. G. Ginott, personal communication, March, 1964.

have raised objections to the use of alternate sessions. It is quite apparent that, if helpful, alternate sessions would constitute an economically desirable regimen. Previous research by Truax and Carkhuff (1965) on a sample of hospitalized patients indicated that the use of alternate sessions was not only nonbeneficial, but led to significantly poorer outcome than regular group psychotherapy, supporting the position taken by Slavson and Ginott. However, since outpatients as a group are in closer contact with reality and more adequate in interpersonal relating, it seems plausible that alternate sessions might prove beneficial with neurotic outpatients even though they might be harmful with hospitalized patients.

Vicarious therapy pretraining (VTP) has been proposed by Truax (1962a, 1962b) to provide standard cognitive and experiential structuring of "how to be a good patient" as a means of quickly engaging the patient in the process of group therapy. VTP simply involves presenting to prospective patients a 30-minute tape recording of excerpts of "good" patient in-therapy behavior. It provides a vicarious experience of how clients often explore their problems and feelings, and how they prove helpful to one another prior to their introduction to group therapy. One study (Truax & Carkhuff, 1965) has indicated modest therapeutic benefit of VTP.

Prior research in individual and group psychotherapy has also suggested that successful patients engage in a greater degree of self-exploration than less successful patients in a wide variety of patient populations (Blau, 1953; Braaten, 1958; Peres, 1947; Seeman, 1949; Tomlinson & Hart, 1962; Truax, 1961, 1962a, 1962b; Truax & Carkhuff, 1963; Wagstaff, Rice, & Butler, 1960). The present study attempted, also, to study the relationship between patient in-therapy self-exploration as it is related to outcome.

The present study, involving a heterogeneous sample of both therapists and patients, was aimed at evaluating the following hypotheses: (a) patients receiving alternate sessions in addition to their regular sessions will show greater evidence of constructive personality change than patients receiving regular sessions only, (b) patients receiving VTP prior to group therapy will show greater evidence of constructive personality change than patients not receiving VTP, and (c) patients in groups that engage in relatively high levels of self-exploration will show greater evidence of constructive personality change than patients in groups that engage in relatively low levels of self-exploration.

METHOD

A total of eight psychotherapy groups, with an initial 10 patients in each group ($N = 80$), were seen by eight different therapists[5] for time-limited group psychotherapy consisting of 24 sessions on a twice weekly basis over a time span of approximately 3 months. The 80 outpatients were assigned to groups from the available populations of the following cooperating institutions: Department of Psychiatry, University of Wisconsin; Counseling Center, University of Massachusetts; Veterans Administration Clinic, Covington, Kentucky; and University of Kentucky.

All group therapy sessions were completely tape recorded to allow for analysis of levels of patient self-exploration occurring in each group. Patients were given a battery of psychological tests pretherapy and posttherapy which served as the basic measures of outcome.

The eight groups formed a 2 × 2 factorial design, with half of the groups receiving VTP and the other half non-VTP, and half of the groups receiving alternate sessions in addition to regular sessions with the other half holding regular sessions only. For those patients receiving VTP, the 30-minute VTP tape recording was presented to the group prior to the first session. The alternate sessions for those groups holding alternate sessions began after the eighth, ninth, or tenth sessions, and continued alternating with the regular sessions until the 24 regular sessions were completed.

Patient Population

The patient population as a whole was a mildly disturbed, neurotic outpatient group. The patients ranged from 18 to 58, with a distribution skewed to the right. Six patients, based on their pretesting, might be labeled schizophrenics.

Therapists

The therapists were assigned to the eight groups within the samples from the participating institutions. In general, they were highly experienced in individual and group psychotherapy. They were quite heterogeneous in orientation, including two therapists who could be described as client-centered, four therapists who could be described as psychoanalytically oriented, and two who would describe themselves as eclectic in

[5]Several groups involved co-therapists in addition to the therapists responsible for the group.

orientation.[6] Of the therapists and co-therapists, four were psychiatrists and seven were psychologists.

The therapists were, in general, positively disposed toward the study. They were optimistic about the usefulness of VTP, and they were interested in the effects of alternate sessions. The latter constituted a minor administrative annoyance, but there was no evidence that therapists felt threatened by their groups' meeting without them.

Measurement of Patient Self-Exploration

The Depth of Intrapersonal (Self) Exploration Scale (Truax, 1962c) was used as the basic measure of patient self-exploration. From the set of tape recordings of regular sessions of the eight groups, one 3-minute sample was selected from the middle third of every other recorded therapy session (89 samples). These samples were obtained by running the tape recorder at rewind to the middle section of the tape and stopping. The 3-minute samples were then taken beginning with the first new utterance by a patient or therapist and continuing for 3 minutes, or until the conclusion of a statement to preserve intelligibility. These samples were rerecorded individually onto small single spools which were then randomly assigned code numbers and presented to the raters in boxes of 12 samples.

Four undergraduate college students who were naïve with respect to psychotherapy theory and practice were trained in the use of the rating scale. A criterion of a correlation of 0.50 for interjudge and rate-rerate reliability on training samples was used to screen the raters. The raters rated the coded samples in different orders of blocks of 12 samples. The mean ratings from the four judges per sample were used in the analyses.

Measurement of Patient Personality Change

Although 80 patients were given pretesting, a number of patients dropped out of group therapy before the tenth session, some refused to participate in testing posttherapy, and for a few the test administrations were judged invalid and discarded without examination of the results because of patient misunderstanding or inability to perform on the measure. Thus,

[6]The present research would not have been possible without the dedicated contribution of the therapists who gave so freely of their time, energy, and talent. Appreciation is very gratefully extended to the following therapists and co-therapists: Arnold Marx, L. Stein, Donald Kiesler, Donald Price, Robert R. Carkhuff, Jerome Sczymanski, Walter A. Dickenson, Joseph Willet, Dean Allen, and Joe Havens.

62 patients were available for data analysis on some measures, while as few as 51 patients were available for analysis on the measures of *Q* sorts for self-concepts.

The test battery in the present study administered pretherapy and posttherapy included the MMPI, with the 10 clinical scales, the Sum of Clinical scales, the Barron Ego Strength scale, the Truax Constructive Personality Change Index, the Welsh Internalization of Anxiety Ratio, Edwards Social Desirability, Sum of Validity Deviations, Welsh's Anxiety Index; the *Q* sort for self- and ideal concept (Butler & Haigh, 1954) with the five specific measures of self- and ideal concepts; and the Finney Palo Alto Group Therapy scale (Finney, 1954).

The 80-item *Q*-sort deck was used for only two sorts (self and ideal) both pretherapy and posttherapy. The five measures obtained were (a) change in the correlation between self and expert *Q* sorts from pretherapy to posttherapy, (b) change in the correlation between self and ideal *Q* sort, (c) change in the correlation between ideal and expert *Q* sort, (d) change in the self *Q* sort adjustment scores, and (e) change in ideal adjustment scores. The "expert" *Q* sort is a *Q* sort representing ideal adjustment made by a panel of 14 experts (Lewis, 1959). The "adjustment" *Q* sorts, both self and ideal, refer to a method of scoring the *Q* sorts on the basis of an imposed true-false type of dichotomy.

The Palo Alto Group Therapy scale consists of a number of true-false items referring to social interaction behavior engaged in by the patient during group psychotherapy itself. It is filled out by the therapist. In the Forsythe and Fairweather (1961) study it was the only measure in a large battery that was predictive of follow-up adjustment posttherapy.

For the most part the outcome battery consisted of self-report measures, however. Ideally, behavioral indexes of change might have been included, such as ratings by *O*s, changes in earnings, grades, etc.; but the heterogeneity of the patient population and geographic dispersion of the groups made this infeasible.

RESULTS

Change scores for each patient on each of the 23 measures of outcome were obtained by subtracting the score earned pretherapy from the score posttherapy. To guard against possible differences between groups in initial status, analysis of covariance was used to partial out the pretherapy level in its effect on measured change.

The basic design of the present study might be described as a 2×2

factorial design with the additional factor of high versus low self-exploration within each cell. Perfect design balance was disturbed, however, by missing data due to invalid testing, refusal to take tests, and premature terminations. As such, cell frequencies were unequal requiring that the unweighted means method for computing the analyses of covariance be used. In addition, since cell frequencies become more disproportionate with finer subdivisions, and since presumably the greater the disproportionality the more questionable the validity of the analysis, the major variables were analyzed separately by one-way analyses of covariance. None of the hypotheses in the study are concerned with interactions of the variables, thus lack of information regarding these is not a great loss.

Table 1 Mean Values and Analysis of Covariance F Ratios: Effects of Vicarious Therapy Pretraining on Outcome.

Measures of outcome	Mean values		Analysis of covariance F ratios	
	VTP	NVTP	VTP-NVTP	Therapists/Cells
Q sort				
Self, adjustment	9.950	4.065		32.745***
Self-expert *r*	0.335	0.138	1.187	34.256***
Ideal, adjustment	0.952	−0.871		53.533***
Self-ideal *r*	0.354	0.177		27.884***
Ideal-expert *r*	0.001	0.003		45.896***
Palo Alto Group Therapy scale	0.490	0.179	4.019	1.475
MMPI				
Sum of Clinical Deviations	23.792	−0.750	8.034*	
Constructive Personality Change Index	14.917	4.125		
Hs	1.125	−1.188	2.033	
D	4.000	−0.125	5.758*	
Hy	3.375	−1.188	19.631**	
Pd	2.042	−0.906	2.958	
Mf	0.792	1.406		1.227
Pa	2.792	0.469		
Pt	4.875	0.313	5.554*	
Sc	6.083	1.250	1.779	
Ma	1.583	0.781		4.191***
Si	5.500	2.531		
Barron's Ego Strength	3.667	1.500		
Edwards' Social Desirability	3.750	2.500		1.124
Sum of Validity Scales' Deviations	3.875	−0.938	2.010	1.072
Welsh's Anxiety Index	7.125	1.906	2.944	
Welsh's Internalization Ratio	0.025	0.016		1.394

*$p < 0.05$, one-tailed test, **$p < 0.05$, two-tailed test, ***$p < 0.01$, two-tailed test.

To test the main effects in each analysis, group or therapist variability within cells was used as the estimate of error. This constitutes a relatively conservative error estimate. Differences in outcome associated with different therapists and therapy groups are assessed by testing between group variability against *S* variability.

Effects of Vicarious Therapy Pretraining

The mean values of outcome measures for patients receiving VTP versus those not receiving VTP (NVTP) is shown in Table 1. There is a striking tendency for VTP to show therapeutic advantage over NVTP. On the 23 measures of outcome, patients receiving VTP showed greater improvement on 21 and less improvement on only two ($\chi^2 = 15.696$, $p < 0.001$). Also presented in Table 1 are the results of the analyses of covariance for the effects of VTP on patient outcome. Patients receiving VTP showed significantly greater improvement than patients not receiving VTP on the following MMPI Scales: *D*, *Hy*, *Pt* and the Sum of Clinical Deviations. Thus, the data tend to provide relatively strong support for the initial hypothesis. It appears that the greatest influence of VTP was on neurotic symptomatology.

Effects of Alternate Sessions

Table 2 presents the mean values on the 23 outcome measures for patients receiving alternate sessions in addition to regular sessions versus patients receiving only regular sessions. Patients receiving alternate sessions showed greater improvement on 17 measures and less improvement on six ($\chi^2 = 2.630$, *ns*); whereas, patients receiving only regular sessions showed greater improvement on only six measures and less improvement on 17.

The results of the analyses of covariance on the 23 measures also appear in Table 2. There it can be seen that the addition of alternate sessions to regular group therapy results in significantly greater outcome on the following MMPI measures: *Hs*, *Hy*, Sum of Clinical Deviations, and the Constructive Personality Change Index.

Thus, the data suggest moderately positive consequences by the addition of alternate sessions to regular outpatient group meetings.

Patient Degree of Self-Exploration

The level of self-exploration was calculated for each group, and then the groups were subdivided into those showing highest versus those showing

Table 2 Mean Values and Analysis of Covariance *F* Ratios: Effects of Alternate Sessions on Outcome.

Measures of outcome	Mean values: Alternate	Mean values: Regular	Analysis of covariance *F* ratios: Alternate regular	Analysis of covariance *F* ratios: Therapists/ Cells
Q sort				
Self, adjustment	8.000	4.048		32.745***
Self-expert *r*	0.260	0.151		34.256***
Ideal, adjustment	−0.226	0.000		37.848***
Self-ideal *r*	0.324	0.125		27.884***
Ideal-expert *r*	0.025	−0.032		40.671***
Palo Alto Group Therapy Scale	0.254	0.421		1.475
MMPI				
Sum of Clinical Deviations	15.290	2.920	11.517**	
Constructive Personality Change Index	12.419	4.200	21.304**	
Hs	1.032	−1.720	7.049*	
D	1.903	1.320		
Hy	2.194	−1.000	23.572**	
Pd	0.387	0.320		
Mf	0.452	2.000		1.227
Pa	1.645	1.240	1.244	
Pt	3.290	1.000	2.923	
Sc	4.290	2.120	2.994	
Ma	0.323	2.120		4.191***
Si	4.484	2.960		
Barron's Ego Strength	3.323	1.320	4.210	
Edwards' Social Desirability	2.903	3.200		1.124
Sum of Validity Scales' Deviations	−0.161	2.720	1.712	
Welsh's Anxiety Index	3.677	4.720		
Welsh's Internalization Ratio	0.043	−0.008		1.394

*$p < 0.05$, one-tailed test, **$p < 0.05$, two-tailed test, ***$p < 0.01$, two-tailed test.

lowest levels of self-exploration. Ratings were made with raters using the Scale of Depth of Self-Exploration (Truax, 1962c).

The mean outcome scores on the 23 measures for patients in groups that engaged in high levels of self-exploration and patients in groups engaging in low levels of self-exploration are presented in Table 3. There it can be seen that patients in groups engaging in high levels of self-exploration showed greater improvement on 15 measures and less improvement on eight ($\chi^2 = 2.130$, *ns*); whereas, for patients in groups engaging in low

Table 3 Mean Values and Analysis of Covariance *F* Ratios: Effects of Depth of Intrapersonal Exploration on Outcome.

	Mean values		Analysis of covariance *F* ratios	
Measures of outcome	High DX	Low DX	High–Low DX	Therapists/ Cells
Q sort				
Self, adjustment	9.233	2.286	4.553*	19.506***
Self-expert *r*	0.293	0.104	3.510	21.961***
Ideal, adjustment	−0.290	0.095		38.288***
Self-ideal *r*	0.330	0.116	6.336*	16.556***
Ideal-expert *r*	−0.024	0.041	2.255	30.675***
Palo Alto Group Therapy Scale	0.283	0.386	1.485	3.233***
MMPI				
Sum of Clinical Deviations	12.533	6.577		1.207
Constructive Personality Change Index	15.833	0.577	4.950*	
Hs	−0.267	−0.115		1.188
D	1.967	1.269		
Hy	1.133	0.346		1.432
Pd	0.233	0.500		
Mf	0.633	1.731	3.377	
Pa	2.067	0.769		
Pt	3.333	1.038		1.017
Sc	4.367	2.115		1.049
Ma	0.167	2.231	1.677	2.577**
Si	5.833	1.462	3.570	
Barron's Ego Strength	3.600	1.077	3.113	
Edwards' Social Desirability	4.533	1.308	2.729	
Sum of Validity Scales' Deviations	0.833	1.462		1.321
Welsh's Anxiety Index	5.500	2.577		
Welsh's Internalization Ratio	0.050	−0.015	2.451	

Note: DX = depth of intrapersonal exploration.
$^{*}p < 0.05$, one-tailed test, $^{**}p < 0.05$, two-tailed test, $^{***}p < 0.01$, two-tailed test.

levels of self-exploration, greater improvement occurred on only eight measures and less improvement on 15.

The results of the analyses of covariance for high and low levels of self-exploration are also presented in Table 3. Differences favoring better outcome with high rather than low levels of self-exploration occurred on the following measures: *Q* sort for self-adjustment, *Q* sort congruence between self- and ideal concepts, and the Constructive Personality Change

Index from the MMPI. These findings give modest support to the hypothesis suggesting greater improvement for high self-exploration groups.

DISCUSSION

In general, the results of the present study lend support to the hypotheses stated at the outset. As such, the study was successful in serving to establish the effectiveness of the variables investigated in producing constructive personality and behavioral change through the treatment known as group psychotherapy.

The effect of inserting alternate sessions with the therapist absent between regular group therapy sessions with the therapist present would appear to be slightly facilitative from the present results. They generally support the recommendations of Wolf (1961) and Wolf and Schwartz (1962), and refute the suggestions of Slavson (1963) and Ginott (see Footnote 3) who have objected to the use of alternate sessions. This finding is of particular importance as the shortage of trained therapists increases. It is an economical procedure since it extends the effectiveness of scarce therapists. It should be cautioned, however, that alternate sessions may not be effective with other types of patient populations. Indeed, it has been found by the authors (Truax & Wargo, 1968a, 1968b) that the use of alternate sessions with hospitalized mental patient groups and with juvenile delinquent groups led to considerably less improvement than did the use of regular sessions only. It may be that patients must be more socially responsible in order to benefit from alternate sessions; indeed, in order to be not harmed or retarded by alternate sessions.

The effects of vicarious therapy pretraining were quite positive. This supports the hypothesis based on earlier suggestions by Truax (1962a, 1962b) that this form of systematic preparation for psychotherapy might well be beneficial to outcome. Again, however, this finding should not be generalized to other patient populations since this same hypothesis is clearly not supported by the findings in the previously mentioned study of institutionalized juvenile delinquents. It does appear, however, that the structuring of patient roles through the use of tape-recorded modeling is facilitative with psychoneurotic outpatients. This procedure is of therapeutic value when incorporated into the treatment of neurotic outpatient groups.

As for the relationship between level of self-exploration and psychotherapeutic outcome, the results of the present study provide modest support for the hypothesis that high levels of self-exploration will be related to high degrees of outcome. It is of particular interest to find that it holds for group therapy, since level of self-exploration in group therapy is determined by the overall level of the group rather than by the levels of self-exploration demonstrated by individual members of the group. It is most likely that there is considerable within-group heterogeneity of self-exploration in most groups. As such, measurement of the variable is gross. At the same time, it is likely that some benefit accrues to the patient who sits quietly but is able to vicariously benefit from the explorations of fellow patients within the group. In this sense, then, the level of exploration manifested by the group as a whole may somewhat accurately reflect the benefit gained by each member individually. It may be that levels of overt exploration on the part of one person leads to greater exploration on the part of the second, even though the second never voices his explorations publicly. Self-exploration, as the name suggests, may be a kind of working through of one's problems and it is in this manner that it may lead to constructive personality change.

A very interesting, but unpredicted finding has to do with the self-concept measures. Tables 1, 2, and 3 show that the therapists-within-cells terms are significant for all five *Q*-sorts measures. (Actually, this term might better be called "therapy-groups-within-cells" for purposes of interpretation, rather than "therapists-within-cells," which is a handier designation.) It appears that there were differences from group to group with regard to the amount of improvement made in self-concept which is not attributable to the variables included in the study. This very specific effect, apparently independent of other personality and behavioral changes, obviously resulted from something occurring in the group process. What this might be is not clear. One might suggest any number of hypotheses, however. A likely explanation has to do with differences between therapists in their reinforcement of self-references. That is, therapists could conceivably condition positive changes in self-concepts through differential reinforcement of self-reference statements. This is likely, since self-reference statements are one indication of degree of self-exploration. This explanation receives some support from the results, presented in Table 3, which show that of the five *Q*-sort measures used, the three which are measures of self-concept against a standard all changed more in high-exploration groups, and two of these were significant. Thus, it would appear that change in self-concept is at least partially related to level of self-exploration in the therapy group.

The present study provides moderate support for the use of two procedures which differ from standard group therapy practice. Further, it suggests some relationship between self-exploration and outcome in group psychotherapy.

REFERENCES

Blau, B. A. A comparison of more improved with less improved clients treated by client-centered methods. In W. U. Snyder (Ed.), *Group report of a program of research in psychotherapy*. State College: Pennsylvania State College, Psychotherapy Research Group, 1953.

Braaten, L. J. The movement from non-self to self in client-centered psychotherapy. Unpublished doctoral dissertation, University of Chicago, 1958.

Butler, J. M., & Haigh, G. V. Changes in the relation between self-concepts and ideal-concepts consequent upon client-centered counseling. In C. R. Rogers & R. F. Dymond (Eds.), *Psychotherapy and personality change*. Chicago: University of Chicago Press, 1954.

Finney, B. C. A scale to measure interpersonal relationships in group psychotherapy. *Group Psychotherapy*, 1954, **7**, 52–66.

Forsythe, R. P., & Fairweather, G. W. Psychotherapeutic and other hospital treatment criteria: The dilemma. *Journal of Abnormal and Social Psychology*, 1961, **62**, 598–605.

Lewis, M. K. Counselor prediction and projection in client-centered psychotherapy. Unpublished doctoral dissertation, University of Chicago, 1959.

Peres, H. An investigation of non-directive group therapy. *Journal of Consulting Psychology*. 1947, **11**, 159–172.

Seeman, J. A study of the process of non-directive therapy. *Journal of Consulting Psychology*, 1949, **13**, 157–168.

Slavson, S. R. *Textbook in analytic group psychotherapy*. New York: International Universities Press, 1963.

Tomlinson, T. M., & Hart, J. T. A validation study of the process scale. *Journal of Consulting Psychology*, 1962, **26**, 74–78.

Truax, C. B. The process of group psychotherapy: Relationships between hypothesized therapeutic conditions and intrapersonal exploration. *Psychological Monographs*, 1961, **75** (7, Whole No. 511).

Truax, C. B. Client-centered group psychotherapy. Workshop at American Group Psychotherapy Association, New York, January 1962. a

Truax, C. B. The therapeutic process in group psychotherapy: A research investigation. Wisconsin Psychiatric Institute, University of Wisconsin, January 1962. (Mimeo) b

Truax, C. B. A tentative scale for the measurement of depth of intrapersonal exploration (DX). In, *Discussion papers*. Wisconsin Psychiatric Institute, Madison: University of Wisconsin Press, 1962. c

Truax, C. B., & Carkhuff, R. R. For better or for worse: The process of psychotherapeutic personality change. In, *Recent advances in the study of behavior change*. Montreal, Canada: McGill University Press, 1963.

Truax, C. B., & Carkhuff, R. R. Personality change in hospitalized mental patients during group psychotherapy as a function of alternate sessions and vicarious therapy pre-training. *Journal of Clinical Psychology*, 1965, **21**, 225–228.

Truax, C. B., & Wargo, D. G. Antecedents to outcome in group counseling with institutionalized juvenile delinquents: Effects of therapeutic conditions, patient self-exploration, alternate sessions and vicarious therapy pretraining. Unpublished manuscript, Arkansas Rehabilitation Research and Training Center, 1968. a

Truax, C. B., & Wargo, D. G. Effects of therapeutic conditions, alternate sessions, vicarious therapy pretraining, and patient self-exploration on hospitalized mental patients during group therapy. Unpublished manuscript, Arkansas Rehabilitation Research and Training Center, 1968. b

Wagstaff, A. K., Rice, L. N., & Butler, J. M. Factors of client verbal participation in therapy. In, *Counseling center discussion papers*. Chicago: University of Chicago Press, 1960.

Wolf, A. Group psychotherapy with adults: The alternate meeting. Paper presented at the meeting of the American Personnel and Guidance Association, New York, January 1961.

Wolf, A., & Schwartz, E. K. *Psychoanalysis in groups*. New York: Grune & Stratton, 1962.

CRITIQUE

1. PHILOSOPHICAL AND THEORETICAL CONSIDERATIONS

One counseling theory from which the authors of this study have drawn most heavily is client-centered therapy. They also appear to have used assumptions generated by their past research.

It should be pointed out, however, that the authors reveal no clearly stated overall paradigm or theoretical structure of the helping process within which their particular study is undertaken. It is difficult to determine the theoretical elements related to clients, the counseling process and counseling outcomes, respectively. It would have been helpful to have had a stronger theoretical basis for VTP and alternate sessions.

2. CRITERIA

Two criteria, self-exploration and constructive personality change, were used. Such self-report types of measures do not include objective behavioral referrents, and the authors acknowledge this problem by stating that the weakness stems from administrative problems in collecting this kind of data. It appears that the criteria follow clearly from the goals.

Constructive Personality Change is defined by the measurements used. Also, the Scale of Self-exploration is the authors' operational definition of the construct (self-exploration), and it is a scale with a good bit of construct validity.

3. RESEARCH DESIGN

The author refers to a 2×2 factorial design, but it is more accurately a $2 \times 2 \times 2$ multiple treatment design. It is difficult to understand the use of this factorial design because interactions, the real strength of such designs, were of no interest in the study. In reality, this design simply involves grouping data in three ways: alternate vs. regular sessions, VTP vs. non-VTP, and high self-exploration vs. low self-exploration. Two additional points may be noted. First, the lack of a control group always raises the question of spontaneous remission. Second, randomization procedures are never referred to in either the design or sampling. Thus, there are important questions about control and internal validity which must be raised. There is also the question of whether or not clients/therapists were assigned randomly to treatment conditions.

On the positive side, there are many advantages to the use of factorial designs in comparing several independent variables, especially in examining important interactions; scheduling time-limited sessions meant that all patients received the same amount of treatment; alternate sessions were equal for the groups scheduled; and there were identical measurement times (pre and post).

4. SELECTION AND SAMPLING PROCEDURES

Sampling procedures of clients or counselors, and assignment of clients/counselors to various treatment conditions is impossible to evaluate because it did not occur. The sampling procedure employed is at best incidental (Chapter 5). There is evidence of the patient uniformity assumption, although the authors do make a point to distinguish between in- and outpatients. We know very little about the subjects in this study. To say that they were mildly disturbed, neurotic outpatient groups, ranging in age from 18 to 58, really tells little. Would not different groups be found at a university counseling center, a V.A. outpatient clinic, and a Department of Psychiatry? Who were the clients at the University of Kentucky? How many were male and female? To assume that all clients needed group therapy, self-exploration and personality change is unwarranted. For example, the college students may have been in more situational circumstances with transitory neurotic concerns; the veterans problems may have been chronic; and the University of Wisconsin group may have been acute and more serious. Describing a group of clients as heterogeneous does not really describe them at all.

The *N* in this research initially included 80 patients, but data from only 51 to 62 were available for analysis. It is obvious that with more subjects, all the "cells" in the design might have been filled and interactions could have been tested.

The selection of the therapists was also part of the incidental sampling procedure. Therapists in the study did not comprise a heterogeneous sample in the literal sense; they were simply available and interested. A heterogeneous sample would have included theoretical orientations representative of more than three self-acclaimed therapeutic approaches and would have been drawn according to some predetermined sampling plan. Moreover, there is no evidence that the researchers attempted a *post facto* examination of the nature of this "sample" and generalization to other therapists or clients is unwarranted.

5. COUNSELING AND THERAPY TREATMENT

Although tapes were made of every session, it is impossible for the reader (or researcher who would want to replicate) to really know what indeed happened in the therapy group sessions. For example, how do client-centered and eclectic therapists differ from one another? How do they go about their work in different ways? And, would not one expect a client-centered therapist to differ his approach with a group of psychiatric outpatients and a group of college students? Not only is the matter of explicating the treatment method the crucial methodological problem in all other counseling research, it is the main problem here. To clarify the point: If one wanted to replicate this study, would it be appropriate to just pick eight therapists who could be described as "two client-centered, four psychoanalytically oriented and two eclectic" in orientation? The obvious answer should be no.

In addition, it might be pointed out that some groups had co-therapists. Were both therapists in each setting of the same theoretical bent? In reality, the co-therapist effect becomes another independent variable in the study.

6. MEASUREMENT

The criterion of Constructive Personality Change was measured by the eight different psychological tests and inventories (MMPI, Barron Ego Strength Scale, etc.). In essence, the authors have defined this criterion by the tests they used. It appears, that the tests defined the criteria rather than vice versa.

The criterion of self-exploration was measured by a rating scale which has been developed and used by the first author in many research projects. Yet, we seriously question the rejection of raters who simply do not seem to agree (at a significant level) with the other raters. Were the ratings done independently? What was the interjudge reliability of the four raters used in this study?

We agree with the authors that it would have strengthened the study to have had some objective, external measure to help establish the criteria of constructive personality change and self-exploration.

Finally, the complete lack of randomization, of course, raises serious questions about the use of statistical procedures where randomization is an important statistical assumption.

7. ETHICAL, PROFESSIONAL, AND LEGAL CONSIDERATIONS

There appear to be no shortcomings in this area. It is assumed that each client had a choice about the tapings and that clear prescriptions were described for the research use of the tapes. The published report does not mention any client names.

On the other hand, since the authors fail to describe in detail their client/counselor communications in subject selection one cannot tell if any ethical factors were questionable. For example, was any pressure used in obtaining *S*'s, particularly in some of these settings?

In viewing the research as a totality, one gets the feeling that the researchers may have attempted to do too much, without conditions or personnel to complete each aspect of the investigation thoroughly. Some details are covered rather lightly, for replication.

8. RESULTS

Although the results are presented clearly, several comments should be made. There was a high attrition rate of dropouts. Almost 23 percent were not available for "some measures," and as high as 36 percent were not available for the self-concept *Q* scores. Which clients did not complete the post-test? Was there some kind of systematic self-selection taking place here? Were there more from one participating institution than another?

A COMPARISON OF THE EFFECTIVENESS OF BEHAVIORAL AND CLIENT-CENTERED APPROACHES FOR THE BEHAVIOR PROBLEMS OF ELEMENTARY SCHOOL CHILDREN[1]

Theodore G. Alper
Stanford Institute for Behavior Counseling at Stanford University
and
Gerald D. Kranzler
Counselor Educator in Eugene, Oregon

This study compares the relative efficacy of client-centered versus behavioral approaches in dealing with the behavior problems of elementary school children. The subjects were 36 children randomly selected from a total population of students referred by their teachers for high-rate "out-of-seat" behaviors. They were then randomly assigned to one of four treatment conditions: (a) client-centered counseling, (b) precision teaching (a behavioral approach), (c) attention placebo, and (d) no-treatment control. The treatment period lasted for four weeks; post-treatment assessments were made directly after the period. Four outcome criteria were used: out-of-seat rate, sociometric choices, Self Social Symbols Task (SSST) scores, and arithmetic computation rates. No significant differences between treatment groups were found. A discussion of the implication of these findings was made in terms of counselor's treating problems outside the classroom environment.

Both in their training and on the job, school counselors utilize a variety of approaches in dealing with problems of children. In order to determine which of these approaches is most effective in helping children, experimental comparisons must be made.

PREVIOUS STUDIES

Much counselor training focuses on "insight"-oriented approaches to counseling (London, 1946, p. 57). Rogerian, client-centered methods of counseling are insight-oriented approaches that have been adopted by many school counselors. Integral to the Rogerian approach is the development of a good relationship between the counselor and client. Since the

[1]Alper, Theodore G. and Kranzler, Gerald. A comparison of the effectiveness of behavioral and client-centered approaches for the behavior problems of elementary school children. *Elementary School Guidance and Counseling*, 1970, **5**, 35–43. Copyright 1970, by the American Personnel and Guidance Association, and reproduced by permission.

inception of client-centered therapy, many studies have been completed that have tried to assess the effectiveness of this approach in helping children. Most of the early research (e.g., Axline, 1947; Bills, 1950; and Cox, 1953) was marked by major faults in design and analysis. Recent studies, even though more scientifically sound, have resulted in contradictory conclusions. Even when the studies have dealt with similar problem populations, results have differed (e.g., Biasco, 1956; Kranzler, Mayer, Myer, & Munger, 1966; Oldridge, 1964). Thus, despite the widespread use of client-centered therapy in training and treatment, evidence concerning the efficacy of this approach is lacking.

In recent years the more "action"-oriented approaches to dealing with behavior and emotional problems of children have become popular (London, 1946, p. 74). Most practitioners of action-oriented approaches describe themselves as behavior modifiers and claim to derive their treatment from modern learning theory. Most of these treatment programs have been derived from operant conditioning paradigms and focus on relatively discrete behavioral acts. Proponents of this system tend to deny the necessity of working with underlying causes or problems and believe that a change in overt behavior is a sufficient indication that their approach has been successful.

A number of studies have been published that support the thinking of the behavior modifiers (Dickinson, 1968; Morice, 1968; Patterson & Ebner, 1966). Published results have been impressive and have indicated a promising future for the system. The vast majority of these studies, however, have been of the single-case-study type. In the absence of a large number of studies with adequate controls, it is impossible to come to any firm conclusions regarding the efficacy of behavioral approaches in dealing with the problems of young children.

The inconsistencies in results of studies evaluating client-centered counseling and the inadequacy of the single-organism designs ordinarily used to assess the behavioral approaches led the authors to conduct the present study. The primary objective was to answer one basic question: Are there differences in effectiveness between client-centered and behavioral approaches in dealing with behavior problems of children? Related to this question was an even more crucial one: Is either of these two approaches more effective than merely paying special attention to children or leaving them alone in a no-treatment control group?

METHOD

Subjects

All subjects were drawn from regular elementary school classrooms, grades one through six. Teachers had indicated on a referral form those children with high-rate out-of-seat behavior problems. From the total population of referrals (N = 42), 36 subjects were randomly chosen.

"Out-of-seat without permission" was chosen as the selective criterion because a great many students referred to counseling evince relatively simple classes of problem behaviors like this. "Out-of-seat without permission" and "talking out inappropriately" are the two most common complaints teachers make about children in their classroom (Lindsley, 1968). The elementary school counselor must be able to deal with problems such as these, in addition to his many other functions, to help the teacher establish adequate learning environments.

Treatments

Three counselors who were enrolled in a Master's program in counseling administered all treatments in this study. Prior to their participation in the study, they were trained to use both client-centered and behavioral counseling techniques. At the time of the study, they were near the end of their Master's program.

Of the 36 subjects, 9 were assigned at random to each of four treatment conditions: (a) client-centered counseling, (b) precision teaching, a behavioral approach developed by Ogden Lindsley (1964), (c) attention placebo and (d) control. Three of the nine subjects assigned to each treatment conditions were assigned at random to each counselor.

Subjects assigned to client-centered and precision-teaching conditions were seen individually, twice weekly, over a period of five weeks. Subjects assigned to the attention-placebo condition were seen in groups of three for equivalent time periods.

In the client-centered condition, the counselors focused on developing a relationship in which subject self-exploration would occur. Each counselor tried to be noncritical, warm, and accepting. The main techniques used were those of reflection, summarization, and clarification of the subjects' verbal statements. No attempt was made to deal specifically with the referral problem unless an individual subject introduced the topic and seemed to want to talk about it.

In the precision-teaching condition, counselors attempted to apply techniques originally developed by Ogden Lindsley (1964). They attempted to focus on the environmental determinants and contingencies of reinforcement controlling the out-of-seat behavior. During the initial session the counselor tried also to determine what types of preferred activities (free time or drawing time) or items (marbles, books, or a softball) each subject would like to learn. A contract was then made in which the subject would receive points towards his chosen activity or object for every day on which his rate of out-of-seat behavior decreased. Time during subsequent interview sessions was spent administering the program and presenting the preferred choices.

In the attention-placebo condition, the counselor read unfinished stories that served as stimuli to group discussions. The stories dealt with problems commonly experienced by children, such as making friends and difficulty with school work. Counselors were instructed not to bring up specific referral problems and to keep the discussion away from the subjects' personal problems. (Incidentally, the counselors reported that subjects in this treatment seemed to enjoy themselves more than did subjects in other conditions.)

The subjects assigned to the control condition were not seen by any of the counselors. Every effort was made to keep them unaware of their participation in the experiment.

Criteria and their measures Because selection of subjects was determined by their having been referred by their teachers for high-rate out-of-seat behaviors, out-of-seat rate was the criterion of most interest in this study. Their teachers observed subjects for 30-minute periods over 10 consecutive days in each of three phases: (a) before treatments began, (b) during treatments, and (c) after termination of treatments. Percentage of inter-observer agreement ranged from 0.81 to 1.00.

Attitude toward self and others was a second criterion. The measure employed was the SSST, a projective test developed by Ziller (1969). Included in the SSST are scales purporting to measure Self Esteem, Self Centrality, Social Interest, and Marginality. Ziller and his colleagues have conducted a number of studies that have demonstrated the reliability of these scales and suggested their viability as measures of personality in young children.

A third criterion was social acceptance and rejection as measured by a sociometric test. Three questions were asked dealing with seating preferences, work preferences, and play preferences. This criterion was administered in each of the subjects' classrooms in the 10 days following treatment.

The last criterion was school achievement, measured by a method that was natural to the setting and sensitive to any changes in achievement that might have occurred. Therefore, a standard academic task was presented to subjects in each of the three phases of the study. In grades one though three, subjects worked on addition fact sheets, and subjects in grades four through six worked on multiplication fact sheets. The daily rate and problems computed were used as the criterion measure.

RESULTS

Conclusions concerning post-treatment differences among means of treatment were analyzed statistically by a simple analysis of variance. All questions were tested in null hypothesis form and were rejected if the results were significant at the 0.05 level. A second analysis that excluded

Table 1 Means, Number of Subjects, Standard Deviations, and F-Ratios of Treatment Group—Post-Treatment Measures of Outcome Criteria.

		Treatment Groups (9 Subjects Each)				
Outcome Criteria	Measure	Client-centered	Precision Teaching	Attention Placebo	Control	F-Ratio
Out-of-seat	M	0.069	0.055	0.157	0.110	
rate	SD	0.059	0.036	0.104	0.123	1.6537
Positive						
sociometric	M	10.333	9.778	11.111	13.889	
choices	SD	8.231	6.610	7.688	8.259	0.5205
Negative						
sociometric	M	18.222	15.222	16.778	12.444	
choices	SD	7.710	6.741	11.649	4.693	0.8314
SSST						
Self-Esteem	M	14.778	13.444	15.667	17.000	
scores	SD	4.604	4.157	3.000	2.000	1.5420
SSST						
Social Interest	M	2.222	3.111	2.333	1.556	
scores	SD	2.539	2.205	2.291	1.810	0.6285
SSST						
Self-Centrality	M	2.111	2.667	2.333	1.444	
scores	SD	1.833	1.224	1.732	1.130	1.0050
SSST	M	1.778	1.889	1.778	3.222	
Marginality	SD	1.922	2.028	1.856	1.302	1.3860

Note: Value of F significant at 0.05 level with 3 and 31 df = 2.92.

control-group subjects was made to determine whether there were differences among counselors or interaction between counselors and treatment conditions. This analysis was made by means of a two-way analysis of variance. Computational formulas for all analyses used were those presented by Hayes (1963).

Table 1 presents the number of subjects, means, standard deviations, and F-ratios for all treatment groups on the outcome criteria. All data were derived from post-treatment measures of criteria.

The computed F-ratios in Table 1 were compared with tabled values of F for the appropriate degrees of freedom (df). None of the F-ratios reached the predetermined level of significance. Thus, it was concluded that the hypothesis regarding no differences among treatment groups would not be rejected.

The analyses of differences among counselors or interaction between counselors and treatment conditions revealed only one significant result. Scores on the Self Centrality Scale of the SSST were significantly different among counselors at the 0.05 level. This difference, the authors believe, is meaningless and should be discarded because it is only one significant difference among the large number of criteria tested; therefore, it was very likely a chance result.

DISCUSSION AND CONCLUSIONS

Failure to reject the null hypotheses of one's study is difficult to accept. It is even more difficult to interpret, however, because the nonsignificant results of an evaluation study such as this one are always open to three equally tangible explanations: (a) the treatments made no difference; (b) the treatments made a difference, but because of research design of measurement devices, the differences that did exist were not found; or (c) (a recently developed explanation) counseling treatments affected subjects for better or worse, resulting in variability within treatment groups but not in significant differences between treatment groups.

Because the results of the present study are so consistent with previous studies of elementary school counseling effectiveness (summarized by Kranzler, 1968, 1969), we have decided that the first conclusion – the conclusion that there was no difference in effectiveness among treatment conditions – is the most tenable.

One of the best known of the modern behavior modifiers, Gerald Patterson, has said that research on behavioral approaches is still at the "Whoopee! We did it again!" stage of development (personal communication). Most behavior modification "research" is really little more than case studies with numbers and graphs. We hope that the present study demonstrates that behavioral approaches are, at best, promising: their value is yet to be demonstrated. Some behavioral techniques seem to us to merit continued experimentation, but to contend that they are revolutionary is to be somewhat grandiose.

We think we have also demonstrated one more time that talking to children in the privacy of the counselor's office is largely a waste of time, no matter what the counselor's theoretical orientation. If one accepts the notion that behaviors such as out-of-seat are much more a function of situational than intrapsychic variables, then treating the problem by removing the child from the situation to talk to him appears to be somewhat absurd.

Recent research on classroom management techniques (Madsen, Becker, & Thomas, 1968; O'Leary, Becker, Evans, & Saudargas, 1969; Thomas, Becker, & Armstrong, 1968) has shown the powerful effects of teacher behavior in controlling and curbing classroom misbehavior. We think that from these studies counselors may learn effective techniques of working directly with the teacher to change both academic programs and reinforcement contingencies in the classroom.

In conclusion, we hope that the results of the present study will help lead to a rapid discarding of traditional conceptions of both the role of the elementary school counselor and the treatment he offers. We view the nonsignificant results obtained in the present study as one more indicator that new directions need to be taken to make more effective the work of the elementary school counselor. New directions can and should be taken because the old ones have not stood the test of experimental evaluation.

REFERENCES

Axline, V. M. Nondirective play therapy for poor readers. *Journal of Consulting Psychology*, 1947, **11**, 61–69.

Azrin, N. H., & Holtz, W. C. Punishment. In W. K. Honig (Ed.), *Operant behavior: areas of research and application.* New York: Appleton-Century-Crofts, 1966, **58**, 143–159.

Biasco, F. The effects of individual counseling, multiple counseling, and teacher guidance upon the sociometric status of children enrolled in grades 4, 5, 6. Unpublished doctoral dissertation, Indiana University, 1956.

Bills, R. E. Nondirective play therapy with retarded readers. *Journal of Consulting Psychology*, 1950, **14**, 140–150.

Clement, P. W., & Milne, D. C. Group play therapy and tangible reinforcers used to modify the behavior of eight-year-old boys. *Behavior Research and Therapy*, 1967, **5**, 301–312.

Cox, F. N. Sociometric status and individual adjustment before and after play therapy. *Journal of Abnormal and Social Psychology*, 1958, **48**, 354–356.

Dickson, D. J. Changing behavior with behavioral techniques. *Journal of School Psychology*, 1958, **4**, 178–283.

Kranzler, G. D. Elementary school counseling: an evaluation. *Elementary School Guidance and Counseling*, 1968, **2**, 286–294.

Kranzler, G. D. The elementary school counselor as consultant: an evaluation. *Elementary School Guidance and Counseling*, 1969, **3**, 285–288.

Lindsley, O. R. Precision teaching. Paper presented at the conference on behavior technology at the University of Oregon, July 1968.

London, P. L. *The modes and morals of psychotherapy*. New York: Holt, Rinehart & Winston, 1964.

Madsen, D., Becker, W., & Thomas, D. Rules, praise, and ignoring: elements of elementary classroom control. *Journal of Applied Behavior Analysis*, 1968, **1**, 139–150.

Mayer, G. R., Kranzler, G. D., & Matthes, W. A. Elementary school counseling and peer relations. *The Personnel and Guidance Journal*, 1967, **46**, 360–365.

Morice, H. O. The school psychologist as a behavioral consultant: a project in behavior modification in a public school setting. *Psychology in the Schools*, 1968, **2**, 253–262.

Oldridge, B. Two roles for elementary school guidance personnel. *The Personnel and Guidance Journal*, 1964, **43**, 367–370.

O'Leary, K. D., Becker, W. C., Evans, M. B., & Saudargas, R. A. A token reinforcement program in a public school: A replication and systematic analysis. *Journal of Applied Behavior Analysis*, 1969, **2**, 3–13.

Patterson, G. R., & Ebner, M. J. Application of learning principles to the treatment of deviant children. Paper presented at a meeting of the American Psychological Association, Washington, D.C., September 1965.

Patterson, G. R., Ray, R. S., & Shaw, D. A. Direct intervention in families of deviant children. *Oregon Research Institute Bulletin*, **8** (No. 9), 1969.

Southworth, R. S. A study of the effects of short-term group counseling on underachieving six-grade students. *Dissertation abstracts*, 1966, **27**, 1271–1273.

Strickler, E. Educational group counseling within a remedial reading program. *Dissertation abstracts*, 1966, **25**, 5129–5130.

Thomas, D. R., Becker, W. C., & Armstrong, M. Production and elimination of disruptive classroom behavior by systematically varying teacher's behavior. *Journal of Applied Behavior Analysis*, 1968, **1**, 35–45.

Ziller, R. Self-other orientation: theory and tasks. Unpublished manuscript, University of Oregon, 1969.

CRITIQUE

1. PHILOSOPHICAL AND THEORETICAL CONSIDERATIONS

The authors have stated very clearly the counseling theoretical orientations which served as a base for this study: a client-centered approach and a behavioral modification strategy based on operant conditioning techniques. The problem under study is stated clearly: Are there differences in effectiveness between client-centered and behavioral approaches in dealing with behavior problems (out-of-seat without permission behavior, more specifically) of school children? This study would have been strengthened by the presence of a paradigm within which one could place the dependent and independent variables as well as the contrasting styles of behavior change. It would also have been useful to know whether any attempt was made to examine the client-centered or precision-teaching practices as being compatible with their respective theoretical origins.

2. CRITERIA

The criterion of central interest in this study was out-of-seat behavior. This follows quite logically from the goals set forth. It is specific, observable, and external to the treatment itself. Since the precision-teaching condition focused specifically on environmental determinants and contingencies of reinforcement controlling this behavior, this is the best criterion. Yet, as one looks at the other conditions especially individual client-centered counseling in which the presenting problem was not dealt with specifically, the criterion of out-of-seat behavior seems to be much less relevant and farther removed.

Three other criteria were used: attitudes toward self and others, social acceptance and rejection, and arithmetic computation rates. Just why these were included is not clear. Was it assumed that if one stays in his seat more frequently, that his skills in arithmetic will increase? Why would a student do better in arithmetic after ten sessions of client-centered counseling? The other two criteria, attitudes toward self and others and social acceptance, might logically be expected to be changed some as a result of self-exploration (as occurred in the client-centered counseling) or even from the group discussions (attention placebo) but not necessarily from the precision-teaching condition. Yet, it is a sound idea to test differing approaches in relation to both intentional and alternate criteria. These two criteria are of the self-report variety and hence are subjective in nature. The arithmetic computation is an objective, external and quite specific criterion.

3. RESEARCH DESIGN

The counselor-researchers utilized a powerful multiple treatment-control group design to focus appropriate factual information in the problem question. The advantage of the multiple treatment factorial design over the classical experimental-control group design is that it removes the need for the "no-treatment" condition (Chapter 3). The factorial design is also advantageous because powerful statistical procedures, e.g. analysis of variance, can be utilized.

Finally, in reference to procedure, there is a question about teachers' knowledge of which students were actually in the study or in different treatment groups. In effect, the researchers ask us to assume teachers did not know the answer to either part of the question, but the opposite assumption is more plausible.

4. SELECTION AND SAMPLING PROCEDURES

Random procedures were used in selecting the 36 subjects from the 42 pupils referred by the teachers and in assigning clients to counselors. This is a highly desirable procedure. Unfortunately, the counselors themselves were not selected in such a systematic way, but this is very difficult to accomplish in reality. And, as noted earlier, their personal counseling biases, sex, and other descriptive information were not included in the report. Assuming most clients and counselors were males, it would seem necessary to wonder about differential sex effects. Such interactions were reported earlier by Krumboltz and others regarding information seeking behavior.

The lack of representativeness regarding counselors, and perhaps clients, raises some question about external validity. This is especially true in light of the sweeping generalizations offered by the authors about the appropriateness of the counselor's role in the elementary school.

5. COUNSELING TREATMENT

The authors are to be commended on trying to explicate the treatment, yet several comments need to be made:

a. Three counselors enrolled in a Master's program administered all treatments. Presumably they were not very experienced in counseling. What were their preferred theoretical orientations? Although the researchers trained them in the use of both treatment methods, we do not know the length or depth of such training. Also, if the counselors' personal orientations differed from the one they administered did they fully co-operate? Most proponents of client-centered counseling maintain there are no techniques in that approach; the crucial aspect is in the attitudinal ingredients of the counselor himself. We might speculate that the results would have been different had experienced client-centered and experienced behavioral counselors been involved.

b. By the way the client-centered counseling is described, it might better have been labeled non-directive rather than client-centered. Why were not the phenomena of genuineness and empathy emphasized and measured? The quality of the relationship established could have easily been measured by the Barrett-Lennard Relationship Inventory or Truax-Carkhuff rating scales. Finally, could not a counselor encounter his client with the presenting behavior (out-of-seat without permission), explain the effect this has on his teacher and others, and deal with it in the session, and still be considered client-centered?

c. In the precision-teaching behavioral approach, each client was seen individually, presumably not in the classroom situation. The most relevant question here is, were these clients *aware* that the counselor was trying to get them to stay in their seats? This cannot be discerned from the study. What connection did they see between the rewards and their own behavior? Who reported on the rate of out-of-seat behavior? Following the dictates of a behavioral approach, the conditioning should have occurred in situ, with the rewards appearing immediately after the desired behavior (not at the end of the day) for maximal results. Although the behavioral counseling research does not put much credence on the relationship between the client and counselor, we wonder about the quality of this relationship, or the rapport, or the attraction between the clients and the counselor in this treatment. Some research seems to indicate that a "good" relationship (that is, a conducive one) must exist before behavior shaping can occur. Finally, although the authors mention the rewards, we wonder if, in fact, those listed were equally reinforcing to all clients. For example, either a marble, a book, a softball, or free or drawing time just might not be a potent enough reinforcer for all of the kids.

d. The attention-placebo condition might have been called group guidance or group counseling. We don't really know what happened in this treatment, except that the discussions were steered away from personal problems.

e. The control group seems to have been a true control group, since efforts were made to keep them unaware of their participation. It is assumed that this group proceeded on a daily activities routine.

In summary, it seems this study could have been greatly strengthened by the use of experienced counselors whose personal counseling style matched the treatment; by establishing the quality of the relationship between clients and counselors in the two experimental and the placebo groups; by applying behavioral techniques in a more systematic, sequential, and in situ way; and by a broader and more contemporary understanding of the client-centered counseling.

6. MEASUREMENT

It appears that the criteria performances are quite clear and follow in a natural way. Out-of-seat behavior seems specific enough, yet we wonder if getting out of one's seat to talk to a friend in the back of the room has the import of getting out of one's seat to pick up a pencil for a neighbor, or to ask the teacher a question. Out-of-seat behavior was measured for 30-minute periods over 10 consecutive days. Was this 30-minute period consistent (that is, the same time of day) each day? The 30-minute period should have been different (i.e., 9:00 A.M. first day, 9:30 A.M. second day, etc.) since it is obvious that elementary children become more restless (and hence, more prone to get out-of-seat) as the school day progresses.

The other three criteria seemed to have been measured in very appropriate and relevant ways. The SSST seems a good measure of attitude toward self and others, and a sociometric test (which one?) is a good measure of social acceptance, especially peer acceptance. School achievement might better have been labeled arithmetic computation achievement. Curiously, the data are not reported for the last criterion (arithmetic achievement) in Table 1.

7. ETHICAL, PROFESSIONAL, AND LEGAL CONSIDERATIONS

Did the control group subjects later have an opportunity to receive some kind of treatment for their problem, getting out-of-seat without permission?

Also, it would have been useful to know how the subjects were approached and their feelings about their involvement. One might question using "counseling" approaches on subjects who apparently have not indicated any obvious need for assistance.

In terms of professional reporting of research some confirmation of the fact that the counselors were "trained to use both client-centered and behavioral counseling techniques" would have aided in replication of the study. How realistic is this assumption? In the same vein the reader may wish to have more data about "precision teaching," i.e., exactly how were "environmental determinants and reinforcements contingencies" really used? The use of the term "attempted" tends to raise some doubts as to the effectiveness of the procedures followed.

8. RESULTS

This section will deal with some of the interpretations of the results, rather than the results, *per se*. And here, we feel the authors have vigorously and fairly pursued this matter. We will, for illustrative and personal reasons, disagree with some of their points.

First, at a very logical level, why would one expect ten sessions of client-centered counseling which would focus on only a few techniques and in which "no attempt was made to deal specifically with the referral problem" to change a student's out-of-seat behavior? Did the students perceive themselves as having a problem, or was it a teacher's problem? Do elementary counselors really have these expectations and implement these strategies? If they do, we need no research to instruct them to desist immediately. Client-centered theorists would make no such claims for their theory. We would have expected some significant results in the area of attitude toward self and others and in social acceptance.

Secondly, it is not understood why the precision-teaching method did not show more conclusive results, except for the remarks made earlier and more probably because of the authors' explanation that some did do better (stayed in their seats more frequently) and some did not, cancelling any statistically significant results. Yet, as a result of this treatment, we would not have expected any changes on the other three criteria.

Thirdly, we can agree that "talking *to* children" is a waste of time, but are unable to conclude, on the basis of this study, that counseling *with* children is not necessarily a waste of time.

Fourth, we cannot agree that "the present study demonstrates that behavioral approaches are, at best, promising." On the basis of this study the one treatment which should logically be expected to show some results is the behavioral one. The results do not show that even this behavioral treatment is promising. The value of behavioral techniques have been proven to be quite successful with certain kinds of clients presenting certain kinds of problems (which, incidentally, they themselves perceive and present), with certain kinds of behavioral counselors and therapists.

Finally, we would re-word the authors' implications to read: New directions probably should be taken because the old ones have not been subjected to adequate experimental evaluation.

In summary, we feel that these authors have done a very good job of experimental counseling research in our present stage of development.

VERBAL-REINFORCEMENT AND MODEL-REINFORCEMENT GROUP COUNSELING WITH ALIENATED STUDENTS[1]

Richard W. Warner, Jr.
Pennsylvania State University
and
James C. Hansen
State University of New York at Buffalo

This research investigates the effects of model-reinforcement and verbal-reinforcement group counseling on alienated high school students. Juniors in three high schools who scored one standard deviation above the mean on a scale of alienation were selected for inclusion in the study. In each school these students were randomly assigned to one of four treatment groups: model reinforcement, verbal reinforcement, placebo, and control. Findings: (a) Both reinforcement counseling groups were effective in reducing students' feelings of alienation. (b) There were no significant differences between the effects of the model-reinforcement and verbal-reinforcement counseling. (c) There was no interaction between counselors and treatments or between sex of student and treatment. (d) The placebo treatment had no significant effect on alienation.

Counselors show increasing interest in the effectiveness of behavioral counseling (Krumboltz, 1966). Available evidence indicates that behavioral counseling can be effective when working toward specific goals, for example, information seeking. Since much high school counseling deals with less specific goals such as problems of a personal or social nature, there is a need to investigate the effectiveness of behavioral counseling with such problems. One such problem facing counselors is the increasing proportion of alienated youth.

Contemporary sociologists describe alienation as an outgrowth of the demands that modern society places on individuals. Seeman (1959) believes that our society so controls the reward system that the individual sees no relationship between his own behavior and his rewards; this is the

[1]Warner, Jr., Richard W. and Hansen, James C. Verbal-reinforcement and model-reinforcement group counseling with alienated students. *Journal of Counseling Psychology*, 1970, **17**, (2), 168–172.

situation which gives rise to feelings of alienation from society. Merton (1949) states that the society not only establishes the goals for which everyone should be striving, but also establishes and controls the acceptable modes for reaching these goals. When the society completely controls the individual, he develops a feeling of powerlessness. When the individual cannot accept the norms of society, he becomes normless; and when both goals and norms of society mean little to the individual, he will feel isolated from society.

Group behavioral counseling promises the possibility of some success with alienated students. Behavioral counseling views client problems as problems in learning, and the counselor needs to "think of his job as one in which he helps his client learn more effective ways of solving his own problems [Krumboltz, 1966, p. 4]." Two methods of behavioral counseling are verbal reinforcement and model reinforcement. Verbal-reinforcement counseling assumes that a positive reward which follows the occurrence of the desired behavior will increase the probability of the reoccurrence of that behavior. Model-reinforcement counseling adds the additional element of imitative or vicarious learning, which is based on the assumption that an individual who observes another individual receive a reward will imitate that behavior in order to receive the reward (Bandura & Walters, 1963). Several studies (Krumboltz & Schroeder, 1965; Krumboltz & Thoreson, 1964; Ryan & Krumboltz, 1964) have demonstrated the usefulness of both verbal-reinforcement and model-reinforcement counseling in groups, when working with problems of a cognitive nature. These investigations left unanswered the question, "Can behavioral techniques be used with more broadly defined affective problems?"

The purpose of this study was to investigate the effectiveness of verbal-reinforcement and model-reinforcement group counseling, in helping students resolve conflicts they have with the social structure. By reducing their feelings of alienation, can they become more fully functioning, participating members of society?

The following hypotheses were investigated:

1. Students receiving either verbal- or model-reinforcement group counseling will show a greater decrease in normlessness, powerlessness, social isolation, and total alienation scores than students in either the placebo or no counseling groups.
2. Students receiving model-reinforcement group counseling will show a greater decrease in normlessness, powerlessness, social isolation, and total alienation scores than will students receiving only verbal-reinforcement group counseling.

3. Differences in treatment effects across counselors will not be significant.
4. Differences in treatment effects across sex of the client will not be significant.

METHOD

Instrument

A scale of alienation developed by Dean (1961) was used to identify alienated students. This scale was chosen because of its division of the concept of alienation into three distinct parts: powerlessness, normlessness, and social isolation. This enabled the counselors to concentrate on specific topics in relation to the general feeling of alienation. Powerlessness is the feeling of not being able to understand or to influence the outcomes of one's own behavior. Normlessness is the feeling that society has no norms to live by or that the norms that do exist do not apply to one's own life. Social isolation is the feeling of being alone; of being separated from society.

The alienation scale consists of 24 items. The student is asked to respond to each statement on a five-point scale. The total alienation score is a sum of the student's responses to all 24 items, with his score on the three subscales being derived from different combinations of the 24 items. The statements in the scale came from 139 statements that Dean had gleaned from the literature. The statements were submitted to seven judges at Ohio State University, five of whom had to agree on the placement of the item before it was included on the instrument. A differentiating power test was applied to each item to determine its validity and whether the item would be retained. Dean tested the reliability (Spearman-Brown) of the scales and the total instrument with a sample of 384 subjects. The resulting reliabilities were: Powerlessness = 0.78, Normlessness = 0.73, Social Isolation = 0.83, and Total Alienation = 0.78 (Dean, 1960).

Sample

The sample of alienated students was drawn from a population of eleventh-grade students in three suburban high schools located in western New York. The schools were located in communities ranging from upper-lower to lower-middle class. Students who scored one standard deviation above the mean on Dean's scale of alienation were considered high-alienation students. In each of the sample schools about 15% of the students so scored. In School A, 65 students were selected at random from 101 students who scored one deviation above the mean; in School B, 65 students were selected at random from 87 that scored one standard deviation above the mean. In School C, a somewhat smaller school, all 50 students who scored on standard deviation above the mean were included in the study.

Models

In each of the three schools two females and two males were selected as models to participate in the model-reinforcement groups. The models were chosen from the junior class because of their overall adjustment to society as rated by their peers and teachers on the following four criteria: the model students must have scored below the mean on alienation; they had to be named at least three times as best liked (and no more than twice as least liked) on a sociogram completed by members of the junior class; they had to receive an overall rating of 3 on a 5-point scale from three teachers on the traits of responsibility, ambition, and emotional maturity; and, the students must have maintained an overall C average.

Counselors

One counselor in each school conducted all group sessions in that school. All three counselors were males with experience in counseling and had completed postmaster's work in counseling. Prior to the start of the investigation, all three counselors preferred an insight-oriented approach to counseling; however, the counselors did complete a training program in behavioral counseling. This training was under the direction of the authors and consisted of readings, discussions, listening to tapes, and role playing. Emphasis was placed on how behavioral techniques could be used with students who were alienated from the society. During the course of the investigation, periodic meetings were held with the counselors, and tapes of the group counseling sessions were played in an attempt to insure that the desired techniques were used.

Procedures

In each school the subjects were randomly assigned to one of four treatments. Each school had two model-reinforcement groups, two verbal-reinforcement groups, one placebo group, and one control group. The data from the pretest of alienation was submitted to an analysis of variance in order to determine that the various treatment groups were not statistically different. This analysis yielded an F value of 0.53 which was not significant.

The students in the model-reinforcement, verbal-reinforcement, and placebo groups met with the counselor for six sessions lasting 40 minutes each. The students in the control group did not meet with the counselor at any time.

In the model-reinforcement and verbal-reinforcement groups two sessions were devoted to each of the three aspects of alienation. The first session dealt with powerlessness, the second with normlessness, and the third with social isolation. This cycle was then repeated. The goal in the model-reinforcement and the verbal-reinforcement counseling groups was to keep the discussion focused on these topics and to give positive verbal reinforcement to statements made by the students which suggested

Table 1 Means and Standard Deviations, by Treatment Group, on Total Alienation and Its Subparts: Powerlessness, Normlessness, and Social Isolation.

Variable	X	SD
Model reinforcement[a]		
Isolation	29.32	4.14
Powerlessness	28.31	4.18
Normlessness	19.56	3.73
Total alienation	77.70	8.05
Verbal reinforcement[b]		
Isolation	31.09	4.61
Powerlessness	29.18	4.72
Normlessness	19.58	3.28
Total alienation	79.86	9.77
Placebo[c]		
Isolation	32.22	4.83
Powerlessness	32.20	4.88
Normlessness	20.95	3.35
Total alienation	85.40	11.24
Control[d]		
Isolation	31.92	3.99
Powerlessness	31.26	3.89
Normlessness	21.30	3.42
Total alienation	84.49	8.41

[a] $n = 37$, [b] $n = 43$, [c] $n = 22$, [d] $n = 75$.

Table 2 *t* Values for Planned Comparisons between Treatment Groups on Total Alienation, Social Isolation, Powerlessness, and Normlessness.

Comparison	*t* values			
	Alienation	Isolation	Powerlessness	Normlessness
Model reinforcement and verbal reinforcement > placebo and control	4.25*	2.63*	3.97*	2.85*
Model reinforcement > verbal reinforcement	1.09	1.93	0.35	0.03
Placebo > control	0.32	0.24	0.80	0.54

Note: $t = 2.326$, $df = 153$, $p < 0.01$ (one-tailed).
*$p < 0.01$.

positive attitudes toward their position in the social structure. The specific aim was to get the students to look at the positive aspects of their situation and to consider positive steps that the students could take to eliminate feelings of powerlessness, normlessness, and social isolation.

The model-reinforcement treatment differed from the verbal reinforcement only in the fact that one male and one female peer model participated in each model group while being unaware that they were acting as models. The student models presumably would act as reinforcing agents that might be more powerful than the reinforcements given by the counselor and through the use of the models the principles of imitative learning and vicarious reinforcement would be operating in the groups. Hence, the alienated students might imitate the behavior of the models because they saw it as a desirable solution to their problems.

The purpose of the placebo group was to control for the Hawthorne effect. The counselor in these groups made no attempt to focus the discussion or to reinforce any statements made by the students.

At the conclusion of counseling, the students in all four treatments in each school were readministered Dean's Scale of Alienation. The data resulting from the students' scores on this instrument were then analyzed to test the research hypothesis. Planned comparisons were used to test the main effect of the four treatments on alienation and its subparts. Planned comparisons are appropriate when the hypotheses are stated in such a way as to indicate the expected direction of the findings, and when the purpose of the investigation is to examine the significance of differences between particular treatments.

The main effect of sex of the student and the main effect of counselors, as well as all interaction effects were analyzed through the use of two analyses of variance. The first analysis was a three-way univariate analysis with the total alienation score as the dependent variable, and the second analysis was a three-way multivariate analysis with the three subparts of alienation: powerlessness, normlessness, and social isolation being used as the dependent variables. The two different analyses were necessary because the sum of the scores on the three subtests equals the total alienation score.

RESULTS

An examination of the means shown in Table 1 indicates that the two groups of students which received either model-reinforcement or verbal-reinforcement counseling had lower feelings of isolation, powerlessness, normlessness, and total alienation at the close of counseling than students who were in either the placebo or control groups. The data also show that students who received the model-reinforcement counseling had scores slightly lower than those students who received the verbal-reinforcement counseling.

In order to test for the significance of differences between the four treatment groups on the variables of total alienation, social isolation, powerlessness, and normlessness, the data on each variable were submitted to three planned orthogonal contrasts. Table 2 shows the results of these comparisons.

Table 2 shows a significant difference in mean alienation scores for students who were in either the model-reinforcement or verbal-reinforcement counseling groups as compared to students in either the placebo or the control groups. The data also indicate that the significant difference between the reinforcement counseling and the other two groups held true across the three subparts of alienation. While the means for the model-reinforcement groups were lower than the verbal-reinforcement groups for all variables, these differences must be attributed to chance as no differences were significant at the 0.01 level. The comparisons between the placebo and the control groups also yielded no significant differences on any of the four variables.

In order to test Hypotheses 3 and 4, the data were submitted to a $3 \times 4 \times 2$ univariate analysis of variance for the total alienation score, and a $3 \times 4 \times 2$ multivariate analysis for the three subparts of alienation. The first analysis examined the effects of counselor, treatment, and sex on the total alienation score. The second analysis examined the effects of counselor, treatment, and sex on the three subparts of alienation as a group.

The data from these analyses indicated no significant interactions between counselors and treatments, or between sex of the students and treatments. The data further indicate that the counselors were not differentially effective across the four treatments, nor was there any indication that one treatment was more effective for one sex than the other. Hence, Hypotheses 3 and 4 cannot be rejected.

DISCUSSION

The results of this investigation demonstrate that both verbal- and model-reinforcement counseling can be effective in reducing students' feelings of alienation. The students in the two reinforcement treatments improved more on the total alienation scale than the students who received either no counseling or who participated in the placebo groups. Both model-reinforcement and verbal-reinforcement counseling were effective in reducing the students' feelings of social isolation, powerlessness, and normlessness. Behavioral counseling techniques may be effective even when the problem under consideration does not concern specific and well-defined behaviors.

The absence of significant differences between the effects of the model-reinforcement and verbal-reinforcement counseling may be a function of the length of time involved in counseling. In order for models to be effective, the subjects must be able to identify the models as either someone they desire to be like or as someone who receives rewards that the subject would like to receive. The short-term (6 weeks) nature of the group counseling may have been too short a time for this identification.

The lack of significant differences between the placebo and control groups suggests that the mere meeting of a counselor with a group of students has little effect on students' feeling of alienation.

The results suggest that behavioral techniques can be effective with high school students of both sexes regardless of counselor personality or philosophical background. Prior to this investigation, the three counselors involved in this study essentially operated from an insight-oriented framework. The results point to the feasibility of training counselors to use behavioral techniques in the schools.

One of the limitations of this investigation must be noted – no measurement of overt behavior was recorded after the completion of counseling. The instrument used to measure alienation was of a self-report type, hence student perceptions of their feelings and behavior, not their actual behavior was the criterion. However, in some situations covert feelings of students must be changed before any overt changes in behavior can be expected. In social learning theory and behavioral counseling a place remains for insight; that is, when counselors are dealing with students whose problems are of a personal or social nature change in the students' feelings may be expected to accompany overt behavior changes. In this respect, the behavioral counseling techniques used in this investigation were successful in bringing about changes in the students' feelings about their relationship with the society.

REFERENCES

Bandura, A., & Walters, R. H. *Social learning and personality development.* New York: Holt, Rinehart & Winston, 1963.

Dean, D. G. Alienation and political apathy. *Social Forces*, 1960, **38**, 185–189.

Dean, D. G. Alienation: Its meaning and measurement. *American Sociological Review*, 1961, **26**, 753–758.

Krumboltz, J. D. *Revolution in counseling.* New York: Houghton Mifflin, 1966.

Krumboltz, J. D., & Schroeder, W. W. Promoting career explorations through reinforcement. *Personnel and Guidance Journal*, 1965, **44**, 19–26.

Krumboltz, J. D., & Thoresen, C. E. The effect of behavioral counseling in group and individual settings on information-seeking behavior. *Journal of Counseling Psychology*, 1964, **11**, 324–333.

Merton, R. *Social theory and social structure.* Glencoe, Ill.: The Free Press, 1949.

Ryan, T. A., & Krumboltz, J. D. Effect of planned reinforcement counseling on client decision-making behavior. *Journal of Counseling Psychology*, 1964, **11**, 315–323.

Seeman, M. On the meaning of alienation. *American Sociological Review*, 1959, **24**, 783–791.

CRITIQUE

1. PHILOSOPHICAL AND THEORETICAL CONSIDERATIONS

The rather amorphous concept of alienation was used as a basis for the dependent variable in this study. While this is certainly a contemporary issue, particularly in our youth oriented culture, it is not reflected in the two references cited by the authors. Is not alienation for today's youth, the generation gap, drug tripping, etc., something different from earlier notions of alienation as they applied to middle-aged Americans? The authors failed to relate the moral revolution, the development of subcultures, etc. to alienation. Which youth are alienated? Why? How? And how will one alienated from society change himself? Maybe society should be changed?

What will he do, how will he behave differently? What are the goals and terminal behaviors for counseling with the alienated?

The authors have anchored their study in a behavioristic mold, and have stated it well. One point needs to be made regarding reinforcement. The authors state, "Verbal-reinforcement counseling assumes that a positive reward which follows the occurrence of the desired behavior will increase the probability of the reoccurrence of that behavior." One interpretation of this might mean that when the subject emits the task behavior or the terminal behavior, then he receives reinforcement. This is incorrect. In operant conditioning *any* emitted behavior which is in the direction of the final desired behavior is evidence for reinforcement. This is Skinner's notion of immediate reinforcement of successive approximations to desired (terminal) behavior, and it is obvious that the authors are using that learning theory rather than a Hullian one, for example.

Another point in this opening section may cause some misunderstanding. The reader might well get the impression that behavior techniques have been used exclusively with cognitive, specific behaviors. It is true that behaviorists emphasize dealing with specific, observable kinds of behavior; however, it is equally true that the earliest work using behavioral techniques was with affective problems. Because the authors have limited their references to the work done by Krumboltz, Thoresen, Ryan, and the Stanford group, they overlook a mass of literature done by other counselors and therapists dealing with so-called affective problems.

The stated goal of this study was to investigate the effectiveness of verbal-reinforcement and model-reinforcement group counseling in helping students resolve conflicts they have with the social structure.

2. CRITERION

The single criterion of this study has to do with alienation, a significant social phenomenon which is most worthy of study in these times. Although the authors have defined this concept and broken it down into three divisions (powerlessness, normlessness, and social isolation), one immediately wonders what it is that people say or do by which we infer they are alienated? Are there different levels, degrees and intensities of alienation?

It is obvious that the authors had a difficult time answering these questions, and this shows most readily when they selected their models for treatment, at which time, they were presumably trying to identify models who were non-alienated from society. They used four criteria for selection: (1) the alienation score, which follows logically; (2) the results of a sociogram which probably indicates likeability or popularity rather than non-alienation; (3) a rating scale used to tap responsibility, ambition, and emotional maturity, all rather irrelevant to non-alienation, e.g., many clinically diagnosed alienated students are quite emotionally mature, and many presumably are quite responsible and ambitious; and (4) grade averages, which are no indication whatsoever of alienation (again, many alienated students are quite bright and have high GPA's). Here the authors seem to make little distinction between adjustment (conformity) and alienation.

3. RESEARCH DESIGN

A strong multiple treatment-control group was used. This factorial design allowed for simultaneous analysis and control of several different kinds of variance, including treatment effects, client, sex and counselor personality on the three component parts of the alienation variable. It is especially commendable that the authors controlled for client sex, because this is one of the most commonly overlooked sources of variance in treatment effects. Examination of the control problems related to design functions (Chapter 3) shows that the counselor-researchers did a good job in designing this study.

4. SELECTION AND SAMPLING PROCEDURES

Most clients in the study were selected by use of a random procedure. The authors note that the schools were representative of the broad range of socioeconomic levels. In terms of the goals and outcomes of this study, this is probably an example of a case where simple random selection was not powerful enough. There is evidence of the operation of a uniformity assumption for alienated clients. There is no recognition of individual differences in why youth compared to adults are alienated, e.g., racism, socioeconomic level, the draft, existential anxiety, drugs, college choice. These individual differences are probably important to treatment effects, but were not controlled in selection. But, there is some comfort in the fact that a variety of social situations are represented in the study. The counselors, however, were all initially committed to "insight therapies," and did not represent any broad spectrum. Unlike many research reports, these counselors were experienced professionals, rather than graduate trainees.

Randomization was also used in assigning clients to treatment-control groups. This is a sound procedure, and the random sampling and assignment procedures are important in meeting basic assumptions for later parametric statistical tests.

The fact that good procedures were used in the design and sampling of this study increases the internal and external validity. Assuming adequate theoretical bases, treatment definition, criterion measurement, etc., the researchers can therefore more confidently assume treatment differences are indeed real.

5. COUNSELING TREATMENT

It is stated that the counselors used in this study initially preferred insight oriented counseling approaches. Which ones – rational-emotive, client-centered, psychoanalytic oriented, trait-and-factor, etc.? This tells us little about their orientations, counseling styles, or competencies. We wonder how the counselors would have scored on the alienation test? It would be nice to know how much experience each counselor had (six months or six years?). The authors are to be commended on conducting training sessions with the counselors to point out some of the behavioral techniques, and to indicate what was expected of them. Did they all have the same amount of training (two hours or two months)? Also, how adequate was the provision of periodic meetings with the counselors to keep them on task?

In the specification of the treatment, the authors have tried to be as explicit as possible. Yet, in the verbal-reinforcement group we are told that the students received positive verbal reinforcement for the emission of verbal statements suggestive of more positive attitudes toward their position in the social structure. This is a tough response class to define, and it would have helped if the authors might have given us several examples of the verbal behaviors which were reinforced. We got the feeling that student statements which were indicative of conformity or, at least, more socially acceptable ways of doing things, were also being reinforced. What positive steps can a black kid from the ghetto see for himself when his whole situation (home, school, community) is, in fact, so hopeless?

The model-reinforcement group "differed" from the one above only because of the presence of the two models. We would suggest it probably differed in many other respects. For example, a completely different group of students discussing different content, with different frequencies and amounts of verbal reinforcement were involved. Tersely put, groups are just plain different from one another in a host of ways, even when the same counselor is administering the same treatment. The placing of two models in the group, just with the hope that something different might happen seems unjustified. Research done in this area suggests modeling works best when the person wants to become more like the model, the prestige of the model attracts the other person, and the payoff (intrinsic rewards) the person is seeking is in acting more like the model. Modeling or imitative learning seldom just happens.

Depending on the model-potency of the counselor and the others in the verbal-reinforcement group, we might speculate that modeling for *some* of the students in that group could have just as well taken place. This, in addition to the interpretation given by the authors, might have accounted for no significant differences between the verbal and model-reinforcement group.

In the placebo group the counselors made no attempt to focus the discussion or to reinforce any statements by the students. This hardly explains what did, in fact, occur in these groups. It is hard to believe that a person trained in counseling could sit in a room with students and not focus the discussion or not reinforce, at least some kinds of behavior. A counselor can focus the content and process of counseling in the most subtle ways—nonverbal cues, questions, explanations of what's going on, etc. Did the counselors here deliberately not focus on alienation-related topics? If the counselor was indeed as blah and passive as this sounds, what did the students think was happening?

Finally, we must question the effects of the relationships which existed between the counselor and the clients and between the clients. The attractiveness of that relationship (rapport, understanding, openness, etc.) could have been as instrumental in the results as either verbal or model-reinforcement. It would have been helpful to have had a reading on this.

6. MEASUREMENT

The goal of this study was to examine the effectiveness of two treatment methods in helping students resolve conflicts they had with the social structure. The criterion was the concept of alienation. The criterion was measured by use of an alienation scale. As the reader can see this does not logically follow. It could be made more clear by stating the goal as reducing feelings of alienation as measured by the Dean Alienation Scale. In fact, the authors did not point out what conflicts the students were having, the nature of them, how they were dealt with in counseling, or any external criterion of conflict reduction or resolution (the last of which is a limitation they point out).

We definitely agree with the authors, particularly in light of the behavioristic rationale for this study, that some baseline data about how these feelings were manifesting themselves in the behavior of these students, along with the use of some external criterion, would have made the study a much more solid one.

7. ETHICAL, PROFESSIONAL, AND LEGAL CONSIDERATIONS

Nowhere in this study can we find a statement about whether or not the students were aware of the goals of the study, or whether or not they had a chance to volunteer to be included. We assume they had no choice, which brings several questions to mind: Does a school counselor have the professional right to attempt to change a student's feelings about alienation? This is not only a value judgment, but is a serious ethical question. Some would suggest counselors ought to spend their time intervening in the social system which breeds alienation, in order to bring about changes.

In the design of the study, as a professional investigation, the researchers leave the reader uninformed on several important matters. Specifically how were the models treated in various groups? Little data is given to how they were oriented, placed, and observed in the groups. What did these models do and was their behavior comparable to non-group (school ground or hall) behavior? Were these models chosen for their non-alienation characteristics or for "overall adjustment"?

8. RESULTS

The results are presented quite clearly. Several comments can be made about their interpretation, however. The authors state that the lack of significant differences for the placebo and control groups suggest that the *mere* meeting of a counselor with a group of students has little effect on the student's feeling of alienation. What professional counselor would assume that it would? Also by insinuation, the authors imply that the placebo group was insight oriented, and hence, behavioral techniques are more effective. This is an exaggeration of a comparison between the two approaches. Insight oriented counselors do focus on the content and process of group counseling, and they do, in a manifold of ways, use behavioral techniques (verbal and nonverbal reinforcement). As noted earlier, it might have been the relationship between the counselor and the clients, and between the clients, which produced the results of lowered scores on the alienation scale.

Because of the lack of specificity of (1) the nature of the response class (feelings of alienation); (2) the reinforcers used (to call it verbal is not sufficient); (3) the frequency of reinforcement; (4) the contingencies of reinforcement; (5) the quality of the relationships established; and (6) the actual effects of the models, we are unable to conclude that this kind of use of behavioral techniques is any more effective than any other approach.

Author Index

Subject Index

TITLES IN THE PERGAMON GENERAL PSYCHOLOGY SERIES

Vol. 1. J. Wolpe—*The Practice of Behavior Therapy*
Vol. 2. T. Magoon *et al.*—*Mental Health Counselors at Work*
Vol. 3. J. McDaniel—*Physical Disability and Human Behavior*
Vol. 4. M. L. Kaplan *et al.*—*The Structural Approach in Psychological Testing*
Vol. 5. H. M. LaFauci & P. E. Richter—*Team Teaching at the College Level*
Vol. 6. H. B. Pepinsky *et al.*—*People and Information*
Vol. 7. A. W. Siegman & B. Pope—*Studies in Dyadic Communication*
Vol. 8. R. E. Johnson—*Existential Man: The Challenge of Psychotherapy*
Vol. 9. C. W. Taylor—*Climate for Creativity*
Vol. 10. H. C. Rickard *et al.*—*Behavioral Intervention in Human Problems*
Vol. 11. P. Ekman, W. V. Friesen & P. Ellsworth—*Emotion in the Human Face: Guidelines for Research and an Integration of Findings*
Vol. 12. B. Mausner & E. S. Platt—*Smoking: A Behavioral Analysis*
Vol. 14. A. Goldstein—*Psychotherapeutic Attraction*
Vol. 15. F. Halpern—*Survival: Black/White*
Vol. 16. K. Salzinger & R. S. Feldman—*Studies in Verbal Behavior: An Empirical Approach*
Vol. 17. H. E. Adams & W. K. Boardman—*Advances in Experimental Clinical Psychology*
Vol. 18. R. C. Ziller—*The Social Self*
Vol. 19. R. P. Liberman—*A Guide to Behavioral Analysis & Therapy*
Vol. 22. H. B. Pepinsky & M. J. Patton—*The Psychological Experiment: A Practical Accomplishment*
Vol. 23. T. R. Young—*New Sources of Self*
Vol. 24. L. S. Watson, Jr.—*Child Behavior Modification: A Manual for Teachers, Nurses, and Parents*
Vol. 25. H. L. Newbold—*The Psychiatric Programming of People: Neo-Behavioral Orthomolecular Psychiatry*
Vol. 26. E. L. Rossi—*Dreams and the Growth of Personality: Expanding Awareness in Psychotherapy*
Vol. 27. K. D. O'Leary & S. G. O'Leary—*Classroom Management: The Successful Use of Behavior Modification*
Vol. 28. K. A. Feldman—*College and Student: Selected Readings in the Social Psychology of Higher Education*
Vol. 29. B. A. Ashem & E. G. Poser—*Adaptive Learning: Behavior Modification with Children*
Vol. 30. H. D. Burck *et al.*—*Counseling and Accountability: Methods and Critique*
Vol. 31. N. Frederiksen *et al.*—*Prediction of Organizational Behavior*
Vol. 32. R. B. Cattell—*A New Morality from Science: Beyondism*
Vol. 33. M. L. Weiner—*Personality: The Human Potential*
Vol. 34. R. M. Liebert *et al.*—*The Early Window: Effects of TV on Children and Youth*